FEMINIST GEOPOLITICS

Gender, Space and Society

Series Editors: Peter Hopkins, Newcastle University, UK and Rachel Pain, Durham University, UK

The series on Gender, Space and Society aims to publish innovative feminist work that analyses men's and women's lives from a perspective that exposes and is committed to challenging social inequalities and injustices. The series reflects the ongoing significance and changing forms of gender, and of feminist ideas, in diverse social, geographical and political settings.

The themes it covers include, but are not restricted to:

- The constitution and transformation of gender in different political and economic regimes around the world.
- Men's and women's lived experiences of femininities and masculinities in diverse spaces and environments.
- The ways in which gender is co-constituted and intersects with a range of other social identities, such as race, ethnicity, nationality, class, age, generation, religion, (dis)ability, sexual orientation, body size and health status in different places and times.
- Challenging distinctions and offering new understandings of the relationships between public/private, economic/social (re)production, geopolitical/intimate and so on.
- Destabilising the binary man/woman, and developing more complex ways of understanding gendered social and spatial relations.
- Developing theoretical perspectives that shed light on the changing nature of gender relations, such as indigenous, postcolonial, queer, Marxist, poststructuralist and non-representational feminist theories.
- Exploring innovation in methodology, praxis, knowledge co-production and activism as means of challenging social injustices.

Feminist Geopolitics
Material States

DEBORAH P. DIXON
University of Glasgow, UK

ASHGATE

© Deborah P. Dixon 2015

All rights reserved. No part of this publication may be reproduced, stored in a retrieval system or transmitted in any form or by any means, electronic, mechanical, photocopying, recording or otherwise without the prior permission of the publisher.

Deborah P. Dixon has asserted his right under the Copyright, Designs and Patents Act, 1988, to be identified as the author of this work.

Published by
Ashgate Publishing Limited
Wey Court East
Union Road
Farnham
Surrey, GU9 7PT
England

Ashgate Publishing Company
110 Cherry Street
Suite 3-1
Burlington, VT 05401-3818
USA

www.ashgate.com

British Library Cataloguing in Publication Data
A catalogue record for this book is available from the British Library

The Library of Congress has cataloged the printed edition as follows:
Dixon, Deborah P.
  Feminist geopolitics : material states / by Deborah P. Dixon.
      pages cm. -- (Gender, space and society)
  Includes bibliographical references and index.
    ISBN 978-1-4094-5546-2 (hbk) -- ISBN 978-1-4724-8020-0 (pbk) -- ISBN 978-1-4094-5547-9 (ebk) -- ISBN 978-1-4724-0356-8 (epub) 1. Women--Political activity. 2. Feminism. 3. Geopolitics. I. Title.
  HQ1236.5.D59 2015
  320.082--dc23

ISBN 9781409455462 (hbk)
ISBN 9781472480200 (pbk)
ISBN 9781409455479 (ebk – PDF)
ISBN 9781472403568 (ebk – ePUB)

Printed in the United Kingdom by Henry Ling Limited, at the Dorset Press, Dorchester, DT1 1HD

For George Henry Dixon

Contents

List of Figures   *ix*
Acknowledgements   *xi*

1. What Can a Feminist Geopolitics Do?   1
2. Imagining Feminist Geopolitics   21
3. Flesh   59
4. Bones   85
5. Abhorrence   113
6. Touch   141
7. Inhabiting Feminist Geopolitics   171

Index   *187*

List of Figures

2.1	*Carte de France Corrigée*, 1693, by Jean Picard and Phillipe de la Hire	27
2.2	*Carte du Pays de Tendre*, from *Clélie*, 1654	29
2.3	The WILPF Congress, 1915, US section	39
2.4	The WILPF Congress, 1915, panellists	40
4.1	Wounds Man, reprinted in Ambroise Paré's *Opera Chirurgica*, 1594	92
4.2	Sketch by Charles Bell, 1815, illustrating a gunshot wound to the skull and trepanning	96
5.1	Engraving by C Huyberts from Frederik Ruysch's *Thesaurus Anatomicus*, 1703	123
6.1	Pink Infrastructure for Climate Adaptation	164
7.1	Details from *NoArk*, 2007-8, produced by TCA	176

Acknowledgements

This book has been a long time in the making. It registers the impact of a host of academics and friends, it responds to what I think have been fundamental developments in the discipline of Geography over the past 20 years as well as academia *per se*, and it draws together seemingly disparate lines of inquiry that I have undertaken on epidemiology and the medicalisation of society, the labouring bodies of migrant women, the differences engendered by a feminist approach to ontology and epistemology, the productive disjunctures of art and science, and the matter-ing of a geographical imagination. What has drawn these issues together is a sustained interest in the imagining and making of worlds, endeavours that have never, for me, been simply an issue of top-down policies and territorial designations, nor of a preconfigured 'globalism' within which events occur. Rather, I have sought to tease out the lived experience of government, science, and the arts, as these all help provide a sense of place for people, and as these proceed to offer constraints and opportunities for reimagining that place. As this book makes clear, I hope, this is politics as power; this is politics as world-making; and, it is politics as being of the Earth.

I am grateful for the opportunity to thank my current and former colleagues at the University of Wisconsin-Madison, University of Kentucky, East Carolina University, Aberystwyth University, and the University of Glasgow for their support over the years and for sharing their own interests with me, in particular: Dan Doeppers, Karl Raitz, John Pickles, Leo Zonn, Holly Hapke, Jeff Popke, JD Phillips, Tim Cresswell, Bill Edwards, Mike Woods, Martin Jones, Gareth Hoskins, Carina Fearnley, Laura Jones, Libby Straughan, Dan Sage, Sarah Mills, Pete Adey, Sallie Marston, Mrill Ingram, Harriet Hawkins, Keith Woodward, Jo Sharp, Carl Lavery and Chris Philo. It is a pleasure to acknowledge Linda Peake, who was persuaded to take me on as a fellow editor of *Gender, Place* and *Culture*; editing this journal had a tremendous impact on my own writing, as well as my understanding of what a feminist scholarship could be. The greatest influence on my work, however, has come from my long-standing collaboration with JP Jones. Together, we have written on the history and philosophy of Geography, always with an eye to the strange and the ironic. I have no doubt that my own warped and scrumpled geographical imagination owes a great deal to JP.

The overarching argument of this book, and much of its empirical grounding and conceptual framing, has been specially written. Material from section one, Chapter 3, on 'Flesh on the Move' has appeared in an earlier version in a 2014 article entitled "The Way of the Flesh: Life, Geopolitics and the Weight of the Future" published in *Gender, Place & Culture* (21.2: 136-51). In this book, it has been reintroduced and reworked as a counterpart to section two, Chapter 3, on 'the Becoming of Flesh.' My thoughts on a history of geopolitics in Chapter 2 were initially given structure in the chapter 'Geopolitics and Critical Geopolitics' in *An Introduction to Political Geography: Space, Place and Politics*, by Martin Jones, Rhys Jones, Michael Woods, Mark Whitehead, Deborah Dixon, and Matthew Hannah (Oxon: Routledge, 2015). This material has been updated and extensively recontextualised. My thoughts on TCA's work, and the relevance of Rancière, were first articulated in "Creating the semi-living: on politics, aesthetics and the more-than-human," in *Transactions of the Institute of British Geographers* (2009, 34.4: 411-25); these have been reworked and recontextualised in parts of Chapters 6 and 7. Five paragraphs from Chapter 6, on a geopolitics of touch, which describe the work of Frances Whitehead, have also formed the basis for remarks given at the launch of the American Association of Geographers' (AAG) new journal, *GeoHumanities*, at the AAG annual conference in Chicago in April 2015. These comments were subsequently printed as part of an Editorial in the first issue of that journal. Advice and help with images in this book was very kindly provided by Ellen Endslow, Francesca Pezzola, Frances Whitehead, and Ionat Zurr.

Chapter 1
What Can a Feminist Geopolitics Do?

Introducing an Approach

The subject of this book is feminist geopolitics, a field of inquiry that sheds light on the lives of people across the globe, which aims to produce knowledge that helps people improve the condition of their lives, and which also draws attention to how those conditions are shaped by all manner of political, economic, cultural and environmental factors. This is a very broad brush opening, and one that I offer cautiously. It does not distinguish feminist geopolitics from other critical fields of inquiry by virtue of its objects of analysis, nor does it direct specific lines of research. In other words, the usual criteria by which we can identify the differences between one field of inquiry and another are absent here. The reason for my caution is that this issue of *difference* is one that feminist scholars have returned to time and again as they work through such thorny philosophical issues as essentialism (that is, difference as a matter of the distinctness and autonomy of objects/events) and transcendentalism (wherein difference emerges from the relations between phenomena), and as they undertake to make a practical difference to people's lives. Eschewing both an originary moment and a narrow substantive focus, feminist inquiry is arguably an approach that feels for the borders of thought and practice. Such a concern for difference – what it is, how it locates people, ideas and practices, and what it implies about these – problematises at the very outset the question of what *is* a feminist geopolitics?

In giving this introductory chapter the title 'What Can a Feminist Geopolitics Do?' what I want to establish is that while it is important to acknowledge how such a mode of inquiry emerged in terms of its identification of forms of oppression and struggle, the conceptual issues that illuminate these, and its articulation of practice, what this emergence reveals, however, is a thoroughly contingent and dynamic field of inquiry that interrogates the conceptual and methodological terrain it stands on, fashioning it anew. This in and of itself is a critical capacity – it is what a feminist analysis can do. Keeping with this critical stance, what, then, can a *feminist geopolitics* do? What can unfold from an engagement of feminist issues, concerns and practices with the geopolitical? How does feminism allow for a reconfiguration of how these two elements, the geo- and the -political, are understood and related? What lines of inquiry can be pursued? What kinds of objects can be located and put into motion? What kinds of relations can be drawn between these? What kinds of practice become valued? And, what is glossed or rendered absent in the process? The aim of this book is to explore these questions, bearing in mind not only the diverse range of feminist thought and practice, but more specifically the work already undertaken by a host of academics writing on a feminist geopolitics. In the next chapter, I go on to outline this body of work.

In this chapter, however, I want to flesh out the chapter title more by drawing attention to the fraught emergence of feminism as a mode of knowing and engaging with the world, but also that of geopolitics. The field of geopolitics is a time and place specific invention. It can be called modern insofar as it emerges amidst: a European rendering of nation and state as two components of an entity (the nation-state) distinguished as much by its holism as by its sovereignty; the rise of industrialism and urbanism, alienation and marginalisation; the rearrangement and resignification of familial and gender relations as productive and reproductive; the far-flung affects of imperialism and the globalisation of markets and labour pools; a pervasive valorisation of the 'West' over and against its purported Others; the bureaucratisation of warfare and the wholesale marking of civilians as targets; and, finally, the compartmentalisation of academia into specialist subjects and expert cohorts, the latter regarded as capable of describing, but also prescribing for, some aspect of the social or natural world. Firmly established by the turn of the twentieth century as the practice of statecraft, geopolitics was at the same time valorised as the study of how and with what effect nation-states compete (in the name of their citizenry) for territory and influence. Geopolitics was both blueprint and framing device for international relations, effectively blurring a distinction between the analytic lens used to study objects and the objects themselves.

There is no doubt that some of those working within geopolitics have regarded themselves as contributing intellectually to a continuing tradition of statecraft, as various international crises are identified, are observed to unfold, and await explanation. Certainly, events such as the fall of the USSR, the 9/11 attacks in the US and an ensuing 'war on terror,' and the re-animation of a Russian nationalism, have prompted calls for a sustained attention to a classical geopolitics that emphasises territorial control over key resources, as well as a rivalry based on nationalistic ideals and imperatives. For Samuel P. Huntington (1993), for example, what the nineteenth century considered the 'clash of race' has become the 'clash of civilisations:' though religious, linguistic and other 'cultural' fault lines may blur the borders of the nation-state, these nevertheless remain the crucial actors on the world stage. Zbigniew Brzezinski (1997) compared territorial conflict to a giant chess game, with Asia as the board. And Robert D. Kaplan's (2012) *The Revenge of Geography* tells us about how the physical parameters of mountains, rivers and heartlands animate past and future conflicts fuelled by fear, self-interest and honour.

Yet, during this same formative period, geopolitics was also to gain a *modernist* dimension, wherein the forms of knowledge that purported to describe international relations were themselves critiqued not only as inadequate but as thoroughly ideological. The works of Pyotr Kropótkin (1902) and Élisée Reclus (1875-94), for example, countered the regressive accounts of human nature, legitimised by a race-based evolutionary theory, that lay at the heart of geopolitics. They proffered instead the notion of a global interdependency made possible by the masses' generosity of spirit, manifest in the work of solidarity in face of oppression, and the fundamental claims of human rights. Such efforts presage a contemporary approach to the field – a 'critical geopolitics' – wherein the fraught relationships between knowledge and power, and between reality and its representation through various modes of expression (popular as well as elite), become viable objects of inquiry in and of themselves. Under the aegis of a critical geopolitics, there have been concerted efforts to reflect upon the *making* of geopolitics as both an academic project and a complex, far-reaching ensemble of discourses and practices, traces and affects, that often exceeds our analytic apprehensions and exertions. As Gearóid Ó Tuathail argued the case, "the conventional symbolic meaning of geopolitics needs to be undone and the term radicalised as geo-politics (with a hyphen), the hyphen opening up the cross cutting of geographical discourse and political discourse to its polyphonic potential" (1994: 229), a potential, he emphasised, that must needs be actualised in a study of the symbol as a psychoanalytic concept as well as a semantic one. For the most part, however, critical analyses have tended to interrogate the discursive architectures of canonical texts, such as academic tomes certainly, but also speeches and policy proclamations, that proffer influential arguments as to the truth of the world. Critical analyses have also sought to undermine the authoritative status of such texts by querying the very notion of an 'origin' to, and subsequent linear development of, the field. Here, other modes of thinking about the geo- and the -political are reprised and, sometimes, legitimised as more progressive and enlightening modes of thinking about a global community.

Alongside a poststructuralism focused on deconstructing the relation between knowledge and power, and a postcolonialism concerned with the epistemic as well as ontological impacts of colonialism and a world-making outside of this, both a feminist political geography, and a feminist International Relations (IR), have helped animate this broad-scale, critical appraisal of geopolitics. And, in Chapter 2, I outline something of their objectives, and mode of interrogation, insofar as these help to contextualise the emergence of a feminist praxis. It is important to observe at the outset, however, that these fields are themselves both a modern invention and a modernist enterprise. That is, they are modern in the sense that they have been forged amidst the political, economic and cultural upheavals noted above, and thus animate a set of concerns that not only speak to some groupings over and against others, but that have been imagined and articulated in response to particular power relations and in light of specific capacities for action. I do not want to pursue an historical geography of Western feminism *per se* in this book: it is illustrative simply to note, for example, that the term *féminisme* was circulated to great effect at the 1892 'feminist' congress in Paris, sponsored in 1892 by the women's group Solidarity. "By 1900," Karen Offen (1998: 128) remarks, "a veritable taxonomy of self-described or imputed feminisms had sprung into being: 'familial feminists,' 'integral feminists,' 'Christian feminists,' 'socialist feminists,' 'radical feminists,' and 'male feminists,' among others." Feminism thus has an historical geography. But also, it must be acknowledged, the criteria by which a particular argument or practice is judged to be feminist are time and place specific.

This modern feminism was very much infused with the universalism and individualism that characterised so much of a Western Enlightenment thought in philosophy and politics, the sciences and the humanities. How these two ideas were understood, articulated and negotiated did differ, however, according to context. Feminism as an Anglo-American social movement, for example, has long been concerned with suffrage, equality in the eyes of the law, the attainment of reproductive rights and responsibilities, and the dissolution of borders that separate people according to gender. While reformist articulations of feminism continue to privilege a corporeal sovereignty that guarantees rights of and over the body, these demands challenge, but do not seek to overthrow, the legal, political and economic apparatus,' from voting to wage-earning, that have permeated, and continue to permeate, not only everyday life in a modernised West, but also those parts of the world where colonialism and neo-colonialism are felt. It would be a mistake to assume, however, that such a liberal formulation need be merely concerned with expanding the range of choices open to women and other oppressed groups. Such calls can be very much predicated on a desire to transform the subject through their acquiring the right to choose, thereby integrating decision-making into the continuing process of self-becoming (see Grosz 2010). In other, revolutionary, articulations, a key concern is indeed the 'system' within which specific forms of exploitation, injustice, marginalisation and violence are enacted and legitimised, however that system may be defined. Such feminisms call out the intersection of gender relations with a host of others, such that the very notion of a gendered subject becomes a relational one.

At the risk of highlighting contrast over commonality, feminism as a European continental movement has dwelt more upon the articulation of womanly differences, particularly around the specific reproductive capacities associated with women's bodies such as 'mothering,' and the notion of liberation as a libidinal, as well as political economic, project. Aware of the politics that underpinned the social coding of different kinds of bodies as superior and inferior, such feminist analyses were nevertheless attentive to the complex, unfolding fleshy materiality to which these significations were attached. For French feminists in the early 1800s, for example, considering a national birth rate that declined more quickly than any other European country, the relationship between sex, sexuality and reproduction was to become an issue alongside that of the 'rights of women' in an unfinished revolution (Moses 1984). In Nordic countries, meanwhile, the emergence of a welfare state helped shape feminist debates on the relationship between women's work in the home and their waged labour outside of it, and the implications of this for a healthy family and citizenry (Von der Fehr et al. 2005). Despite such differing responses to what the 19th century termed 'the woman question,' there nevertheless emerged what Bell and Offen (1983) describe as loose international alliances in the form of overseas conferences and tours, letters, pamphlets, newspapers and telegrams, as well as the circulation of books by celebrated feminist authors from

Mary Wollstonecraft to Camilla Collett, whose words not only helped bring into being a far-reaching community concerned with improving the lives of women, but invoked a 'public sphere' charged with taking such a project seriously for the benefit of society as a whole.

The manner in which such feminist work conceived of a global politics is something I will return to in the next chapter. What I want to emphasise for the moment, however, is that these examples help illuminate the significance of context for understanding the differing priorities undertaken by feminists. And, they help us to understand why it has sometimes been difficult for feminists operating in one context to translate materials from another and to work through them. In recent decades, for example, we can look to the difficult reception afforded the writings of Simone de Beauvoir, Julia Kristeva, Hélène Cixous and Luce Irigaray, with their complex corporeal cartographies, by feminists more used to advocating for women's rights in the form of a sexual indifference (see Chanter 1995). What they also point to, however, is feminism's own *modernist* heritage insofar as it sought to recognise and challenge the conceptual architectures that legitimised gender-based inequalities as either common sense or necessary. One of the key planks of the post revolutionary women's education movement in the US, for example, was the Enlightened contention that while male and female bodies may be differently suited to particular forms of labour (not least of which was nation-building), the mind was nonetheless unsexed: *contra* long-held beliefs as to the feeble-mindedness of the female sex, reason was a property of both men and women and should be cultivated as such (see Baym 1991). The rise of freethinking feminism in mid-nineteenth century Britain, meanwhile, identified the heterosexism of Judeo-Christian Scripture as the "founding text of female subordination – from which flowed all modern laws discriminating against women" (Schwartz 2010: 780). This interrogation of knowledge and power has formed the backbone of an academic feminist inquiry into the twentieth century and beyond.

Whilst not alone in critiquing the association of the modern era with progress and emancipation, as well as such 'core' academic principles as categorisation and objectivity, some forms of a Western feminist critique have sought to link these modes of thought to a 'masculinism,' wherein good sense and reason are denoted as male attributes, whilst their oppositions – particularism, relationality, and subjectivity – have been constituted as the domain of female faculties driven by mere sensibility (see Dixon and Jones 2015). A major area of such feminist research, therefore, has involved charting the ways and means by which this gendering of epistemology took place, and an assessment of its repercussions in terms of the marginalisation of women within and beyond academia (see Rose 1993). Configured as an explicitly political project, one of the key objectives of this line of inquiry is to explore the hitherto unrecognised capacities of women and other marginalised cohorts as a means of constructing knowledges that enable these groups to improve the condition of their lives.

In developing lines of inquiry that are sensitive to the context and situation of subjects, however, feminists have staked larger claims to the challenges and limitations of, as well as opportunities for, knowledge making. Certainly, one of the key conceptual objectives to emerge within feminist thought has been to confront and counter oppressive formulations of difference apparent in, for example, the dialectics of Self and Other that have helped shore up not only an Enlightened reason, but also a raced, classed and heterosexed Anglo-American and European subjectivity. In querying the positioning of 'woman' as the complementary (not to say inferior) form of man, feminists have returned time and again to the question of how to imagine, occupy and narrate a location that is not only outside of this dualism, but exists aside from its critical function as a constitutive outside. For Rosi Braidotti (2008: 13), it is this quest – to articulate a more progressive account of difference around figurations such as "the womanist, the lesbian, the cyborg, the inappropriate(d) other, the nomadic feminist and so on" – that helps to characterise feminist thought, but that also brings it into alignment with critiques from postcolonial and poststructural literatures that do similar kinds of work. The common point of reference, she argues, is that such critiques rework difference from a materialist as well as relational perspective. That is, the figurations posited,

> Express materially embedded cartographies and as such are self-reflexive and not parasitic upon a process of metaphorisation of 'others.' Self-reflexivity is, moreover, not an individual activity, but an interactive process which relies upon a social network of exchanges ... On the creative level, they express the rate of change, transformation and affirmative deconstruction of the power one inhabits. 'Figurations' materially embody stages of metamorphosis of a subject position towards all that the phallogocentric system does *not* want it to become. (ibid., emphasis in original)

Importantly for Braidotti, these figurations are also what she terms 'conceptual *personae*,' by which she means capable of illuminating not only the power relations within which specific subjects are located, and within which they locate themselves, but of expressing how far distant each subject has come from the norms and mores desired by the state, capitalism and a phallogocentric order. As people across the globe experience a neoliberal orthodoxy, she argues, wherein difference becomes a matter of re-entrenched nationalisms allied with a fetishisation of personal responsibility, these figurations become all the more significant as harbingers of possible, alternative futures.

Such a critical enterprise upends the question of what a feminist thought and practice – and by default a feminist geopolitics – *is*, as though these could be defined according to past priorities, or from an adding up of substantive concerns and techniques. By all means influential texts such as Cynthia Enloe's (1989) *Bananas, Beaches and Bases* can be identified that have ushered in self-proclaimed feminist lines of inquiry that focus on the experiences of women. Tendencies within given bodies of work to revolve around concepts such as embodiment, the everyday and so on can also be highlighted; these flesh out our understanding of how 'women' and 'womenly spaces' emerge as gendered within various contexts, from diplomatic circles and relief offices to children's textbooks and popular magazines. In similar vein, methodological stances, such as reflexivity and partial truths, can be discerned; these acknowledge the manner in which research does not so much 'reveal' such objects of analysis as help call them into being. But, these subjects, concepts and stances are by no means specific to feminist work on geopolitics; nor do they exhaust the possibilities of what a feminist geopolitics can be.

For me, it is the materiality that Braidotti (2008) draws attention to that offers a fascinating series of openings in regard to geopolitics. That is, I am interested in the ramifications of such a material-orientated approach for an object of analysis – the body – that, whilst preoccupying geopolitical writers and practitioners since its emergence as a modern-day project, has nonetheless been considered as something to be overcome, transcended even, and put to one side as having been dealt with before the proper work of geopolitics can take place. This matter-ing of the 'geopolitical body' as an object of analysis has emerged in large part from the extension of feminist analyses of embodiment to the role of the state therein. And, what such a line of analysis can do is redraw the body as 'distributed' insofar as the Self is understood as socially situated, for example, while the fleshy corporeality of the body is variously: the target of inscription and enrolment; the site of resistance to the same; the locus of myriad struggles to realise equal access to liberal notions of rights to the body, such that access to the flesh becomes possible as a choice by the Self; and the marker of all manner of politico-ethical systems that contest and rework such liberal accounts.

What I would like to emphasise, however, is that feminist analyses of the matter, affect and meaning of a corporeality are themselves embedded within a broader feminist exploration of materiality, manifest in feminist philosophies and economics, feminist literature and ecologies, and feminist arts theory and practice. Such fields are not usually enrolled as part of a feminist geopolitics insofar as their concerns do not immediately resonate with those signified under the prefix geo- by classical or critical geopolitics. That is, they are not state-centric, nor are they space-centric; though, I would argue, both state and space are implicitly enrolled time and again. Here, state and space are not afforded the status of what Isabelle Stengers (2013) calls a 'major key' around which other permutations must dance. Instead, this is a constellation of work (not limited to academia, and by no means operating *in toto* conceptually or politically) that is concerned (without a fixed conceptual grounding) with differential orderings of and access to life on Earth, and especially the matters of sex, sexuality and reproduction; and, more specifically, with a concern for differential renderings of a corporeal vulnerability and obduracy; and, the articulation of these *alongside* the building of a practice-based ethics.

For me, this attentiveness to the matter of life on Earth, and the myriad workings of power that enable, accrue to, and ensue from life, usefully returns our attention to the biological formulations that helped to underwrite a classical geopolitics. Certainly, Geography's turn of the twentieth century's politicians, as Richard Peet (1985) amongst many others points out, sought to ground their work as scientific via reference to prevailing evolutionary ideas on both race and conflict, thereby helping to legitimate the conquest of some societies by others. And, a systematising explanation for the relations between such groupings, and their relation in turn with the environment, was proffered under what came to be called social Darwinism. Here, human bodies were simultaneously part of an all-encompassing Nature, and *malleable*, such that they could rise above Nature's ordainments. Geography's grand strategists were obsessed with the 'upwelling' of a primordial flesh and the need for its containment. At home and abroad the flesh was to be quelled via a combination of reasoned discourse and industriousness, the *cordon sanitaire* and purification, and the development of military rules of engagement alongside the use of armaments (such as the Dum Dum bullet and aerial bombardment) that were blunt enough to 'shock' especially unruly flesh into quiescence.

Such a marking of the unruly potential of bodies must also, I want to insist, be traced back further as part and parcel of the 'founding' ways of knowing the world that animated classical geopolitics. It must be traced back to the burning of carnal bodies in the witch hunts that cauterised Christian Europe, and a middle-class dismissal of feeble minds in feeble bodies in the eighteenth century, manifest in the denotation of inferior physiognomies and sensibilities, as well as the reasoned triumph of human understanding over the visceral. All of these fleshy geographies and more can be invoked in a discussion of the emergence of Westphalian state ideals, the gathering pace of colonialism and imperialism, the taxonomic renderings of a Natural History, the rapid prototyping of capitalism, and the fast-paced topologies of globalisation. Indeed, it has been argued by Barbara Hooper (2008) that the metaphysical foundations of the *polis* – classical foundations taken time and again to be both originary and globally relevant – are predicated on what she calls a parting of reason from the flesh.

The 'Earthliness' underpinning feminist materialism eschews the evolutionary biology and environmental determinism that helped underwrite classical geopolitics – one may well remember Ellen Churchill Semple's (1911: 1) hymnist observation that "Man is a product of the Earth's surface ... dust of her dust" – but does not devolve bodies so easily into social materials. That is, there is an attentiveness to the social construction of biological and environmental knowledges, certainly, but also an acknowledgement of the anthropocentrism (a 'for me-ness') that underpins ontologies predicated upon sharp-edged taxonomies and the ready substitutability of matter within these. Of course, there is a vulnerability associated with the taking on board of a term – Earthliness – that has been used as a signifier for the inferiority of various cohorts over the centuries (Federici 2004). The implication time and again has been that such cohorts have not risen above the flesh when compared with others, and so are not capable of entering into a politic community (Longhurst 2001). What is more, in recent years it is often in defence of 'life on earth' – a 'Mother Earth,' one might say – that various state efforts have targeted poor farming communities as disposed through ignorance to harm the environment via their land use. For me, however, the term invokes a sustained body of feminist work that is concerned with the import of both Biology and Environmental Science, but which takes both under critical consideration according to how and with what import such knowledges are, and can be, put to use. With regard to this latter point, I would add that such work is open to the notion of experimentation with the unknown underwriting the natural sciences, but also the specialised experimentations of philosophy and the arts.

What an emphasis upon an Earthliness also allows for, however, is renewed attentiveness to the geo- in geopolitics. Feminism has obvious implications for how the -politics part of this term is to be problematised and reconfigured with an eye to exclusions, othering and the possibilities and violences of sameness. Politics can no longer be conceived of as a mere constitutional or institutional edifice; it is a matter of deeply felt power relations. And in this vein feminist thought very much resonates with a critical geopolitics. The simplistic and deterministic accounts of the physical landscape manifest in the work of Semple and others have been disavowed by generations of geographers, while the topographic accounts of international rivalries put forth by geopolitical writers such as Huntington and Kaplan have been criticised as dismissive of the complex social geographies that underpin international relations and events. What a critical geopolitics has usefully acknowledged instead is the making and unmaking of social bodies, and the making corporeal of gender, as well as race and class. Indeed, a critical geopolitics has arguably become a matter of inquiring into socio-spatial relations, in the form of encounters, conjunctions, engagements, negotiations, resonances and congruencies, as they become manifest in the making and unmaking of borders, boundaries, territories, terrains, and volumes. But, what of the geo- here?

A feminist materialism presses upon this issue of the geo- and, in so doing, offer new possibilities for how it can be brought into conjunction with such a power-laden -politics. That is, the geo- here is not a matter of the inscription of gender upon an otherwise passive flesh, nor is it the cumulative impact of environmental *effects* upon bodies. Instead, a feminist material approach, as articulated by Braidotti (2008) for example, asks questions of the body as existing in and for itself, as well as part and parcel of a web of relations that stretch well beyond the social realm. Such an approach recognises the movement within social theory more broadly to reassert the body as pertaining to the action of knowing, as well as being an object of knowing. Indeed, it is with this context in mind that a feminist materialism is, on the one hand, concerned to establish the conceptual thresholds of such a body-aware social theory, and, on the other hand, to set in motion a feminist articulation of the same. At the risk of over-simplifying, what is at issue here is a social theory that, when it universalises an imaginary body schema, must needs locate the same as 'surficial.' A universal body schema can only be understood as enrolling difference when it is *inscribed upon* by socially-derived laws, moralities, norms and expectations, or when the body *pushes back* against the same (see Cheah 1996). A feminist materialism, by contrast, sees the lived body as always already sexually situated by virtue of a raft of androcentric anatomical imaginaries (medical, psychoanalytic, legal and political) and as an excess to the same. An adequate response to such a situatedness is not to offer a feminist subjectivity as a supplement to a universal schema, nor as a neutralising intervention. An adequate response needs must highlight the work of such imaginaries, explore the materiality of the body in and for itself, and offer new modes of knowledge production that allow space for bodies to stand distant from a phallogocentric order.

There are three important points to be made here concerning such a feminist understanding of bodies. First, an attentiveness to materialism does not thereby indicate a Romanticised, purely 'Natural' being; as Elizabeth Grosz notes in her configuration of 'volatile bodies,' "The body is not opposed to culture, a resistant throw-back to a natural past; it is itself cultural, the cultural product" (1994: 23). The ontological openness of organic processes to cultural intervention, she goes on to argue, must be acknowledged. Such a materialism can hence problematise the knowledges and practices (across academia, and beyond) that locate emotion and affect as belonging to or impacting upon an individual, for example, by offering other imaginaries, such as a co-constitution of corporeal bodies and the environments within which they emerge and transmogrify. Second, in identifying a productive and inclusive series of inter-relationalities within which bodies 'become,' such a materialism does not thereby assume that all components are thus substitutable in the sense that they are equally causal. Quite to the contrary, each is singularly capable of expressing particular capacities for action. Third, and following on from this, such a materialism does not thereby presume that all is subsumed under the domain of a vast inter-relationality, whereby every particle and experience is understood to be thoroughly concerned with the production of body and environment, Self and Other. On the one hand, there is the danger here of affirming the transcendental force of a relationality, as well as a ubiquitous form of vitalism, over and against the singularity of things. On the other hand, such a materialism pays serious attention to its own conceptual thresholds; that is, to the way in which, in describing the work of the world in such detailed fashion, the excess to such labour is configured in anthropocentric terms as very particular forms of absence (such as that which cannot be thought or felt). Indeed, perhaps the key 'lesson' reiterated by a feminist materialism is that we must be wary of the tendency to grant more reach to our imaginaries than they warrant.

Importantly for this reconfiguration of the geo-, all of these de-centering moments draw attention not only to the complex interrelations that continually rework the corporeal geographies of the body, but also other temporalities, such as the evolutionary tempo of species and the deep history, or 'Earth history,' within which all life, as well as the materials that enable and aver this combination, is embedded (Dixon et al., 2012). It can reference the capacity of corporeal bodies to undertake work, for example, a capacity enabled and limited by their interaction with other bodies, some human, most not. And, it can prompt explorations of the plurivitality of the corporeal body, taking into account, for example, the work of inherited DNA, epigenetic influences, microbial viruses and bacteria, neural receptors, kinaesthetic sensitivities and so on, all of which subvert the idea of a sovereign subject in a fleshy container. As Braidotti (2008) observes, all manner of 'earth-others' have been just as much a part of the specular economy of the modern subject as Woman, and the ethnic or racialised Other; and, while it is important to acknowledge how these differences have been rendered as deviant, or 'monstrous,' as well as critical responses to the same, it is nevertheless important to articulate a more progressive account of difference that is materially grounded.

The implications of a feminist material approach are far-reaching, not least in regard to how the planet itself has come to be configured as a geopolitical body. In the more traditional sense of the term geopolitics, there is no doubt that the Earth has become an intense object of concern for nation-states that contribute to a 'global environmental governance.' From the 1980s onwards, for example, we have been witness to: the United Nations (UN) General Assembly signing the Montreal Protocol (1987), which addressed the declining ozone layer; the publication of the Brundtland Commission Report on *Our Common Future* (1987) and the introduction of sustainability; the establishment of the Intercontinental Panel on Climate Change (1988) as an expert monitoring and advisory board on the state of the planet; the UN Conference on Environment and Development (or 'Earth Summit,' 1992) and the associated Framework Convention on Climate Change (1992-1994); and the proliferation of environmental security and resilience rhetorics by policy-making agencies, non-governmental organisations and funding agencies operating with international, national, and subnational territorial remits. Indeed, it is almost impossible at this point to think the system of nation-states as somehow operating outside of a planet-scale ecological context as, on the one hand, climate change, loss of biodiversity and environmental degradation have all become articulated as complex, wicked problems that require cross-border cooperation and, on the other hand, nation-states have taken to articulating their *raison d'être* as essential mediators between an errant Nature and a vulnerable population. From a classical perspective, it is now more urgent than ever to strategise how such global issues are dealt with through foreign policy initiatives, such as contributing (or not) to an environmental diplomacy, as well as domestic policy and practice.

Yet, if we take a feminist materialist approach to heart, then there is much more to be said concerning the making of differentiated geopolitical bodies here. It requires that we pay attention to how a classical geopolitics has helped to develop, visualise and animate a God's-eye view of Earth not only as a game-board upon whose surface events transpire, but as a readily traversable globe, with points A though Z laid out in systematic coordinates. As numerous geographers have pointed out (e.g., Katz 1994), this is a topographic imaginary that very much lends itself to the parcelling of space by both state and capitalism, and a top-down mode of calculation and governance. In critiquing such a modern imaginary it is important, as Gayatri Chakravorty Spivak (2003) argues, not to simply substitute a 'better' one in its place – such as a topological imaginary, for example, that envisions space as a series of folds and twists – but to acknowledge the singularity of those bodies which, in concert, make up that planetary body some call Earth. For Spivak, it is important to keep this 'concert' in mind, despite the attendant pitfalls of an anthropocentrism, because it is a useful prompt to action based on a feeling of connectedness with, and responsibility to, a non-human world.

Spivak's concern for 'planet' over and above 'globe' is a generalisation, to be sure, and is one that speaks loudest as a response to a topographic tradition that emerged in a particular time and space, and an accompanying Society/Nature dualism that needs be queried. It certainly speaks to the continued unfolding of a modern, Western critical geopolitics. Following this train of thought, what such an approach requires is that we understand how an androcentrism has not only externalised an overly profligate Nature, but in doing so has implicated relationships between particular bodies and Nature according to gender and sexuality, as well as class and race, and disavowed others such that a Society/Nature dualism can be upheld. It requires that we acknowledge how bodily capacities for 'managing' environmental crises are differentially valued and put into practice. It requires examining the repertoire of a formal geopolitics, such as borders and sanitation policies, not simply as diplomatic tools, but as ways of understanding and dealing with particular bodies that are understood to be *too* vulnerable to an externalised environment, such that these also become sources of an excess difference. It requires that we track the mobilisation of affects and emotions that, because they emerge as embodied, can further serve to 'naturalise' the order of things, including people, and the power relations within which they are embedded. And, it requires that we attend to the question of what it is about bodies (and the socio-temporalities that adhere to their 'stuff') that allows for the unfolding of social as well as biological processes. All of this, in turn, requires an analytic approach that eschews the modern delineation not only of geopolitics as a form of statecraft, but of the arts and sciences as creative and analytic silos. And, which recognises that the summing up that emerges from such an analysis is not thereby complete, or sufficiently reflective of a complex reality, but is itself contingent upon what has come before and the futurities that this has allowed for.

Feminist Geopolitics/Material States

The aim of this book is to explore what a feminist geopolitics can do. In Chapter 2, *Imagining Feminist Geopolitics*, my intent, therefore, is not to describe the conceptual lineage of a feminist geopolitics as linear and teleological, but rather to gather materials that together help me articulate an answer to this same question. My approach is to take the two parts of a geopolitics – the geo- and the -political – as entry points and interpret them in such a way as to allow me to identify and track particular ways of knowing and doing that work to worry away at the difference-making configurations (or 'imaginaries') that are either posited or glossed by a classical geopolitics; these differences turn time and again on gender and sex, but also other ordered subjectivities such as class, race and species. In keeping with a feminist material approach, what I mean by imaginary in this context is not an ideational account, which would simply reiterate a Cartesian mind/body split, but rather the ways in which bodies are configured as having a particular place not only in relation to other bodies but in the world at large (see Bray and Colebrook 1998). As I go on to argue in Chapter 2, such a materialism emerges in large part as a reaction against a philosophical and political history that has not only rejected the body as the antithesis of a masculinised, classed and raced thought, but has also negated the making of sexual difference in these bodies by assuming an androcentric corporeality. Feminist imaginaries also constitute bodies, of course, but do so with an attentiveness to the differences thereby implied, and their import for particular well-beings.

What I want to undertake in Chapter 2 is a querying of the 'common sense' character of a classical geopolitics, which dictates what is and what is not appropriate to its subject matter, but also the privileging of the state as central to the making of a geopolitics. I do not mean to suggest that the state is thereby unimportant, but rather that its importance does not negate other dimensions of a geopolitical imaginary; nor, one might add, does it stand apart from these. That is, imaginaries that envision politics as emerging from some other guiding principle, for example, or that consider some form of global connection outside of an internationalism predicated on relations between states. In order to flesh this point out, I focus on two examples of a feminist imaginary that help to contextualise a feminist politics of the global. The first emerges from the same modern foment that wracked the Low Countries of Europe and produced the 'foundation' of a classical geopolitics; namely, a Westphalian framing of nation-states, sovereignty, conflict and diplomacy. By contrast, there also emerged an imaginary that centred not on military confrontation, and a balance of power, but on another cartography entirely, that of a reasoned and emotionally sensitive society predicated on companionship and discourse, and populated by denizens whose relations of kinship and affinity extended well beyond that of the liberal model citizen. At first blush, such an imaginary seems to be so tangential as to be inappropriate to such a subject. Yet, this same sense of distance between a Westphalian doctrine and the literary salon of Madelaine de Scudéry tells us a great deal not only about the narrow substantive constraints set around what is considered to be a formal geopolitics, but also how we expect such a geopolitics to be expressed. The second imaginary I focus on emerges during the height of imperialism, when competition between nation-states became configured as a geostrategy animated as much by social Darwinism as a *realpolitik*. I focus on the contemporaneous emergence of another mode of being 'international,' one that often spoke to a prevailing nationalism, to be sure, but which also allowed for a subject identity outside of this. In outlining the objectives and practices of a feminist internationalism, I want to stress efforts to transcend borders in search of a new, more progressive, more peaceful, global identity. It is with these two imaginaries in mind that I go on to outline more recent, feminist articulations of the geo- and the -political, drawing on International Relations and Geography respectively.

Chapter 2 culminates in a discussion of feminist materialism, and an outline of three related points as to the value of such an approach in engaging with geopolitics. I argue, first, that such work queries not only the realism that adheres to geopolitics, but its broader, metaphysical underpinning; that is, a feminist materialism targets a classical, Western framing of a body politics by emphasising how this is constructed, in large part, from imaginaries of sexual difference. Second, in noting how an androcentrism has allowed for and justified the making of entire sections of living beings into subsidiary and disposable bodies, such an approach prompts us to look at the role of the non-human in the proffering of freedom, autonomy and agency as political concepts, and, subsequently, the role of the non-human in a newly forged body politic. And third, whilst acknowledging the singular presences that emerge from material differentiation – a movement that transverses bodies/territories and their interiors/exteriors – a feminist materialism is nonetheless sensitive to the work of a classical geopolitics that seeks to order, smooth, and make sense of difference. Taken together, what these points allow for is, certainly, an acknowledgement of how a classical geopolitics proceeds to demarcate and place people and things, and the relations between them, and the import of this for the production of difference. In similar vein, they highlight the reordering work of a feminist geopolitics. But, what these points also allow for is an attentiveness to how a classical geopolitics, and a feminist geopolitics, are themselves always and already historically and geographically *located*; a term that, in the context of a feminist materialism, refers to an unfolding within particular conditions.

The bulk of the book is an animation of these three points. Using a wide range of empirics and literatures, I frame the following chapters around geopolitical bodies that have become strange or unfamiliar, a process that, to be sure, speaks to the smoothing work of a classical geopolitics. Such bodies – specified here in terms of their capacities and their afterlives – also speak, however, to the conditions that allow for their emergence, conditions that, when made visible, provide a sense of the contingency of such a geopolitics. Importantly, such contingencies are more than mere reminders that things may have been otherwise, and the vested interests that shaped events; they also serve as a reservoir of feelings and phenomena, discourses and objects, that can be displaced and relocated within a feminist geopolitical imaginary.

I begin this project of displacement and relocation in Chapter 3 by looking to disassociated flesh as a form of global life, insofar as its material expressions and the potential capacities and thresholds associated with these are the product of an Earthly evolution. Some flesh are also, arguably, global citizens, insofar as the particular capacities they realise emerge from their extra-corporeal existence under conditions of a complex and dynamic international regulatory environment. Stem cells, for example, are the product of a well-funded, intensive medical research endeavour that seeks out sites of little or no regulation; they undergo an intricate series of mobilities and pauses as they traverse sub- and international orders whilst 'secured' against contamination and leakage; and they are afforded a particular set of rights to preservation insofar as there is the promise of an eventual return to the corporeal body. As a life form, they are subject to intense surveillance procedures, but also exceed any easy classification in commercial, legal or medical terms. They are of the human, yet simultaneously *in*human, insofar as they do not strive to live, to actualise, as part of a bodily collective. How can such a geopolitical body – existing without a corporeal whole – shed light on that key object of inquiry proffered by a classical geopolitics, the border? And, how can such a geopolitical body shed light on one of the enduring mythologies of geopolitics, that of women as mothers of the nation?

In Chapter 4 I delve more deeply into the making of a classical geopolitics using as an entry point the often taken for granted, 'end product' of a militarised international relation: bones. Rather than query the canonical status of key geopolitical texts as a means of decentering its authority, a deconstructive project that has been well carried out elsewhere, I take this hybrid material, at once organic and steeped in dense emotional experiences of trauma and suffering, and expand upon how bones have come to be located and scrutinised as tangible objects of analysis that help make up what is appropriate (and not) to the world of war, conflict and international relations. I acknowledge the emergence of an intimate knowledge of bones that has, to be sure, proceeded alongside warfare, such that it is their particular vulnerabilities that are both targeted from an offensive point of view, and denoted as problematic from a defensive position. And, I go on to note how such knowledges very much helped constitute a burgeoning European Enlightenment that sought to explain the human condition, and the place of human beings within the natural order of things, via the cultivation of centres of collection, calculation and examination. I also emphasise, however, how this knowledge making proceeded alongside the halting, also increasingly mechanised assembling of a knowledge of female bones, particularly as they related to the supernatural and a heterosexual reproduction, such that two sets of anatomical expertise, highly gendered and understood to exist in counterpart to each other, emerged. While male bones remain visible (whether collected or remaining in the ground) as testament to the carnage of warfare, these female bones are afforded a circumscribed afterlife. They are testament to a concerted political, medical and legal effort to successfully reproduce a healthy population, but are yet demarcated as supplemental to the matter of geopolitics.

In Chapter 5 I continue to explore the making of a knowledge of bodies that underpins a classical geopolitics, a knowledge constituted in large part from the abstraction and systemisation of information pertaining to a 'population,' certainly, but also from often emotionally intense encounters between bodies. Indeed, I want to argue that such visceral encounters, often dismissed as peripheral to the real work of geopolitics, have been profoundly significant in shaping knowledge of Self and Other, us and them, over here and over there. Not only do particular encounters mobilise emotions, but these emotions in turn help to mark out what is significant from what is insignificant in the world, and can even serve to 'naturalise' particular forms of response precisely because they are 'felt.' The particular corporealities that I focus on are 'monsters,' a term that has become, on the one hand, a fraught indicator of unrelatable emotions prompted by a visceral encounter with Otherness, and, on the other hand, a well worn trope within popular culture, signifying a pleasurable fear. Where classical monsters were portentous because of their singular materiality, later figures were understood to exhibit a distributed monstrousness, all the more threatening because of their capacity to hide in the midst of crowd. I want to dwell on how these rare and aberrant fleshy/ boney presences are rendered significant as tangible expressions of a normative social body, such as a populace, and a deeply felt *wrongness* that provides insight into what the world *should* look like. Such monstrous forms have become crucial points of reference for a highly conservative, xenophobic, Gothic politics that both posits and fears the irruption of the primitive and the chaotic in the midst of civilisation. To be sure, such a politics has often been undertaken in concert with a social Darwinism – a scientific *cum* popular knowledge acknowledged as a key component of a classical geopolitics – but, what I want to emphasise in this chapter is a much more complex relationship between sense-making, biology, global imaginaries, and nation-building. That is, the Enlightenment proponents of teratology (the systematic study of the monstrous) were also inclined to favour a profligate Nature, as well as a biologically diverse citizenry, both of which could be usefully understood and augmented in the making of a prosperous and progressive nation.

In Chapter 6 I develop what has been so far an ancillary theme, that of an externalised and pathologised Nature, in this wide-ranging discussion of geopolitical bodies made strange. At one level, my intent is to emphasise how a contemporary geopolitics concerned with security continues to: place the Self as immersed in an excessive, profligate environment; problematise those corporealities considered to be more open to its touch, such as the Third World farmer, the climate refugee, and the lax traveller; and valorise hard-edged bodies guided by a gnostic knowing of such a world. In counterpoint to these, I go on to stress how an attentiveness to touch can help animate a feminist geopolitical imaginary that welcomes a material differentiation. Here, I look to the critical politics of art and performance, and the manner in which specific art projects hinge on a generosity of touch that not only acknowledges the presence of what has been termed a 'more-than-human' world outside of our explanatory modes, our intent and our desires, but also an ethical stance in regard to the same. What is more, in their insistence upon the mobilisation of emotive aspects of touch – the feeling of being in touch/out of touch – and how these interconnect with the 'exterior' work of sensation, these artworks raise the question of how a human subjectivity emerges in the midst of, rather than in spite of, such porous, permeable relations. At a broader level, though, I am concerned with the import of such a mode of inquiry for thinking the Earth as a vast and complex geopolitical body, especially in light of an Anthropocene that sees our carbon-centric culture as a geologic force operating alongside that of an evolutionary reproduction.

Chapter 7 is very much a culmination of the proceeding discussions, taking elements from all of the chapters to develop feminist geopolitical figurations – and adding thereby to Braidotti's (2008) conceptual *personae* – that do not fold back into a sameness, nor lurk in the shadows as outliers, but register through their disturbing, even uncanny, form the divergence of all bodies from state, capitalistic and phallogocentric norms. In keeping with a feminist materialism outlined above, such figurations are no mere 'utterances,' or rhetorical schemata. They unfold within particular, material conditions that allow for their legible articulation, as well as their expression as felt states, as tangible and intangible presences, and as political performances that press back against their subsumption within master narratives. In ontological terms, all of these capacities and more help to mark out the material differentialities distributed across geopolitical bodies. But also, as Nancy Fraser (2008) makes clear, such figurations have profoundly practical implications for how bodies affect others, insofar as they help animate a framework of comprehensibility and normality within which bodies operate, effectively opening up or stifling potential becomings. In offering these as part and parcel of what a feminist geopolitics can do, however, I am also concerned to outline more of the context within which such figurations 'make sense;' that is the monstrous landscape that animates these, and across which they traverse and reverberate. Such a ter[r]aformation, I argue, is important not only for grasping how the categorical imperatives of a Westphalian sovereignty and an allied Natural History are called into question, but how we can configure Earthly geographies as a material becoming democratically inclusive of all.

References

Baym, Nina. 1991. Between Enlightenment and Victorian: Toward a Narrative of American Women Writers Writing History, *Critical Inquiry* 18.1: 22-41.
Bell, Susan G. and Offen, Karen M. (eds). 1983. *Women, the Family, and Freedom: 1750-1880*. Stanford, CA: Stanford University Press.
Braidotti, Rosi. 2000. Teratologies. In Buchanan, Ian and Colebrook, Claire (eds) *Deleuze and Feminist Theory*. Edinburgh: Edinburgh University Press, pp. 156-72.
Braidotti, Rosi. 2008. *Metamorphoses: Towards a Materialist Theory of Becoming*. Cambridge: Polity Press.
Bray, Abigail and Claire Colebrook. 1998. The Haunted Flesh: Corporeal Feminism and the Politics of (Dis)embodiment, *Signs* 24.1: 35-67.
Brundtland, Gro Harlem. 1987. *Report of the World Commission on Environment and Development: Our Common Future*. New York: United Nations.
Brzezinski, Zbigniew. 1997. *The Grand Chessboard: American Primacy and its Geostrategic Imperatives*. New York: Basic Books.
Chanter, Tina. 1995. *Ethics of Eros: Irigaray's Re-writing of the Philosophers*. New York: Routledge.
Cheah, Pheng 1996. Mattering, *Diacritics* 26.1: 108-39.

Dixon, Deborah P. and Jones III, John Paul. 2015. Feminist Geographies of Difference, Relation and Construction. In Aitken, Stuart and Valentine, Gill (eds) *Approaches to Human Geography*. London: Sage, pp. 42-56.

Dixon, Deborah, Hawkins, Harriet and Straughan, Elizabeth R. 2012. Of Human Birds and Living Rocks: Remaking Aesthetics for Post-human Worlds, *Dialogues in Human Geography* 2.3: 249-70.

Dixon, Deborah P. and Straughan, Elizabeth R. 2010. Geographies of Touch/Touched by Geography, *Geography Compass* 4.5: 449-59.

Enloe, Cynthia. 1989. *Bananas, Beaches and Bases*. London: Pandora Press.

Federici, Silvia. 2004. *Caliban and the Witch*. Brooklyn, NY: Autonomedia.

Fraser, Nancy. 2008. Abnormal Justice, *Critical Inquiry* 34.3: 393-422.

Grosz, Elizabeth. 1994. *Volatile Bodies: Toward a Corporeal Feminism*. Indianapolis, IN: Indiana University Press.

Grosz, Elizabeth 2010. Feminism, Materialism, and Freedom. In Coole, Diane and Frost, Samantha (eds) *New Materialisms: Ontology, Agency, and Politics*. Durham, NC and London: Duke University Press, pp. 139-57.

Grosz, Elizabeth. 2011. *Becoming Undone: Darwinian Reflections on Life, Politics, and Art*. Durham, NC: Duke University Press.

Hooper, Barbara. 2008. Dialegesthai: towards a Posttranscendent Politics – or, Let's Talk about Bodies, *Environment and Planning A* 40.9: 2562-77.

Huntington, Samuel P. 1993. The Clash of Civilizations? *Foreign Affairs* 72.3: 22-49.

Kaplan, Robert D. 2012. *The Revenge of Geography: What the Map Tells Us About Coming Conflicts and the Battle against Fate*. New York: Random House.

Katz, Cindi. 1994. Playing the Field: Questions of Fieldwork in Geography, *The Professional Geographer* 46.1: 67-72.

Kropótkin, Peter. 1902. *Mutual Aid: A Factor of Evolution*. London: William Heinemann.

Longhurst, Robyn. 2001. *Bodies: Exploring Fluid Boundaries*. London: Routledge.

Moses, Claire G. 1984. *French Feminism in the 19th Century*. Albany, NY: SUNY Press.

Offen, Karen. 1988. Defining Feminism: A Comparative Historical Approach, *Signs* 17.1: 119-57.

Peet, Richard. 1985. The Social Origins of Environmental Determinism, *Annals of the Association of American Geographers* 75.3: 309-33.

Rose, Gillian. 1993. *Feminism and Geography: The Limits of Geographical Knowledge*. Minneapolis, MN: University of Minnesota Press.

Reclus, Élisée. 1875-1894. *La nouvelle géographie universelle, la terre et les hommes* (*Universal Geography*). London: Virtue & Co.

Schwartz, Laura. 2010. Freethought, Free Love and Feminism: Secularist Debates on Marriage and Sexual Morality, England c. 1850-1885, *Women's History Review* 19.5: 775-93.

Semple, Ellen Churchill. 1911. *Influences of Geographic Environment, on the Basis of Ratzel's System of Anthropo-geography*. New York: H. Holt.

Spivak, Gayatri C. 2003. *Death of a Discipline*. New York: Columbia University Press.

Stengers, Isabelle. 2013. Introductory Notes on an Ecology of Practices, *Cultural Studies Review* 11.1: 183-96.

Tuathail, Gearóid Ó. 1994. Critical Geopolitics and Development Theory: Intensifying the Dialogue, *Transactions of the Institute of British Geographers* 19.2: 228-33.

Von Der Fehr, Drude, Jonasdottir, Anna and Rosenbeck, Bente. 2005. *Is there a Nordic Feminism?: Nordic Feminist Thought on Culture and Society*. Taylor and Francis ebook.

Chapter 2
Imagining Feminist Geopolitics

Introduction

In setting aside the question of what a feminist geopolitics is, in favour of what a feminist geopolitics can do, there is a challenge in regard to assembling and contextualising the ideas and concerns that shape an exploration of this question without recourse to an essentialising discourse that takes these as definitive. So much of academic debate is articulated along the lines of a 'pinning down' of one approach or another such that an alternative can be launched with sufficiently different premises from what has gone before. A modernist account of knowledge and power, Isabelle Stengers (2010) observes, while sceptical of proffered truths, yet holds to a Platonic disavowal and a 'rising above' of ambiguity or instability, qualities captured, aptly enough, in that problematic citizen of the Greek city state, the sophist. What follows in this chapter, I want to emphasise, is not intended as a reform of classical geopolitics via the positing of a new canon and conceptual lineage that more accurately captures the key dimensions of real world events and situations. Nor is it intended to sum up a feminist geopolitics as one more critical account of the regressive nature of such a geopolitics, though such a critical stance is certainly a large part of what a feminist geopolitics can do. Both of these approaches are problematic for me, insofar as they would exhaust feminist geopolitics as the Other or constitutive outside to a classical geopolitics.

While it must be acknowledged that feminist imaginaries of the geo-, and the -political emerge within the same modern upheavals as a classical geopolitics, and work in large part as a 'response' to the same, or as an 'intervention,' it is important not to thereby understand these imaginaries as forming a mere counterpoint to a modern-day geopolitics. Such an account underplays the wide-ranging context within which such feminist imaginaries emerged, and in particular the ways in which such imaginaries were animated by a series of concerns, and designed to achieve a host of objectives. They did, and continue to do, an immense amount of work in the sense that they guided personal trajectories, expressed all manner of anxieties and hopes, and helped people make sense of an often turbulent world, to name just a few. To be sure, these imaginaries were more often than not disparate, fleeting, suppressed and undervalued, and as such did not tend to display the same centralising tendencies as a classical geopolitics. But, these are limitations only in the sense that they do not add up to a formal, systematic mode of knowing the world predicated on truth.

In accounting for a feminist geopolitics in this chapter, then, my concern is not for a retrieval of past truths that taken together make up a better way of knowing the world, but for the continuing invention of a feminist geopolitics. And, it is with this temporality in mind that I take the two parts of a geopolitics (the geo- and the -political) as entry points and interpret them in such a thoroughly contingent way that they allow me to identify and track particular imaginaries that can be considered feminist in the sense that they worry at the differences that are either posited or glossed by a classical geopolitics; but also because they formulate difference anew. These differences accrue around gender, sex and sexuality, but, as will be shown below, they also speak to other axes of purported difference, such as class, race and even species.

What this approach does, of course, is not only query the essentialist work of a classical geopolitics, which dictates what is and what is not appropriate to its subject matter, but also a relational approach that, recognising the contingency of classical geopolitics, nevertheless takes as its guiding coordinates for analysis the centrality of the state to a notion of global politics. To be sure, one cannot ignore the profound significance of the state, however it has been historically and geographically articulated; the state has an ontological surety that is socially (as well as materially) produced. But, one can also be open to recognising, describing and thinking about approaches that imagined the geo- and -politics in ways that did not take the state for granted: that is, imaginaries that envisioned politics as emerging from some other guiding principle, or that considered some form of global connection outside of an internationalism predicated on relations between states. That there is currently a difficulty in thinking about such imaginaries and their mode of expression as pertaining to geopolitics says a great deal about how our analytic field of vision has progressively become narrowed.

That said, in this chapter I do want to acknowledge how a classical geopolitics as a mode of knowing does rely upon an originary narrative and established core texts that structure a slew of academic courses on international relations, as well as confirm the authoritative role of 'public intellectuals' who proceed to help shape national and international policy. Such a geopolitics was and is underpinned by realism, for example, which assumes an inevitable conflict between individuals and peoples, and which emphasises *realpolitik* as both a fact of life and an admired form of statecraft. Such an acknowledgement is important not because it outlines the repertoire of concepts – namely, geostrategy, environmental determinism and social Darwinism – of a classical geopolitics, a repertoire that a broad-based critical effort, including that by feminist scholars, has sought to de-center. Rather, it is in juxtaposing these over and against contemporaneous feminist work, emerging in much the same social context, that the latter's efforts to query difference can be highlighted. These efforts should not be neatly summed up as performing a contrast to a classical geopolitics, nor are they interventions from the margins; though certainly they have been deployed as a contrast, and they have been marginalised. As I hope to show below, these imaginaries allow for all manner of work to be undertaken. And, one of the things they provide for is a reservoir of concerns, thoughts and practices that can be reappropriated to flesh out what a feminist geopolitics can be.

In what follows, I intimate something of this complex entanglement of ideas and practices – sometimes resonant, sometimes polarised – by sketching out two tumultuous periods and places in the formation of a classical geopolitics, and a feminist geopolitics. The first is denoted time and again as the origin point for an articulation and shared understanding of the state that sits at the heart of a classic geopolitics, namely a Westphalian politics. As Simon Dalby (2010) observes, there remains a prevailing tendency in foreign policy discussions today to view matters through 'Westphalian lenses,' despite the many, contemporary agencies, such as the United Nations, and actions, such as an extra-territorial 'war on terror,' that hollow out the notion of state sovereignty. What I would like to stress, however, is the contemporaneous emergence of a feminist political imaginary from the same modern foment that wracked the Low Countries of Europe. This was a seventeenth century imaginary that centred not on military confrontation, and a balance of power between competing states, but on another cartography entirely, that of a reasoned and emotionally sensitive society predicated on companionship and discourse. What is more, this imaginary brought a scepticism to the Cartesian model of the thoughtful human subject that so neatly meshed with a Westphalian politics, emphasising instead complex relations of kinship and affinity between the knower and the known. At first blush, such an imaginary seems to be so far-fetched from the geopolitical coordinates set out by a Westphalian doctrine that it must needs occupy another, purely fictitious world – Madelaine de Scudéry's land of *Tendre* – with little rooting in the realities of political, economic and religious upheaval. And yet, I want to insist, it is this very same sense of 'distance' that tells us a great deal not only about the substantive constraints set around what we now consider to be appropriately political, but how we consider a politics to be expressed.

My second period ranges from the end of the nineteenth century through World War II, a period often denoted as the height of European imperialism (see Gilmartin and Kofman 2004), but which has also been called *La Belle Époque* of an international feminist movement by such writers as Gisela Bock (2002). It is in the midst of imperialism that some of the key features of a classic geopolitics were to emerge. A fundamental state of competition between nation-states for resources and markets, a geographically-aware foreign policy, an academic sector geared towards the imperial project at home and abroad, the reasoned explanation of military intervention and conquest as the prerogative of the civilised, and a cartography of key sites and zones of conflict, were all proffered as the building blocks of geopolitics. As Rosi Braidotti reminds us, the legitimating tales of nationhood and conquest that helped animate such a geopolitics, "have been constructed over the body of women, as well as within the crucible of imperial and colonial masculinity" (2000: 1062). Again, what I would like to stress, however, is the contemporaneous emergence of another mode of being 'international,' one that often spoke to a prevailing nationalism, to be sure, but that also allowed for a subject identity outside of this. Karen Offen (2014) points out that a great many of the histories of feminism have centred on struggles carried out in a national context. And yet, in recent years there has been increasing recognition of what she calls a transnationalism that picks out the efforts by some to articulate a feminism that transcended borders in search of something better. In similar vein, Verta Taylor and Leila Rupp (2002) rediscover a *fin de siècle* rendering of a transnational identity that is feminist insofar as it dealt with the notion of gender and sex-based difference, but was also feminist by virtue of its enrolment of explicitly emotive expressions. That is, feminist activists worked to stage, "public rituals of reconciliation between women who stood on opposite sides of national conflicts"; formed "intense affective ties across national boundaries"; and, last but not least, drew on "the emotional template of mother love" as a founding edifice for social relations (ibid.: 141).

With this more extensive accounting of feminist imaginaries of a global political geography in mind, I turn in the last section to more recent Anglo-American feminist articulations of the geopolitical, articulations that have substantially impacted my own work. Admittedly a wide-ranging field of inquiry, one can discern many of the same issues and problematics in the feminist analyses of the past few decades as were apparent not only at the turn of the twentieth century, but in the Parisian salons of the 1600s. An emphasis on the ways in which territorial rivalries, family structures, and the negotiation of sexuality, for example, all intersect, featured in the philosophy of Madelaine de Scudéry, and very much remains pertinent to feminist efforts to understand the differential power relations within which subjects are embedded. One might also note that shared conversation and dialogue, as opposed to an explanation of truth, remain key components of a feminist analysis. Similarly, the tensions between activism at the national level, and the forging of a global awareness and ethics of care, are just as much a preoccupation of twenty-first century feminist scholars as they were in the nineteenth century. And, the transformative politics that early transnational feminists advocated – a politics that offered meagre space to postcolonial calls for justice – are arguably echoed by current concerns that a feminist praxis of 'becoming' glosses the different levels of trauma that accrue from a colonial history, and the lived memory of this. Indeed, what I hope will become apparent over the course of this chapter is how a making intimate of geopolitics as both thought and practice, unto the fleshiness of the body and the interiority of the psyche, as well as an inventiveness in the means of articulating such an intimacy, emerge time and again not only as contrasts with classical geopolitics, but as modes of knowing and practice that helped people make sense of the world they lived in, and to imagine the world they wanted to live in.

Imagining the Politics of the State

Westphalian States

As Jan Nijman (2007) writes, the Treaty of Westphalia (1648) has long been hailed as inaugurating a new, European political order predicated upon the notion of a sovereign state governing a given population and territory independently of other states, in concert with the promotion of an economic protectionism and public credit. To be sure, the treaty marked a profound moment in European politics insofar as the rights to govern territory were redistributed. At the outset of the sixteenth century, the Low Countries were the inherited territories of the Holy Roman Emperor Charles V (Carlos I of Spain), whose domains extended across Western, Central, and Southern Europe, as well as the new Spanish colonies in America. Maritime, cosmopolitan cities such as Antwerp had gained tremendously from the burgeoning transatlantic sugar trade, housing refiners from Italy and Germany, as well as the pepper trade. And, profits here enabled the growth of a financial sector that loaned money across Europe, particularly to the English government, such that these cities became central to the entire international economy. As Pepijn Brandon (2007: 116) remarks, though, "The relative openness of Dutch society, its urbanisation and its strategic position at a nodal point in the European exchange of both material goods and ideas, made it exceptionally susceptible to the spread of Reformation ideologies." Anabaptist and Calvinist protests were to periodically erupt through to the 1560s amongst urban artisans, small traders, and fishermen, who provided support to members of the nobility, such as William of Orange, in rebellion against the Spanish Crown. Many of these Reformist protestors were women.

Six of the northern provinces of the Netherlands signed the Union of Utrecht in 1579, in which they promised to support each other in the face of the Spanish, and the Act of Abjuration in 1581, which declared their independence from Spain. With the sacking of Antwerp in 1576 by a Spanish army, and an enforced clearing of the city of 'undesirable' elements over a two year period, a commercial dominance shifted northward to Amsterdam. Indeed, Amsterdam became the main clearing house for trade between the Baltic and the Mediterranean, and between Europe and Asia. Here, as Nijman (2007) writes, "it was hard to distinguish between local merchants, the city's burgomasters, and the members of the embryonic parliament in The Hague." Its republicanism, he adds, preceded, "the treaty of Westphalia that is often seen as the moment of the institutionalization of the state across Western Europe" (1997: 97).

The Treaty of Westphalia, signed in 1648 under the direction of France's Cardinal Mazarin, ended this sustained conflict between the Empire and what was to become the Dutch Republic by formally recognising the latter's independence. Key, then, to the 'Westphalian doctrine' was respect for the territorial integrity, and independence from interference, of European states. In effect, the doctrine proffered the state as the principal actor in international relations and, moreover, marked each state as equal in regard to these legal criteria. In the nineteenth century, this valorisation of the state as a recognised entity amongst other states was considerably enhanced via reference to nationalism, by which was meant a populace united by culture, particularly religion and language. The 'nation-state' became the ideal mapping of a homogenous populace onto a sovereign state and territory, and vice versa. Events in Westphalia also ushered in, however, a particular understanding of how states should apprehend and respond to these new international relations via international diplomacy, or 'statecraft.' This was an understanding, moreover, that emphasised a visual rendering of states as laid out across a map, and whose contours could be overlain by military advances.

In the decades following the 'Peace of Westphalia,' universalism (a doctrine that advocated the reconciliation of diverse populations under Christianity) was countered by the idea of a necessary 'balance of power.' Here, it was assumed that, whilst states were in a state of competition with each other, it was in the interest of each that no one state should have the capacity to overwhelm all others. As such, each state needed to consider its place amongst this new community, and negotiate allegiances such that potential threats from opposing 'power blocs' were curtailed. Formally recognised in the Treaty of Utrecht (1713), which ended the Spanish War of Succession, the balance of power became an axiom of diplomatic strategy, and a reference for military coalitions throughout the nineteenth century. Cartographic renderings of these shifting 'power blocs' emphasised the vulnerability of contiguous borders and coastlines, the strategic importance of key towns, and the utility of transport networks for troop movements. In France especially, which Cristine Petto (2007) calls the 'King of Cartography,' with Paris the undisputed centre of the commercial map trade, a number of stylistic conventions were to become 'authorial' modes of representing a governed territory. Panoramic vistas that immersed the viewer in a scene were replaced by vertical bird's-eye views; topographic features were picked out by shading, hachuring, and (eventually) contour lines; and signs, letters, and numbers were used to identify especially significant details.

As early as the mid-sixteenth century, Henry II (King of France 1547-1559) had sought to instrumentalise cartography as a military tool at home and abroad, an impetus continued by Henry IV's (reigning 1589-1610) corps of engineers. Under Louis XIII (1610-1643), an atlas of 58 maps of the Western Mediterranean was produced, and used to help plan for the 1629 war of the Mantuan Succession, which saw France compete with the Habsburg Empire for control of Northern Italy. By the reign of Louis XIV (1643-1715), map-making was firmly aligned with state colonial and military interests, with a sustained mapping project developed by the *Académie des Sciences* (est. 1666) predicated on astronomical observations (to construct accurate topographical surveys) and a French prime meridian that ran through Paris. An early product of this project – the *Carte de France Corrigée* 1693, by Jean Picard and Phillipe de la Hire – redrew France's coastline (Figure 2.1). And yet, there was to emerge from the same foment as had the Westphalian doctrine another French cartographic rendering, one that, utopic in form, was predicated on a vision of society as an ensemble of amiable relations nurtured and maintained by scientific curiosity and mutual respect, allied with a concern for the vitality of the non-human. It is towards this other rendering of a politics that I now turn.

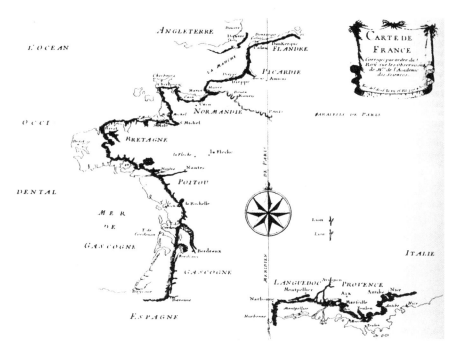

Figure 2.1 *Carte de France Corrigée* **1693, by Jean Picard and Phillipe de la Hire**

Source: http://fr.wikipedia.org/wiki/Carte_de_Cassini#mediaviewer/File:France_cotes_academie.png.

Le Pays de Tendre

It is only very recently, and then only within literary studies and the legal humanities, that the political imaginary advanced by writers such as Madeleine de Scudéry (1607-1701) has been taken seriously as such. This despite the fact that in her day Scudéry was the most popular novelist in France; moreover, her novels were read in instalments across Europe, and translated by her admirers into English, German, Italian, and Arabic (Donawerth and Strongson 2004). Scudéry was the most celebrated of *les precieuses*, what Peter Goodrich (1997: 1) calls, "a short-lived radical movement of separatist women who endeavoured to found and govern an oppositional feminine public sphere within the patristic autarchy of the civil society of their time." In the midst of an absolutist French state, and expounded in the Enlightenment venue of the literary salon, he continues, these aristocrat women envisioned a social edifice founded on sentiment and friendship, administered by women, and enacted through aesthetic tropes such as the love letter.

Arriving in Paris in 1637, Scudéry established her own salon – the *Société du samedi* – that brought together men and women in the discussion of the new philosophies such as Cartesianism, and in the invention and playing of literary games. As Joan DeJean (1991) observes, Scudéry was very much a product of the wealthy Parisian court, insofar as she had access to and time enough to engage with these philosophies. But she was also a revolutionary sympathiser, whose novels did much to romanticise the female leaders, or 'Amazons,' such as the Duchesse de Montpensier, of *La Fronde*, the civil wars that shook France between 1648 and 1653. While the authority of the Emperor was to be finally thwarted in the Low Countries, in France King Louis XIV was to emerge triumphant from his struggle against rebellious nobles acting in concert with cities and towns eager to retain some degree of autonomy.

The clearest demonstration of Scudéry's support for *La Fronde* was the dedication of her romance novel *Artamène, ou, Le Grand Cyrus* (published in ten volumes over the course of the conflict) to the *frondreuse* the Duchesse de Longueville. The book itself is also important, DeJean argues, not so much because the novel as a literary form was a female invention, nor even because it could be used to convey feminist sentiments, but because its means of expression were radically political. The aestheticisation of power it allowed for, wherein the mythic narrative that lay at the heart of the novel was understood to mirror real world protagonists, both contributed to and helped to shape broad-scale debates not only on the rights and wrongs of *La Fronde* itself, but a host of other tensions, such as the contested nature of marriage, and the affective bond of the nuclear family. Within the pages of the novel, these were to intersect time and again. The mode of expression used by Scudéry, then, was very much a part of her politics: despite the varying mediums deployed, DeJean notes, "Activity in the public domain of court politics and activity in the more private literary sphere can ultimately be seen as functionally equivalent" (1991: 6).

It was the King's eventual triumph, according to DeJean, that persuaded Scudéry that power must be exercised through conversation, and its attendant tropes and subjective dispositions, rather than military might. At the close of the conflict in 1654, six years after the signing of the Treaty of Westphalia, Scudéry published the first part of her novel *Clélie*, which contained within it a map of *Le Pays de Tendre* (Figure 2.2). Intended as an allegorical depiction of amiable (as opposed to passionate or sexual) relations that enabled her own salon to work, the map depicted a landscape that centred on her heart, and provided a means of navigating towards this. As Gloria Feman Orenstein describes it,

> Each pretendant, male or female, would begin the journey to Tendre at New Friendship (Nouvelle Amitie), located at the southern mid-point of the map, and then could follow one of three routes first traveling north towards Tendre. One might follow the route of Esteem, and arrive in Tendre-Sur-Estime or the route of Recognition, and arrive at Tendre-Sur-Reconnaissance, or the route of Inclination, and arrive at Tendre-sur-Inclination. Each of these routes is depicted as a river: Estime, Reconnaissance, and Inclination, so that Mlle. de Scudéry 's heart, or the capitol of her country and the location of her salon was a port to and from which immigrants and emigrants flowed on a constant basis ... A person might choose

the wrong route, an eastern trajectory, for example, and wander into the Lake of Indifference, or into Forgetfulness or Luke Warmth (Tiedeur), or Negligence. On the western side of the map, one might choose more wisely and wander through Submission, Obedience, Sensibility, or Constant Friendship, and find oneself arriving in Tender more rapidly than expected. [Scudéry] ... however, was always the one in charge of the narrative. She was the authorial voice, describing the route that had been followed, thus controlling the nature of the friendship she would bestow on the person who sought to win her heart. (2002: 56)

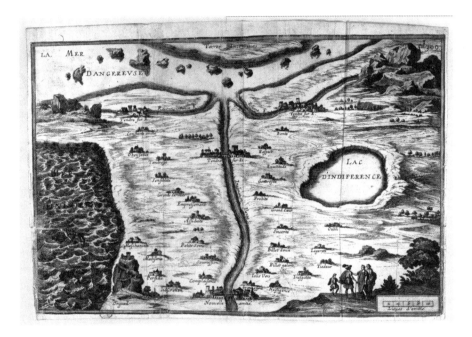

Figure 2.2 *Carte du Pays de Tendre*, **from *Clélie*, 1654**

Source: http://upload.wikimedia.org/wikipedia/commons/6/6b/Carte_du_tendre_300dpi.jpg.

For contemporary admirers of the quick-witted salons, which stood in stark contrast to the arid debating rooms of a university scholasticism, the sociability expressed in these sentiments was a suitably feminine mode of knowledge production, insofar as the softer flesh of the female mind allowed for both the imprint of memory and a subtle imagination (see Daston 1992: 216). As allegory, however, the map had implications for social mobility within France, as her salon offered its bourgeois members a navigable route to its very heart; it operated, Orenstein comments, as, "a kind of training ground for developing an aristocracy of the spirit and the soul – rather than that of an inherited lineage" (2002: 65). Anne Duggan goes further, arguing that Scudéry's mapping was, "an extensive attempt to formulate a utopic model for social and political relations within a salon or state, a model that was to challenge those being proposed by proponents of patriarchy and the absolutist state" (1996: 15). What is more, the amiable relations Scudéry so valued, wherein it is the practicing of a conversation between equals that wins adherents citizenship in *Tendre*, countered the micro-political unit of the patriarchal household that, Duggan observes, was increasingly proffered by an emerging cadre of Natural Historians as a fundamental component of a modern state. In doing so, Scudéry's work and practice spoke to more than the place of women in French society; she formulated concepts and discourse that, "would define the social, political and gender identity of both male and female members of their class or condition" (Duggan 2005: 17).

Consider, for example, Scudéry's comments on glory. In advising what the appropriate conduct of a prince is, she writes,

> the glory of conquerors is only a false glory; because their valour is but a greater kind of injustice... [A prince] never makes war but when tis just, and for the Preservation of the Laws; who knows how to restrain himself in the midst of his Prosperity and when he could carry all, yet contents himself with much less than belongs to him, to spare his Subjects, his Neighbours, and all Europe, from a long and bloody war. (1708: 9-10)

Couched as a matter of moral behaviour, princely duties as recommended by Scudéry are very much at odds with those listed in the now 'iconic' essay *The Prince* by Italian diplomat Niccolò Machiavelli (1532), which describes a politics of what needs to be done, rather than an idealised version of what should be done. Scudéry's comments, however, and regardless of their rationale, were by no means out of place amongst past and contemporary discussions on the nature of rule, as Machiavellianism was condemned in the sixteenth century as a plague upon the body of the Kingdom, and critiqued as unbecoming to an Enlightenment ruler in the seventeenth and eighteenth century. Yet, by the nineteenth century his *realpolitik* was pronounced a pragmatic adaptation to things as they were by such key European players as the Austrian diplomat Prince von Metternich and the Prussian Chancellor Otto von Bismarck. In the absence of appeals to a greater good, the wielding of power via state policy was to be justified solely as a means of buttressing the legitimacy and reach of the state itself which, by this period, had become synonymous with the national interest.

Scudéry's romance novels, as well as her published salon conversations and monologues, frequently touched on the turbulent state of affairs in Europe, narrating these in terms that revolved around a civilised intercourse, as she saw it. But, and importantly for my broader argument on imagining a feminist geopolitics, they also eschewed a prevailing Cartesian separation of the knowing mind from the known world, and the social from the natural; separations that stood at the heart of Enlightenment thinking not so much on the state as on the citizen subjects believed to form its backbone. To a large extent, and somewhat ironically, the very existence of women-led salons in Paris were a consequence of the influence of

Cartesianism. As Erica Harth (1991) observes, the separation of mind and body that Descartes expanded on allowed for the operation of the intellect to be untainted by physical frailties; hence, intellectual discourse could be considered as very much open to women. "Seventeenth-century literature by and about women," she writes, "included variations on the theme, 'the mind has no sex';" indeed, "this phrase became something of a feminist rallying cry" (Harth 1991: 149). Nevertheless, it was precisely Descartes' separation of the living, feeling body from a thinking subject that *salonnieres* such as Scudéry contested. For Harth, Scudéry presents a feminist critique of Descartes' mechanism, as well as Natural Historians' pretensions to a mind-ful objectivity, in her 1688 *Histoire de Deux Cameleons* (*Story of Two Chameleons*). Here, Scudéry writes of her salon's research into and conversations around the gift of two chameleons sent to her in 1672 by the Consul of Alexandria. Contrary to anatomist Claude Perrault's (1669) *Description Anatomique d'un Cameleon* (*Anatomical Description of a Chameleon*), published under the auspices of the exclusively male *Académie des Sciences*, Scudéry's text deploys metaphor to explicate the soul of the animal, as well as her own feelings whilst researching their nature. "The relation between the human and the animal is not that of thinking subject to soulless object," she concluded, "as in Cartesian mechanism, but an empathic one between creatures of Nature" (Hearth 1991: 163).

It is Perrault's observational approach that presages the taxonomic efforts of an international cohort of Enlightenment *savants* who desired to systematise the abundant detail of Nature and, in so doing, establish the unique place of Man over and against such a diversity. Certainly in the context of a French science, Perrault's approach was very much in accord with the collection practices of *Le Jardin du Roi*, established in 1635, and its later incarnation as the National Museum of Natural History; experts here identified themselves as connoisseurs of the natural world and as such, as Emma Spary (2010) notes, suitable advisors to the state on how to manage Nature to the benefit of an increasing population. Meanwhile, though she remained an immensely popular writer in her day, Scudéry was to be ridiculed for her plainness, her spinsterhood, and her views on women's education, whilst her written works were quickly ensconced as part of a fictional, romance genre regarded as having but little relevance to the formal world of politics and statesmanship. Molière's satirical play *Les Précieuses Ridicules*, for example, premiered in Paris in 1659, carried the content and critique of Scudéry's *oeuvre* firmly into the realm of an apolitical aesthetics, as his two female protagonists are mocked for their precocious love of books and conversation, and their disregard of suitable marriage partners. It is no small wonder, perhaps, to find that more recently her mapping of amiable relations has been disparagingly referred to as an "aristocratic diversion" (McDonough 1994: 60), and a cartographic pornography that fetishises the female body (Edney 2008).

Imagining an International Politics

Classical Geopolitics

Both the Westphalian doctrine and a *realpolitik*, introduced above, are realist in the sense that they presume not only the sovereignty of states, and their mutual recognition, but also their intrinsic competition with each other. Whilst there is a very real apprehension of the importance of control over territory here, and a cartographic impulse to map that control, a critical appraisal of the role played by geography in international relations was to be provided by the concept of geopolitics. Though it was the Swedish political scientist and conservative politician Rudolf Kjellén who was to coin the term in the early nineteenth century, there is no doubt that the key ideas pertaining to what we now consider a classical geopolitics emerged from the rapidly developing, systematising world of academia then being institutionalised in the modern universities of Germany, Britain and the US. At these sites of power, a confluence of theoretical analysis, military training and statesmanship was being formulated. Geopolitics was to become constituted from three overlapping strands – geostrategy, environmental determinism, and social Darwinism – each buttressed by reference to academic authority, and put into practice as a matter of state policy.

A sustained acknowledgement, for example, of the crucial role of physical geography in international strategy – a geostrategy – was proposed by Admiral Alfred T. Mahan of the US Navy. Inspired by the naval victories of Britain during the nineteenth century, Mahan, in books such as *The Influence of Sea Power upon History, 1660-1783* (1890), argued that if a post-Civil War United States of America was to achieve its 'manifest destiny' – a term usually associated with an overland, Westward expansion – then strategic control of seaborne commerce in both the Pacific and the Atlantic was required. Wary of possible attack strategies by both the United Kingdom and Japan, Mahan advised that naval bases be built in the Caribbean as well as Hawaii in order to achieve a balance of naval power. To be sure, Mahan's geostrategising was to have a significant impact upon the imperial plans of the US, but also, ironically, that of the UK, Japan and Germany (Evans and Peattie 2012).

For the British government, struggling to hold together a vast Empire by the end of the nineteenth century, the nature and probable site of the threat posed by its competitors was of great interest. According to Halford Mackinder (Reader in Geography at Oxford, Director of the London School of Economics, and co-founder of the Geographical Association), Asia was key. In his 1904 paper to the Royal Geographic Society on 'The Geographical Pivot of History,' Mackinder emphasised that Britain's might as a sea power was potentially on the wane insofar as the land-based powers, and in particular the Russian-ruled 'Heartland,' which stretched from the Himalayas to the Arctic, and from the Volga to the Yangtze, had immense resources and hence capacity for economic development. This capacity, he argued, could feasibly be projected as military might across Europe. In his 1919 book *Democratic Ideals* and *Reality*, Mackinder summed up his argument as,

> Who rules East Europe commands the Heartland;
> who rules the Heartland commands the World-Island;
> who rules the World-Island controls the world. (p. 106)

For Mackinder, a British geostrategy would need to bear in mind the geography of the area, by which he meant its physical landscape (icy waters to the north and mountains and deserts to the south), as well as the presence of transport networks, which, he believed, helped to open up the possibility of invasion.

Though Mackinder's arguments were to have a negligible impact upon British policy of the day, they were afforded a reanimation not only in the German geopolitics of the 1930s and 40s, but also US rhetorics on a balance of power doctrine and interventionism during the same period. Key here was the work of political scientist Nicholas Spykman, Professor of International Relations at Yale University. In *America's Strategy in World Politics* (1942), Spykman argued that a policy of isolationism would leave the US, as an ocean-power, both 'impotent' and open to attack, whilst his *Geography of the Peace* (1944) turned to the balance of power in the Heartland, and the implications for the US of international rivalries here. Contrary to Mackinder, however, Spykman saw the Heartland as very much open to invasion from the sea-powers.

As Neil Smith (1984) observes, also more influential than Mackinder was Isaiah Bowman, Director of the American Geographical Society, President of John Hopkins University, chief territorial adviser to US President Woodrow Wilson at the Paris Peace conference ending World War I, and advisor to the US Department of State during World War II. With a background in Geology, Bowman had, prior to the Paris Conference, been convinced of the causal effect of the physical landscape upon society. Persuaded as to the lack of new frontiers to conquer, however, Bowman had come to the conclusion that a country's future well-being depended upon its control over economic resources and markets (see Smith 1986; 2003). And these, he argued, in *The New World* (1921: v), were accomplished by a policy of interventionism. "Whether we wish to do so or not," he wrote in the introduction, "we are obliged to take hold of the present world situation in one way or another."

In articulating their geostrategies, Mahan, Mackinder, and Spykman eschewed a simple form of environmental determinism, arguing rather that the effects and constraints of physical landscapes upon a state's military might were mitigated by dynamic social geographies of transportation and commerce, but also, importantly for them, a strong leadership, expertise and vitalism of spirit amongst a population. Such a concern for the environmentally embedded nature of populations was pervasive in Anglo-European academia at the turn of the twentieth century, as imperial conquest not only continued to make visible a wide diversity of cultural behaviours and physical characteristics, but also raised tempestuous issues around the longer term impacts of colonialism. The underlying question here was what happened to European bodily types living in non-European habitats? Geographers such as Ellen Churchill Semple, who had studied under Friedrich Ratzel, worried at the possible physical and moral degeneracy of Europeans in such circumstances.

As Richard Peet (1985) explains, Semple, alongside other geographers, sought to ground her analyses as scientific via reference to contemporaneous realist and evolutionary ideas on conflict, thereby helping to legitimate the conquest of some societies by others. Friedrich Ratzel's (1901) organic theory of the state, which strove to advance in the face of intense competition, was to provide an organising conceptual schema for a great deal of this work. As Sarah Danielsson (2009) observes, alongside the geopolitical theorising of von Richtofen, for example, Ratzel's book was to be swiftly translated into genocidal practices by German imperialist forces in Southwest Africa.

"The need to escape from guilt over the destruction of other peoples' lives," Peet argues, "a guilt that survived even in a racialist view of the world, meant that the motivations for actions had to be located in forces beyond human control – 'God,' 'Nature,' or some amalgam of the two" (1985: 311). And, in order to explain the mechanisms by which Nature shaped society, environmental determinists drew upon social Darwinism. That is, within environmental determinism there was the assumption that populations could be considered largely homogeneous by virtue of their racial character and, moreover, that an evolutionary biology could be usefully applied to studies of the reproduction of such groups. This sustained racialisation of humanity can be traced back to numerous antecedents. But, it is in the 1870s that a systematising, academic explanation for the relations between such groupings, and their relation in turn with the environment, is proffered under social Darwinism. The reference to Charles Darwin here ensues not so much from his *Origin of Species* (1860), which described natural selection and species differentiation under conditions of changing environments and limited resources, but from his later two-part book *The Descent of Man,* and *Selection in Relation to Sex* (1882), which addressed the issue of what he called the 'weaker' members of society and their impact upon Mankind as a species. Though Darwin himself advised that the 'strong' members of society manifest their humanity by displaying sympathy for its weaker members, a number of other scholars, such as the sociologist Herbert Spencer who coined the phrase 'survival of the fittest' in his *Progress: Its Law* and *Cause* (1857), lamented the unrealism of this sentiment. Spencer invoked the demographic principles of Thomas Malthus, and the spectre of overpopulation and scarce food resources, to argue that such charity would only exacerbate such problems. The answer for many on the Left as well as the Right to such a looming catastrophe was eugenics.

Social Darwinism was as committed to the idea of humans as naturally competitive as *realpolitik*, and it is no surprise to find that nation-states, as the embodiment and will of their *volk*, as Kjellén (1916) expressed it, were urged to expand their territory at the expense of their weaker neighbours in order to increase their carrying capacity. Whilst *realpolitik* decried a moral imperative, social Darwinism, however, was to be justified via reference to the health and betterment of a racialised populace. As Gearóid Ó Tuathail (2013: xx) notes, an ensuing "social Darwinism on a map," was manifest, for example, in the Nazi *Generalplan Ost* (Master Plan East) of 1940, which anticipated the ethnic cleansing of Central and Eastern Europe, and the 'Germanisation' of those remaining, supplemented by colonisation from good, solid Aryan stock, or *Volksdeutsche*.

In staking so much on the mothers of the next generation, social Darwinism also had, of course, profound repercussions for how women were to be regarded as political subjects. Traditionally conservative accounts of women's place in the home and outside of it, particularly in the context of education, were, as Carol Dyhouse (1976) notes, to become couched in racialised, social Darwinian terms in the late nineteenth century. Where critics of the Parisian, female-led salons had once propounded on the indecorous, even unnatural, nature of women who sought to participate in philosophical discussions, critics from the 1880s onward now also pointed to the detrimental effects of such efforts on the health and progress of the nation, as well as the deleterious impacts of an increased female labour-force working outside of the home. The UK's Interdepartmental Committee on Physical Deterioration Report (1904), for example, written following concerns from the Director General of the Army Medical Services over the lack of physically fit men for the Boer War, firmly tied an imperialist agenda to reproduction. Whilst its authors refused the idea that the British race as a whole was degenerating, they went on to identify the problem as a failure in mothering, evidenced by the decrease in breast-feeding and the raising of children amidst squalid conditions by working class women. For feminists advocating increased support for these impoverished women, such a nation-building imperative became yet one more reason to put in place a state-led welfare. As outlined by Dora B. Montefiore (1904: 555), this would include "every mother, whether married or unmarried," who should be "entitled in every civilised State for fulfilling a State function which conscious motherhood will only fulfil in the future under the State guarantee that the offspring she brings into the world shall be insured, from the moment of its birth, against the uncertainties of existence which obtain under the present economic regime." By 1912, Dr Elizabeth Sloan-Chesser had firmly identified the home as the key site wherein imperialism was borne and nurtured; it was, she wrote, "the cradle of the race" (1912: 54).

In Germany, meanwhile, Kaiser Wilhelm and his wife were widely reported as advocating the four Ks, of *Kinder*, *Küche*, *Kirche* and *Kleider*. What Hitler's Nazi regime brought to the table, according to Elizabeth Harvey (2012), in addition to the notion of mothers as the begetters of the race/nation, and their responsibility for its future vitality, was how women were now to be regarded, "as fellow-fighters in a struggle to redeem and renew the nation. Fascist ideology fetishised the nation and represented it as being threatened by multiple enemies: above all by Bolshevism, also often by Jews, but also by other nationally-specific internal and external agents and influences" (2012: 143). Yet, amidst such purification measures, there were also efforts to foster political relationships that stretched beyond the borders of Germany. In October 1941, for example, the leader of the *Reichsfrauenführerin* convened the *Internationales Frauentreffen* (International Women's Meeting) over five days. As Harvey (2012: 141) describes it, the foreign delegates thus assembled represented women's organizations from 10 different European countries aligned with or occupied by Nazi Germany. Through the succession of lunches and receptions, Italian Fascist inspectresses mingled with leaders of the Dutch and Norwegian Nazi women's organizations, representatives of the welfare organization set up by the wife of the Romanian dictator Ion Antonescu, and officials of long-standing patriotic women's organizations from Bulgaria and Finland. [These were women] ... with whom Germany sought to work to bring about the 'New Order' in Europe.

At once visibly nationalistic in their display of indigenous costumes and other folkloric elements, the meeting nevertheless positioned women as sisters united by their defense of home, family and race. This, its members asserted, was a new model of national-led, cross-border sisterhood, one that supplanted the old-fashioned, liberal feminism that had so far dominated feminist practice.

Feminist Internationalisms

In some ways, the nationalism expressed by the members of the *Internationales Frauentreffen* echoed, rather than departed from, an attentiveness to both national identity, and an underlying presumption of the nation-state as a central form of political organisation, that preoccupied the same older, liberal movement they condemned. That is, for many adherents of this older tradition, the very notion of transcending nationalism via some form of global presencing of women's issues assumed, as Leila Rupp (1997: 225) puts it, "an independent, secure, and perhaps even powerful national existence," while the opportunity to participate itself "depended heavily on the ability to travel, to speak and understand one of the three official languages, and to be accepted as part of the 'international family.'" The fact that key organisational movements such as the International Council of Women (ICW), established in 1888, were predicated on the representation of sovereign, national-level organisations by their delegates meant that a sense of how women's issues were inflected by, and impacted upon, national concerns, was actively nurtured. As Susan Zimmerman (2005: 90) observes, for example,

> the international women's movement contributed to, and in many cases actively promoted, the country-wide organization of women's associations that had hitherto barely existed, promoting a trend of nationalization through internationalization, or inter/nationalization.

This mode of inter/nationalisation was certainly evident in the early years of the feminist movement when women's suffrage at the national level became key. While the first *Congrès International du Droit des Femmes* (International Congress of Women's Rights), convened in Paris to coincide with the 1878 International Exposition, confirmed the beliefs of its members (drawn from France, Switzerland, Italy, Holland, Russia and the United States) that men and women were equal members of the human race, and should be treated as such, it avoided the question of women's right to vote. It was this avoidance of suffrage that prompted Hubertine Auclert to publish a call for equal civic and political rights in 1882 in *La Citoyenne*, using in the process the terms *féminisme* and *féministe* to denote an active campaigning for women's emancipation. Such feminists would encourage and support each other across borders, but the primary focus of activity remained the manner and function of the nation itself. In similar vein, the first quinquennial International Congress of Women, held in Chicago in 1893 to coincide with the World's Columbian and International Exposition, raised the issue of racial discrimination as a fundamental impediment to the realisation of an American nation-state. Denied space at the Chicago World Fair itself to present on the accomplishments of African American people in the making of the Americas, six women went on to address the ICW-sponsored event, arguing that one could not imagine a 'progressive women's' cause without taking the experiences of women of colour into account (see Rief 2004). At the next such meeting in Berlin, in 1904, Rief (2004) notes, invited presenter Mary Church Terrell, speaking in German, exhorted feminists abroad to support the national rights of African American women. "If I could succeed in interesting only a few women outside North America in the struggle of the colored woman of the US," she told her audience, "then my mission would be filled here in Berlin" (cited in Rief 2004: 207-8).

Nevertheless, as Zimmerman (2005) goes on to note, while the ICW did not seriously question the place of the nation-state as a political ideal, it undertook to engage with the tumultuously unfolding world of international relations, a world that included not only political subjects who struggled for recognition within a US federal society riven by racism, but also those who laboured within an ageing Habsburg Empire, and as part of a decolonisation movement. It is these engagements that prompted considerable debate on how (as well as if) to acknowledge entities that did not accord with a national/supranational dichotomy predicated on the sovereignty of the nation-state. And, moreover, that allowed for the imagining of an international feminist subject not only founded on ties other than those of an inter/nationalism, but manifest in avowedly emotive terms. These emotions eschewed the patriotic jingoism of the imperial era, and dwelt instead on a shared suffering and loss in times of conflict, as well as an intimate 'sisterly' bond that both crossed borders and supplanted the micro-politics of the idealised nuclear family.

Certainly, there was scope for such a formulation in the ICW's constitution, which presented the organisation as, "a federation of women of all races, nations, creeds and classes to further the application of the Golden Rule to society, custom and law: Do unto others as ye would they should do unto you." And, at the Paris 1878 conference, a delegate from Poland – then partitioned between Prussia, Austria and the Russian Empire – was recognised. It was only after 1899 that a more *realpolitik* strategy became apparent at the ICW as it struggled to square the claims of feminists from Central Eastern Europe with the representativeness required of its 'Austrian' members; for these, Austria was synonymous with the

Habsburg Empire as a whole. Similar issues were to emerge in regard to the founding of the Australian Commonwealth in 1901, the establishment of Norway in 1905, and the erasure, and reassertion, of Finland's autonomy between 1899 and 1906 (see Zimmerman 2005). All of these events triggered debate on the defining characteristics of the nation-state, as well as the representativeness of a federation built on national delegations; debates that become the particular remit of the ICW's committee on 'Races and Nationalities' formed in 1904 in Berlin.

At the same 1904 ICW event, a new international feminist organisation more closely concerned with suffrage was established, the International Woman Suffrage Alliance (IWSA). Despite its commitment to the making citizens of women, and hence a national-level drive to raise the issue, the IWSA was also, however, undergirded by a commitment to the self-government of nations, regardless of their association with a sovereign, autonomous state. The one stipulation here was that such nations had the power to enfranchise its women as citizens. What this meant, in effect, was that its members could be joined in international sisterhood – what US suffragette leader Carrie Chapman Catt called in 1908 "our world's army" (cited in Rupp 1994: 1576) – outside of the Westphalian parameters that contemporaneous geostrategists such as Mackinder were working within. The notion of sisterhood here, of course, was still open to interpretation. Did the call for women as equal political subjects with men necessarily equate with a recognition of a universal human being-ness?

It has been noted by some that iconic women's rights activist Catt, for example, while she may have decried racism in some contexts, was nevertheless willing to ally women's suffrage with a strengthening of white supremacy if need be in order to gain support (see Munns 1996). For Kevin Amidon (2007), this allusion to race was more than mere *realpolitik*. While noting several trajectories in her speeches and writing, Amidon argues that Catt's work was very much predicated on the prevailing evolutionism of the latter half of the nineteenth century, insofar as feminism was understood by Catt to be a harbinger of a more advanced, civilised mode of being human. For instance, when asked to define what she meant by feminism, Catt replied that this was an evolution, like enlightenment, or democracy (cited in Amidon 2007: 308). Nevertheless, she also adhered to the notion of a biological differentiation within this evolutionary process, a differentiation that was the product of sex and race. It is this emphasis upon a particular racial 'heredity' that allowed Catt to identify and 'explain' degrees of primitivism and civilisation amongst various, racialised cohorts; an explanation that did not diverge in any significant way from that of Ellen Churchill Semple, as noted earlier. What is more, Charlotte Weber (2001) argues, whilst feminist leaders such as Catt sought to expand membership outside of North America and Europe by going 'on tour' and appealing to the shared oppression of women, their exposure to Middle Eastern societies did not prompt them to re-evaluate the relative merits of their own; "ultimately, the belief of Western feminists in the superiority of European culture proved stronger than their belief in 'global sisterhood'" (Weber 2001: 129).

The well publicised horrors of World War I were to disabuse many of the notion that humanity was moving steadily forward to a more civilised state. It is perhaps not surprising, then, to find that the most explicit commitment to the notion of an international (rather than inter/national) feminist subject was to emerge from the International Committee of Women for Permanent Peace (later, the Women's International League for Peace and Freedom, or WILPF). Founded in the midst of conflict, at the Congress of Women at The Hague in 1915, with over 1,300 members from Austria, Belgium, Britain, Canada, Denmark, Germany, Hungary, Italy, Netherlands, Norway, Sweden, and the US, these "women of the world" set themselves the goal of rising "above the present hatred and bloodshed, and however we may differ as to means we declare ourselves united in the great ideals of civilization and progress" (cited in Rupp 1994: 1576; see Figures 2.3 and 2.4). With the close of World War I, at the 1919 Zurich Congress,

> German women denounced the invasion of Belgium, and Allied women spoke out against the blockade of Germany. [Later] When Japan invaded Manchuria in 1931, the Japanese section apologized to their 'Chinese sisters' for their country's actions ... In this way, members validated their identity as internationally minded women. (ibid.: 1590-91)

Figure 2.3   The WILPF Congress, 1915, US section
Source: WILPF.

Figure 2.4 The WILPF Congress, 1915, panellists

Source: WILPF.

On the one hand, this 'rising above' allowed space for the articulation of a new geopolitical identity, one forged on a sisterly love over and against hate, and relations of mutual support and empathy rather than competition. To be sure, such sentiments were largely understood in essentialist terms, insofar as women's biological capacity for reproduction was understood to make them inherently pacifistic. For South African author and anti-War campaigner Olive Schreiner, for example, writing in 1911, women were intimately aware of what she called 'the history of flesh,' by which she meant the physical and emotional trauma that accompanied birth. Men, by contrast, had a destructive propensity for barbarism and violence, often expressed in times of conflict against women. Time and again, Rupp notes, within these movements women identified themselves as '"guardians,' 'nurses & preservers,' 'Mothers of the Human Race,' 'carriers of life,' 'MOTHERS OF THE NATIONS,' 'guardians of the new generations'" (1994: 1583). But, motherhood could also be couched as a socialising task,

> as illustrated by an appeal in 1920 'To the Women of Palestine Who Love Peace.' It called on women as the socializers of children to use their power to help 'their sons and daughters grow up free from religious and racial prejudice, free from all that is dwarfing in the wrong kind of patriotism'. (ibid.)

On the other hand, such a stance made the claims for justice from women from colonised or newly independent parts of the globe difficult to deal with insofar as these were deemed to be 'nationalistic,' a critique that paradoxically overlooked the sovereign status of ICW member's own 'home' countries. The speech of the philanthropist Huda Sha'arawi, for example, who attended the International Woman Suffrage Alliance Congress in Rome in 1923, identified a specifically Egyptian idea of feminism, buttressed by her reading of the Koran, that explicitly linked women's emancipation with the removal of British Rule. For many years a political activist for independence, on returning from the conference she founded the Egyptian Feminist Union (EFU) while continuing to serve on the board of the International Woman Suffrage Alliance (see Badran, 1995). By the 1930s, however, as the situation in Palestine continued to become more tumultuous, Sha'arawi was to become sceptical of the politics posited by such feminist movements, emerging as they did from an imperialistic Anglo Western context, and looked instead to the possibilities afforded by a pan-Arab configuration, manifest most clearly in her helping to found the All Arab Feminist Union in 1945.

The legacy, then, of feminist internationalisms is a complex one, as befits a richly detailed historical geography that this section has only lightly touched upon. Over the past two decades, detailed archival analyses of the work of the ICW and other organising movements have drawn out how such activism was often, to be sure, the prerogative of privilege, racial as well as class-based, such that the feminist subjectivities that emerged were very much shaped by modern European colonialism and anti-colonial struggles. A sense of feminist belonging more often than not proceeded alongside a national identification that was also 'civilised' (Burton 1994; Grimshaw 2001). They have also traced, however, how rhetorics and practices of solidarity, often undertaken at great personal cost, emerged not only in response to particular events, but as part of a long-term commitment to a new form of global citizenship (Hewitt 2001). It is this configuration of a global citizen that marks another form of geopolitical differentiation to that offered by a classical statecraft. Participants in a feminist transnationalism may well have considered themselves as fellow diplomats in a global community of nation-states, even unto the practice of a *realpolitik*; nevertheless, the bonds of sisterhood often eschewed a competitive realism in favour of relations of mutual support and affection.

The Difference a Feminist Geopolitics Makes

Following the defeat of Germany and Japan in World War II, geopolitics, and political geography more broadly, largely fell into disfavour. It was not until the 1970s that the term geopolitics once more came into vogue, though references to a geopolitics as geostrategy were certainly present in the 1950s and 1960s, not only in the US, but also in Francoist Spain, Portugal, and Turkey, and throughout South America. This reanimation of a geostrategy eschewed the biological underpinnings of a classical geopolitics, while retaining the notion of an intrinsic competition between cultures. As Gerry Kearns (2009) points out, once again statesmen and their advisors looked to the power plays of the Great Game, albeit focused this time on Latin America as well as the Heartland. These: were sceptical of international law via the United Nations; concerned with balancing and containing power blocs; debated land versus sea power; located choke points such as oil, gas and mineral production sites; and displayed a willingness for military intervention in the pursuit of national interest.

Whereas at the turn of the twentieth century an imperialist balance of power had been concerned with the control of resources, the capturing of markets, and the projection of military might, the Cold War was, of course, animated as much by a desire to promote particular socio-political systems, such as 'democracy,' over and against others. Whilst exceptional events such as then President Nixon's 1972 diplomatic trip to the People's Republic of China evidenced a *realpolitik* awareness of the need to work within extant conditions, for the most part the Cold War period can, perhaps, be more usefully described as a return to realism. Indeed, Simon Dalby (1991) has referred to this period as 'neorealist' in that a belief in the inevitability of competition and conflict was axiomatic not only within the professional world of statecraft, but also the mainstream academic world of an Anglo-US International Relations (IR). By the 1980s, however, Marxist, poststructural and postcolonial, as well as feminist, approaches were by now just as entrenched within academia. And, numerous scholars in Geography as well as IR were concerned to unpack the assumptions underlying realism, in addition to bringing attention to how and with what effect it underlay various forms of statecraft, from the planning of military operations to their legitimation via the media.

Certainly, feminist analyses of the scope and analytic potential of International Relations (IR) have, according to J. Ann Tickner, worked to decentre realism by bringing back people's specific experiences into the field, and by taking gender, "which embodies relationships of power inequality – as its central category of analysis" (1997: 614). This has required working within a discipline constituted from what Tickner calls, "methodologically conventional IR scholars – whom I define as realists, neorealists, neoliberals, peace researchers, behavioralists, and empiricists committed to data-based methods of testing, rather than with recent critical approaches" (ibid.: 612); and, she adds, one that assumes a community of states rather than people, such that geopolitics occurs above and beyond the corporeal. Nevertheless, a feminist IR critique of realism has called attention to a prevailing and paradoxical tendency to gloss over women's presence in geopolitics, while simultaneously invoking a weak, fragmented and even chaotic feminine subject identity against which the 'man-craft' of statecraft can be valorised. As Anne Sisson Runyan and V. Spike Peterson put it,

> On the one hand, 'woman' has no place in the grand narrative and high politics of anarchical interstate relations. In this reading, she is a 'domesticated' figure whose 'feminine' sensibilities are both at odds with and inconsequential to the harsh 'realities' of the public world of men and states. On the other hand, the patriarchal construction of 'Woman' as madness, the other, the outsider, which

is coterminus with the way realism defines international relations, gives rise to the need to 'tame' and 'domesticate' her – to bring her under control because she can never aspire to having 'reason' herself. (1991: 68-9)

What such a critique can do, of course, is to highlight the differential impact of foreign policy on women's lives: as Robert Keohane (1989: 248) points out, for example, avowedly empirical feminist analyses can reveal how, "women have been victims of patriarchal states and that major aspects of modern international relations – its institutionalisation of warfare and its reinforcement of state sovereignty – have had harmful, and often disastrous, effects on women's lives." For Cynthia Enloe (1993), it is clear that the individuals lumped together under the identity 'womenandchildren' have been rendered passive, and their politics denied relevance. In similar vein, Christine Sylvester observes how,

> Women who deviate from the norms of IR wander the field unnoticed and untheorised – as the Chiquita Bananas of international political economy, the Pochahanteses of diplomatic practice, the companions for warriors on military bases, the Beautiful Souls who weep at the walls of war and then retreat to their proper place elsewhere, or the abstract 'mother countries' that comprise the international system. (1994: 315-16)

But, as all of these authors go on to note, a feminist IR also questions the way in which seemingly neutral concepts disseminated within and by IR, such as territories and borders, sovereignty and security, are rendered in highly masculinised ways, such that they come to denote control, domination, and sameness. Thus for Dalby (1994), for example, it is important to unpack the conceptual baggage that has accrued to these terms, and their long-lasting import, such that, for example,

> If one looks to the genealogy of 'national security,' the highest value of the apparatus of state, it takes one back at least as far as the rationalisations for Leviathan in Thomas Hobbes's writings on such themes. The social contract implicit in his formulation of the rationale for the absolutist state was a clear derogation of responsibility for the provision of security and 'order' to the apparatus of the state in the person of the sovereign in exchange for the liberty of property owners to dispose of their property as they saw fit. The autonomous individuals of the modern state are autonomous only within the constraints of security. And the individuals in these schemes are nearly always men. (1994: 604).

For Dalby, such a critical accounting of the state – a political geography – is a necessary component of a more targeted deconstruction of geopolitics as both a field of inquiry and arena for practical statecraft. And, such an approach has certainly animated a great deal of feminist geographic work on politics, so that Eleonore Kofman, for example, envisions a "global political geography" that, in denying the centrality of a geopolitics undertaken by what she called the "most repressive elements of the state" (1996: 218), is yet able to acknowledge the agency of those against whom the state operates. This is a political geography that, as Jan Kodras (1999) intimates in her critical analysis of the journal *Political Geography*, must needs eschew the political as a capacity endowed by the state, in favour of politics as the realm of power geographies that are identifiable as such because they enrol, demarcate, highlight and obscure all manner of everyday events, objects, emotions and corporeal states that speak to race, sexuality and gender as well as class. This is a political geography that disassembles the state as a monolithic institution, locating it rather, as Alison Mountz (2004), for example, illustrates in her work on refugees, as a set of settled, though often conflicting, interests, and routinised yet adaptive practices, that are enacted by and on people. This is a political geography that recognises the 'small stories' of everyday transformation that, as Fiona Smith (2001) demonstrates in regard to the reunification of Germany in 1990, together constitute the grand narratives of revolution. And, this is a political geography that acknowledges the complex spatialities, material as well as metaphoric, involved in the practice of geopolitics. As Kofman (2008) observes, for example, while women were indeed just as undertheorised in political geography as they were in IR through to the 1980s, what a feminist geographic accounting of the state draws attention to is the work of professionalised women in the formation and maintenance of key sites of power, from agencies such as the CIA to passport offices. For Anna Secor (2001), similarly, lived space matters to the performance of a geopolitics, such that Islamist politics, for example,

> is thus understood to comprise multiple arenas of political behaviour, encompassing not only 'formal' and 'official' modes of political behaviour (such as voting), but also the less formalised politics of women's everyday activities and encounters with Islamism in the city. (2001: 192)

In such a political geography, a classical geopolitics is critiqued for its depopulation of subject matter, but also for an accompanying despatialisation of these same subjects.

Arguably, what holds these global political geographies in tension with each other as 'feminist' is a desire to call out and work against the force relations that operate through fleshy bodies, and that are shaped in turn by those corporealities. As Dixon and Marston (2011) note in their introduction to a themed issue on feminist engagements with the geopolitical in the journal *Gender, Place* and *Culture*, this work exposes,

> the proliferating bodies of geopolitics, not simply as the bearers of socially demarcated borders and boundaries, but as vulnerable corporealities, seeking to negotiate and transform the geopolitics they both animate and inhabit. (2011: 445)

Lorraine Dowler and Joanne Sharp's (2001) call for an avowedly feminist geopolitics, for example, hinges on the way in which it can illuminate all manner of practices – including representation – through which people become enrolled in a geopolitics. Practice, here, is very much taken to mean a (humanly) embodied activity; thus, practice through the medium of the body 'grounds' an otherwise abstract geopolitics. What is more, their body-aware argument intimates, the singular, physical corporealities that adhere to such people, as well as their subjectivities, are usefully considered a complex, dynamic topography, belying any easy notion of gender, race, sexuality and so on as inscribed into a passive flesh. Though they do not reference the work of Elizabeth Grosz (1990) in constructing this argument, her comments are very much to the point here. The body is a target for inscription, she writes, and yet,

> As well as being the site of knowledge-power, the body is ... also the site of resistance, for it exerts a recalcitrance, and always entails the possibility of a counterstrategic reinscription, for it is capable of being self-marked, self-represented in alternative ways. (Grosz 1990: 64)

It is not surprising to find that for Dowler and Sharp it is thus a reflexive ethnography that offers itself as the most 'exciting' methodological approach to be taken by feminists engaging with geopolitics. Certainly, Carolyn Gallaher's (2003) evocative depiction of the global imaginaries produced by one of the US Patriot Movement's militias, which dwells not only on the emotional articulation of these *in situ*, but on the varied anxieties involved in undertaking research, as a feminist scholar, on this group, amply demonstrates the kind of surprising insights that such a methodology can produce.

Gallaher's analysis is not unique insofar as many feminist analyses have tended to worry away at the many different understandings of the global in a geopolitics, noting in the process how the singular conditions of the site in which the researcher is engaged help specify the power relations that are at work, and the ways in which the individuals who variously traverse or occupy such sites experience and embody such relations. As Rebecca Patterson-Markowitz, Elizabeth Oglesby, and Sallie Marston (2012: 86-7) describe the majority of these efforts, feminist geopolitics continues to grapple with an Enlightened, Western ethnocentrism that both helps animate and justify a 'modern-facing' politics and economy. That is, feminist scholars are attentive to the pressures and strains associated with the continuing reconfiguration of societies across the globe, yet eschew the notion that modernisation can thus be posited as 'global' over and against a reified localism. These analyses present,

> ethnographies of groups as they maneuver differential access to resources through agents of state power including bureaucrats and electioneers ... familial, community, and neighborhood organizations ... legal and judicial institutions ... NGOs, non-profits and international organizations ... and the police, military and

security forces... Much of this literature is directed at exposing contemporary forces of neoliberalization that aim to 'modernize' and reconfigure subjects and subjectivities – oftentimes through extreme violence – around more highly regimented work routines, standards-oriented educational curricula, privatized resources previously communally held, and transformed social relations such as native cultural practices, kinship, marriage and childbearing and the complex relations of difference that transect gender in the constitution of these practices. Importantly, the fieldwork that contributes to this scholarship routinely focuses on non-western populations, often rural and involved in conflict or in post-conflict situations.

For Jennifer Hyndman (2007: 36), such an approach is predicated on acknowledging particular problematics, and hence is, "contingent on context, place, and time, rather than a new theory of geopolitics or a new ordering of space." It is also, she emphasises, a *materialist* conception of geopolitics that, though it (rightly) calls out the role of the internationally-active state in both legitimising and obscuring various forms of violence upon the body, nevertheless refuses to view the state as an always central component of the social realm, nor an autonomous one (Hyndman 2004). Feminist analyses can call attention to the situatedness of those who benefit from such state activity, certainly, but can also recognise situated views that may well, "have the potential to subvert dominant geopolitical narratives, actions that might have concrete effects on the lives of people who are players in such events" (2004: 309). The latter, Paul Routledge (2003) suggests, may perhaps be more usefully described as an 'anti-geopolitics.'

What this approach has enabled is a material unpacking of just such an embodied view, such that seemingly neutral concepts such as security are not only acknowledged as having conceptual baggage, but are reconfigured in visceral terms as the generation and experience of violence, terror and anxiety. As Laura Jones and Dan Sage (2010) write, we can thus examine how, for example,

> indeterminate and spontaneous performances of bodily violence and the threat of violence to life across a range of quotidian and exceptional spaces can be directly connected to the ways in which supposedly civil or judicial forms of government organize and command global space. [We can think about] ... how individual bodies and bodily potentialities literally become expressions of geopolitical space and authority at a time when, in the aftermath of 9/11 and the ensuing 'global war on terror,' the dovetailing of grand geopolitical discourse and lived, quotidian geographies of the home, the street, the border, the combat zone, the factory or the prison camp have been drawn into sharp focus, both inside and outside academia. (2010: 316)

And, as Sara Koopman (2011: 277) has demonstrated in her work on actively building, in concert with other bodies, "alternative nonviolent securities" such as "sanctuary" for those often at the sharp end of policies aimed at securing the state, it is possible to work against the authoritative difference implied in this 'inside'/'outside' boundary and forge instead a broad-ranging yet site specific project that she calls an 'alter-geopolitics.' In similar vein, Rachel Pain and Susan Smith (2008) introduce a complex geography of fear that, far from forming a free-floating 'global culture' in a post-9/11 world, is a matter of percept, affect and emotion, and that circulates in and through the everyday experiences of people variously embedded in raced, gendered and classed relations of power, including the researchers themselves. My own research on the experiences of Mexican migrant women working in the North Carolina crab industry attempts to track the changing configuration of flesh, muscle and bone, as body parts are variously used and valued. Observing the connections made between bodies, tools and objects, I detail how the migrant working body is not somehow 'reduced' through labour, but remains eroticised in that its sensual experience always approaches site specific social and cultural boundaries on form and expression (Dixon 2003: 119).

Such work can do many things, not least of which is a querying of the scalar logics that have for so long underpinned geopolitical descriptions of a community of nation-states. In light of this wealth of feminist work, the geo- in geopolitics can no longer be conflated with a 'global-level' series of relations between nation-states that reaches down to touch the lives of people in various ways. Nor can the geo- be read simply as the prerequisite of an elite echelon, whose global imaginaries make up the substance of a geopolitics. But, what such work can also do, I want to emphasise, is query the geo- from another direction. That is, by invoking geopolitics as an assemblage of site-specific practices, grounded through bodies, this approach opens up space for an inquiry into the very nature of those bodies. This is an inquiry that reiterates a number of problematics in feminist thought and practice that have been articulated in philosophical, political, aesthetic, biological and ecological, as well as geographic, terms, and that revolve around the import of sexuated and species-led differences. These problematics are by no means recent phenomena, insofar as Scudéry's seventeenth century critique of Cartesianism, for example, as noted earlier, worked to query an anthropocentrism that denied not the agency of the animal world, understood in a mechanical sense, but a kinship with and a creativity therein that could, in turn, allow for a more caring relation of 'regard' to emerge. Yet, these problematics have arguably been placed to one side as not immediately relevant to discussions of the geo- in geopolitics, which, certainly in geography at least, have, as with much of its critical theory since the 1970s, tended to turn around a socio-spatiality.

To understand the geo- in light of these problematics is to place the matter-ing of the body at the forefront of analysis; or, as Judith Butler (1993: 9) puts it, to begin with the body as, "a notion of matter, not as site or surface, but as a process of materialization that stabilizes over time to produce the effect of boundary, fixity, and surface we call matter." Boundary, fixity, and surface all speak to a material differentiation, albeit actualised in a number of ways. And, it is this issue that has preoccupied a number of feminist philosophers such as Luce Irigaray, Rosi Braidotti and Elizabeth Grosz. To be sure, such work, particularly that of

Irigaray, has been critiqued for bringing back either an environmentalism or a uterine essentialism in discussions of sexual difference. And Butler's (1990: 30) caution over a, "return to biology as the ground of a specific feminine sexuality or meaning," is well worth noting, insofar as anatomy cannot be granted the criterion of an irrefutable truth. In response, one can point to a "rhetorical essentialism" in Irigaray's prose, as Spivak (1993: 17) does, that constructs the category of Woman only to deconstruct it, but one can also note more generally that far from being subsumed by Biology, such work speaks with, as opposed to, for, or even back to, numerous strands in the Biological and Earth Sciences that emphasise uncertainty and complexity in ways that blur the notion of cause-effect relations both propping up and operating across a Nature/Social boundary. There are many things that a feminist materialism can do, but here I want to emphasise the relevance of three related dimensions of this work to a configuration of a feminist geopolitics.

First, such work queries not only the realism that adheres to geopolitics, but its broader, metaphysical underpinning; that is, a feminist materialism targets a classical, Western framing of a body politics by emphasising how this is constructed, in large part, from imaginaries of sexual difference. Rosalyn Diprose (1987), for example, acknowledges, as does Michel Foucault, the importance of Plato's meditations on the making of a reasoned, disciplined (adult male) citizen via a self-discipline that is derived from an active virility obsessed with penetration and the (dis)possession of a libidinal energy. She goes on, however, to note that the 'art of living' that Foucault draws from this example is already disposed to favour particular corporealities and exclude others; specifically,

> the legitimation of modes of subjectivity proceeds through the denigrating re-constitution of others via normative criteria that favour the production of a specific kind of male body... Women, therefore, are not simply excluded from the position of ethical subject. Woman's body, re-constituted as 'other' to authentic identity, provides the ground for an ethic that cannot, in turn, represent her pleasures – a feature of Plato's discourse that is reflected in contemporary social structures. (1987: 101-2)

It is important to point out that such exclusions do not need centre on women's bodies *per se*, but rather on those bodies deemed to be Other in some way from a masculine ideal; all manner of bodies, as Shane Phelan (2007) observes, can thus be 'feminised' in the sense that they come to symbolise difference. It is these imaginaries of the body politic, he writes, that, "express and construct new opportunities and threats to political units, including states, nations, and social movements. The trope of the body structures concerns for (among others) integration, boundaries, power, autonomy, freedom, and order..." (2007: 58). For Diprose (1997), it is not surprising to find that fundamental political concepts such as 'freedom' are thus bound up in considerations of sexuality and desire, insofar as the self-discipline of citizenship is a form of immunisation against the unruly flesh. In Western metaphysics, she writes, freedom is registered as, "the conscious pursuit of projects by a self-contained self" (1997: 278); interpersonal relations, therefore, are predicated on a Self/Other formulation that involves two, often competing, centres of freedom. Desire, because it taints reason, must needs also pose a threat to freedom. It is desire, Diprose concludes, that "reduces one's body and that of the other to flesh" (ibid.).

In similar vein, Moira Gatens (1996), drawing on the work of Spinoza, as read through Deleuze, argues that this framing of Woman as actualising a lack is no mere outcome of a male-dominated philosophy or political theory, but emerges from a deeply felt metaphysical substratum in Western thought that has had, and continues to have, profound impacts on the way we conduct ourselves as political and ethical subjects. "It is important," she writes to, "draw out the connections between the supposed moral and political autonomy of rational man and the supposed autonomy of the political body" (1996: x), particularly insofar as Woman has been granted a tenuous link to the political, understood as a product of masculine reason. This is an androcentric political imaginary, she argues, invoking Luce Irigaray, that is no mere fantasy, but is a matter of images, symbols, metaphors and representations through which we locate and make sense of bodies, including their differentiation. For Irigaray, Gatens argues, the prevailing Western discourse on sexual differentiation is anal, in the sense that it interprets and portrays sexual difference as though there were only one, and that male, and which, moreover, contrasts with a lived, more complex reality. For Irigaray, it is the apprehension of this 'gap' that prompts a feminist contestation. For Gatens, in contrast, there is no lived reality outside of multiple social imaginaries that are dynamic and subject to transformation. Hence, different "aspects of contemporary liberal sociabilities jostle against each other, create paradoxes of all kinds, and present opportunities for change and political action" (ibid.: xi).

Second, in noting how an androcentrism has allowed for and justified the making of entire sections of living beings into subsidiary and disposable bodies, such an approach prompts us to look at the role of the non-human in the proffering of freedom, autonomy and agency as political concepts, and, subsequently, the role of the non-human in a newly forged body politic. As Braidotti (2008) argues, it is important to recognise that the philosophy of difference that allowed a Western humanism to assert a masculine reason as the norm turned on the presumption of a transcendental, spatio-temporal continuum that eschewed the embodied and embedded liberal subject. In bringing the mattering of the body to the fore we must needs pay attention to what she calls the, "empirical foundations of the subject ... which are mostly related to biology, but also include affectivity and especially memory and desire" (2008: 62). Such an immanent subject no longer sits in a purified socio-temporal continuum, but is in a state of always 'becoming' through and amidst territories, resources, locations and forces. There is, Braidotti intimates, a geography to such becomings. As An Yountae (2014) adds, in the context of a human becoming, it would be a mistake, however, to associate this with "the active deployment of agency" to transform a lived experience into "a fertile horizon," or an unqualified, joyful affirmation of multiplicity, for this would fall back into a universalising of the political subject. Specifically, this would deny the particularity of lived experiences, such as the trauma of colonialism, wherein, "Before the sweeping hail of loss, the means of transformation are not sought in assured terms as if one possesses power and control over the reality" (2013: 10-11).

The becoming that both Braidotti and Yountae point to is thoroughly situated; and, is read to a large extent through the geophilosophy of Deleuze and Guattari (1987). What such a becoming can do, as Elizabeth Grosz (2008), in her work on Deleuze and a 'framing of the earth,' demonstrates, is to highlight how a sexuated mode of reproduction not only increases a biological differentiation – it is, she writes, the "very machinery for guaranteeing the endless generation of morphological and genetic variation" (ibid.: 6) – but possesses an excess to this that also proliferates difference. There is, for example, "an 'art' in the natural world," she continues, "from the moment there is sexual selection, from the moment there are two sexes that attract each other's interest and taste through visual, auditory, olfactory, tactile and gustatory sensations" (ibid.: 7). Both the material experimentation of sexual reproduction, and the artistry that exceeds it, cross species, and, she argues, allow for a frame of reference that brings the houses we build and the bowers of birds into alignment. Importantly for Grosz, the implication of this line of argument is that the 'territory' appropriated and claimed by humans and birds cannot thus be simply described as the control over a patch of land exercised by a sovereign entity, but is rather an extension of this material experimentation. Territory is where an artistic body both merges with and distinguishes itself from its environment, such that it is:

> an external synthesis, a bricolage of geographical elements, environmental characteristics, material features, shifted and reorganised fragments from a number of milieus ... that create both an inside, an outside, a passage from the one to the other, and a space that is annexed, outside, contestatory, a resource: a cohesion inside, a domain outside, doorways from one to the other and energy reserves to enable them to reconfigure or reorchestrate themselves. (Grosz 2008: 47)

Though posited by Grosz in relation to the de-centering of a sovereign (human) body, this articulation of territory as a matter of insides and outsides, passages and doorways, has considerable valency in regard to the making of a body politic, insofar as it also depends on a provisional stability of bodies drawn together into a populace, the "congealing of a bloc of space-time, and a rhythm, the emergence of a periodicity (2008: 47). Territory is a 'touching' of the body to the chaos of the universe according to the body's needs and desires, but it is also, Grosz avers, a matter of simultaneous deterritorialisation, "of breaking up systems of enclosure and performance, traversing territory in order to retouch chaos, enabling something mad, asystematic, something of the chaotic outside to restore itself in and through the body..." (2008: 18).

As I have argued elsewhere (Dixon et al. 2012a), and drawing on Irigaray's (1991) thoughts on an elemental genealogy, there is also, of course, the matter of air, rock and water to be considered, not only in regard to a sexual reproduction, but other modes of (asexual) biological differentiation. In Irigaray's discussion of the 'tomb-robbing earthworm,' for example, there is a mutual co-constitution of matter, elements and life that also relies on energy reserves to enable a reconfiguration or reorchestration of each of these. We thus gain something of a sense from both Irigaray and Grosz of the deep 'Earth History' within which all life, as well as the materials that enable and aver this combination, is embedded (Dixon et al. 2012b). There is no easy resolution to the question of what remains of the human here, as various defining characteristics, such as artistry, and associated concepts, such as territory, become redistributed. Nor is there a resolution to the question of what constitutes the *in*human; that is, one might say, matter that is not untouched by human hands and breath, but that is allowed an existence outside of the conceptual confines of a 'becoming.' Nevertheless, what has usefully emerged as a problematic, for the purposes of my argument, is a focus on 'geopower.'

Drawing on Grosz's argument as to the composition and continuing differentiation of life as a movement, Katherine Yusoff (2013) has sought to sketch out the mineralogical dimensions therein, bearing in mind the reach, temporal as well as spatial, and import of a carboniferous capitalism. The inhuman geologic forces that compose Earth's deep time, and the genomic transformations that mark an evolutionary time, become entangled in processes of material differentiation, or 'becoming' to return to that term. As Yusoff's (2012) roundtable with Elizabeth Grosz makes the case, a geopower speaks to this differentiation in a way that highlights how it allows for the possibility of new forms of being, as well as worlds to inhabit. In similar vein, Stephanie Clare (2013: 61) refers to geopower as a productive engagement with matter. She uses as a ground for her argument, however, the work of philosopher and revolutionary writer Frantz Fanon, whose humanism, she argues, recognises how, "resistance emerges not simply in life itself, but in life as it engages with land. Fanon thus figures a distributed form of vitality that recognizes how life exists between the living and the earth." For Clare, concerned to explicate the situatedness of Fanon's argument specifically, but also the importance of situatedness more generally in deploying such a term as geopower, matter is also appropriated, insofar as "[i]t is transformed into territories, such as the territory of the nation-state" (ibid.). Echoing Yountae's (2013) comments, noted earlier, she is keen to stress that while an emphasis on the becoming of life usefully draws attention to how matter is forceful in itself, there are geographies of appropriation to be considered, of colonisation and decolonisation, "that make clear human life's dependency on land and the violence of expropriation" (2013: 62).

Clare's argument brings me to my third and final point on the relevance of a feminist materialism for an expanded configuration of the geo- in geopolitics. That is, whilst acknowledging this material differentiation – a movement that transverses bodies/territories and their interiors/exteriors – there is nevertheless a classical geopolitics, manifest as an ensemble of authoritative, common sense, and practical knowledges, that seeks to order, smooth, and make sense of difference. This smoothing is no mere intransigence in the face of progressive alternatives, however, but is itself predicated on a continual experimentation with life and death. Consider, for example, the emergence and reach of a carbon-based economy and ecology over the last two hundred years. For Dalby (2007), it is clear that we are living amidst what he calls 'Anthropocene geographies,' wherein violent conflict in various parts of the globe is inextricably linked to carboniferous capitalism, such that, for example, it is petroleum from the Gulf that ignites neo-imperialist, strategic interventions here, but which also,

> both fuels the contemporary transformation of the human condition and threatens, when it is turned into air in furnaces and internal combustion engines, to alter the basic composition of the planetary atmosphere which will change in one way or another the conditions of human life. (2007: 111)

He advises against a tendency to read the geo- in geopolitics as a matter of an externalised environment – this is a 'terrestrocentrism' – and for new vocabularies that help us visualise the nature of this Anthropocenic condition, and in particular the flows of materials that cut across borders, bodies, species, and systems. Both an experimental biopolitics (the nurturing of particular forms of life via the exercise of sovereignty, governance and discipline) and necropolitics (the nurturing of particular forms of death), can usefully be brought to bear here. As governmental discussions on climate change increasingly turn to security, Dalby (2013) goes on to argue, in the form of mitigating the threat to the nation-state from migration and conflict over resources, and environmental disasters such as Hurricane Katrina are understood to offer opportunities for a retrenched neoliberalism, new imaginaries that can both illuminate and step outside of this terrestrocentrism become all the more urgent.

The new geopolitical vocabularies that Dalby desires can certainly emerge from a feminist materialism, insofar as figures such as the 'artist,' for example, help to illuminate the inhuman power relations within which specific bodies are located, and within which they locate themselves. This field of inquiry can offer another dimension to Dalby's Anthropocenic geographies, however, in that such figures can express how far distant each is from the norms and mores desired by the state and capitalism, but also a phallogocentric order. Security, to be sure, is a matter of filtering borders such that the interior remains stable, but the corporealities that enact such measures are hard-bodied, technologically enhanced and masculine, whilst their counterpart are the feminised, unruly, fleshy bodies that require control. Moreover, if we take these figures as harbingers of possible, alternative worlds, then the bodies they are manifest through are intense sites of contestation, as a phallogocentric order, alongside the state and capitalism, seeks to diminish this same distance. Such bodies – the inattentive traveller, the climate refugee, the Third World farmer and so on – are pathologised in ways that speak variously to their sexuated differences and reproductive capacities. They can be denoted as overly productive of a material difference, for example, such that this proliferation becomes the threatening outside to the biopolitical taxonomies that order a populace; or, they can be marked as overly bound to an externalised Nature, such that their lives and those they beget are not adaptive enough to allow membership in a new, resilient global citizenry.

These three dimensions of a feminist materialism offer myriad lines of inquiry, prompted by a wide range of problematics. More pointedly, however, they offer a concerted questioning not only of what an object of inquiry indeed is, but of how we understand the knowing subject also. That is, there is an attentiveness here to the import of the conceptual thresholds established though the research process, particularly in regard to what is rendered absent, as well as a sensitivity to the affective capacity of the researcher, and the manner in which power relations shift and recompose as the research unfolds. In the chapters that follow, what I hope emerges is a sense of how this sustained, feminist attention to a key object of analysis for geopolitics – that of the body – allows for particular insights to emerge not as 'interventions,' or 'correctives,' to a classical mode of inquiry, but as part and parcel of a broad-based feminist imaginary of the world and the place of ourselves and others within that. A feminist geopolitics can, certainly, become a means of critiquing practices that reify subjectivities, exploit corporealities, and produce vulnerabilities. But also, it can offer new becomings, premised on a generosity and openness.

References

Amidon, Kevin S. 2007. Carrie Chapman Catt and the Evolutionary Politics of Sex and Race, 1885-1940, *Journal of the History of Ideas* 68.2: 305-28.
Badran, Margot. 1995. *Feminists, Islam and Nation: Gender and the Making of Modern Egypt*. Princeton, NJ: Princeton University Press.
Braidotti, Rosi. 2000. Once Upon a Time in Europe, *Signs* 25.4: 1061-4.
Braidotti, Rosi. 2008. *Metamorphoses: Towards a Materialist Theory of Becoming*. Cambridge: Polity Press.
Brandon, Pepijn. 2011. Marxism and the 'Dutch Miracle': The Dutch Republic and the Transition-Debate, *Historical Materialism* 19.3: 106-46.
Bock, Gisela. 2002. *Women in European History*. Oxford: Blackwell.
Bowman, Isiah. 1921. *The New World: Problems in Political Geography*. Yonkers-on-Hudson, NY: World Book Company.
Burton, Antoinette. 1994. *Burdens of History: British Feminists, Indian Women, and Imperial Culture, 1865-1915*. Chapel Hill, NC: University of North Caroline Press.
Butler, Judith. 1990. *Gender Trouble and the Subversion of Identity*. New York and London: Routledge.

Butler, Judith. 1993. *Bodies that Matter: On the Discoursive Limits of 'Sex'*. New York and London: Routledge.
Chesser, Elizabeth S. 1912. *Perfect Health for Women and Children*. London: Methuen and Co.
Clare, Stephanie. 2013. Geopower: The Politics of Life and Land in Frantz Fanon's Writing, *Diacritics* 41.4: 60-81.
Dalby, Simon. 1991. Critical Geopolitics: Discourse, Difference and Dissent, *Environment* and *Planning D: Society and Space* 9.3: 261-83.
Dalby, Simon. 1994. Gender and Critical Geopolitics: Reading Security Discourse in the New World Disorder, *Environment and Planning D: Society and Space* 12.5: 595-612.
Dalby, Simon. 2007. Anthropocene Geopolitics: Globalisation, Empire, Environment and Critique, *Geography Compass* 1.1: 103-18.
Dalby, Simon. 2010. *Post-Victorian Geopolitics in the Anthropocene?* Paper presented at the GEOPOL2010 conference, Virginia Tech, Alexandria Campus.
Dalby, Simon. 2013. Biopolitics and Climate Security in the Anthropocene, *Geoforum* 49: 184-92.
Danielsson, Sarah K. 2009. Creating Genocidal Space: Geographers and the Discourse of Annihilation, 1880-1933, *Space and Polity* 13.1: 55-68.
Darwin, Charles [1859] 1991. *On the Origin of Species by Means of Natural Selection*. London: Murray.
Darwin, Charles. [1871] 2009. *The Descent of Man, and Selection in Relation to Sex*. London: Murray.
Daston, Lorraine. 1992. The Naturalized Female Intellect, *Science in Context* 5.02: 209-25.
DeJean, Joan E. 1991. *Tender Geographies: Women and the Origins of the Novel in France*. New York: Columbia University Press.
Deleuze, Gilles and Guattari, Félix. 1987. *A Thousand Plateaus: Capitalism and Schizophrenia*. Translated by Massumi, Brian. Minneapolis, MN: University of Minnesota Press.
de Scudéry, Madeleine. 1708. *An Essay upon Glory. Written... by... Mademoiselle de Scudéry ... Done into English by a Person of the Same Sex*. London: J. Morphew.
Diprose, Rosalyn. 1987. The Use of Pleasures in the Constitution of the Body, *Australian Feminist Studies* 2.5: 95-103.
Diprose, Rosalyn. 1997. The Generosity of Feminism, *Australian Feminist Studies* 12.26: 275-82.
Dixon, Deborah. 2003. Working with Crabs. In Cloke, Paul (ed.), *Country Visions*. Harlow: Pearson, pp. 116-35.
Dixon, Deborah and Marston, Sallie. 2011. Introduction: Feminist Engagements with Geopolitics, *Gender, Place and Culture* 18: 445-53.
Dixon, Deborah, Hawkins, Harriet and Straughan, Elizabeth. 2012a. Golem Geographies, *Dialogues in Human Geography* 2.3: 292-5.

Dixon, Deborah, Hawkins, Harriet and Straughan, Elizabeth. 2012b. Of Human Birds and Living Rocks: Remaking Aesthetics for Post-human Worlds, *Dialogues in Human Geography* 2.3: 249-70.
Donawerth, Jane and Strongson, Julie. 2004. The Other Voice. In *Madeleine de Scudery: Selected Letters, Orations and Rhetorical Dialogues*. Edited and translated by Jane Donawerth and Julie Strongson. Chicago, IL: University of Chicago Press, pp. 1-7.
Dowler, Lorraine and Sharp, Joanne. 2001. A Feminist Geopolitics? *Space & Polity* 5.3: 165-76.
Duggan, Anne E. 1996. Lovers, Salon, and State: *La Carte de Tendre* and the Mapping of Socio-Political Relations, *Dalhousie French Studies* 36: 15-22.
Duggan, Anne E. 2005. *Salonnières, Furies, and Fairies: The Politics of Gender* and *Cultural Change in Absolutist France*. Newark, DE: University of Delaware Press.
Dyhouse, Carol. 1976. Social Darwinistic Ideas and the Development of Women's Education in England, 1880-1920, *History of Education* 5.1: 41-58.
Edney, Matthew H. 2008. Mapping Empires, Mapping Bodies: Reflections on the Use and Abuse of Cartography, *Treballs de la Societat Catalana de Geografia* 63: 83-104.
Enloe, Cynthia. 1993. *The Morning After: Sexual Politics at the End of the Cold War*. Berkeley, CA: University of California Press.
Evans, David C. and Peattie, Mark. 2012. *Kaigun: Strategy, Tactics,* and *Technology in the Imperial Japanese Navy, 1887-1941*. Annapolis, MD: Naval Institute Press.
Gallaher, Carolyn. 2003. *On the Fault Line: Race, Class, and the American Patriot Movement*. Lanham, MD: Rowman & Littlefield.
Gatens, Moira. 1996. *Imaginary Bodies: Ethics, Power and Corporeality*. New York: Routldege.
Gilmartin, Mary, and Eleonore Kofman. 2004. Critically Feminist Geopolitics. In Staeheli, Lynn, Kofman, Eleanore and Peak, Linda (eds) *Mapping Women, Making Politics*. London: Routledge, pp. 113-26.
Goodrich, Peter. 1997. Epistolary Justice: The Love Letter as Law, *Yale Journal of Law and the Humanities* 9.2: 245-93.
Grimshaw, Patricia. 2001. Reading the Silences: Suffrage Activists and Race in Nineteenth Century Settler Societies. In Grimshaw, Patricia, Holmes, Katie and Lake, Marliyn (eds) *Women's Rights and Human Rights: International Historical Perspectives*. London: Palgrave, pp. 31-48.
Grosz, Elizabeth A. 1990. Inscriptions and Body-Maps: Representations and the Corporeal. In Threadgold, Terry and Cranny-Francis, Anne (eds) *Feminine, Masculine and Representation*. Sydney: Allen & Unwin, pp. 62-74.
Grosz, Elizabeth A. 2008. *Chaos, Territory, Art: Deleuze and the Framing of the Earth*. New York: Columbia University Press.
Harth, Erica. 1991. Cartesian Women, *Yale French Studies* 80: 146-64.

Harvey, Elizabeth. 2012. International Networks and Cross-Border Cooperation: National Socialist Women and the Vision of a 'New Order' in Europe, *Politics, Religion and Ideology* 13.2: 141-58.
Hewitt, Nancy. 2001. Re-Rooting American Women's Activism: Global Perspectives on 1848. In Grimshaw, Patricia, Holmes, Katie and Lake, Marilyn (eds) *Women's Rights and Human Rights: International Historical Perspectives*. London: Palgrave, pp. 123-37.
Hyndman, Jennifer. 2004. Mind the Gap: Bridging Feminist and Political Geography through Geopolitics, *Political Geography* 23.3: 307-22.
Hyndman, Jennifer. 2007. Feminist Geopolitics Revisited: Body Counts in Iraq, *The Professional Geographer* 59.1: 35-46.
Irigaray, Luce. 1991. *Marine Lover of Friedrich Nietzsche*. Translated by Gill, Gillian C. New York: Columbia University Press.
Jones, Laura and Sage, Daniel. 2010. New Directions in Critical Geopolitics: An Introduction. *GeoJournal* 73: 315-25
Kearns, Gerry. 2009. *Geopolitics and Empire: The Legacy of Halford Mackinder*. Oxford: Oxford University Press.
Kjellén, Rudolf. 1916. *Staten som lifsform [The State as a Form of Life]*. Stockholm: Hugo Gerbers Förlag.
Kodras, Janet E. 1999. Geographies of Power, in *Political Geography*, *Political Geography* 18.1: 75-9.
Kofman, Eleonore. 1996. Feminism, Gender Relations and Geopolitics: Problematic Closures and Opening Strategies. In Kofman, Eleonore and Youngs, Gillian (eds) *Globalization: Theory and Practice*. London: Pinter, pp. 209-24.
Kofman, Eleonore. 2008. *Feminist Transformations of Political Geography*. Los Angeles, CA: Sage.
Koopman, Sara. 2011. Alter-Geopolitics: Other Securities are Happening, *Geoforum* 42.3: 274-84.
Machiavelli, Niccolò [1532] 1975. *The Prince: Transl. with an Introduction by George Bull*. London: Penguin Books.
Mackinder, Halford. 1919. *Democratic Ideals and Reality*. London: H. Holt.
Mahan, Alfred Thayer [1890] 2010. *The Influence of Sea Power upon History 1660-1783*. Vol. 116. BoD – Books on Demand.
McDonough, Thomas F. 1994. Situationist Space, *October* 67: 59-77.
Montefiore, Dora. 1904. *New Age* (1 September): 555-6.
Mountz, Alison. 2004. Embodying the Nation-State: Canada's Response to Human Smuggling, *Political Geography* 23.3: 323-45.
Munns, Roger. 1996. University Honors Suffragette Despite Racism Charge, *Los Angeles Times* 5 May, available at http://articles.latimes.com/1996-05-05/news/mn-677_1_iowa-state. Last accessed 3 December 2014.
Nijman, Jan. 2007, Place-particularity and 'Deep Analogies': A Comparative Essay on Miami's Rise as a World City, *Urban Geography* 28.1: 92-107.

Offen, Karen. 2014. Understanding International Feminisms as 'Transnational' – an Anachronism? May Wright Sewall and the Creation of the International Council of Women, 1889-1904. In Janz, Oliver and Schönpflug, Daniel (eds) *Gender History in a Transnational Perspective: Networks, Biographies, Gender Orders*, pp. 25-45.

Orenstein, Gloria Feman. 2002. Journey through Mlle de Scudéry's *Carte de Tendre*: A 17th-Century Salon Woman's Dream/Country of Tenderness, *FEMSPEC* 2.2: 53-66.

Ó Tuathail, Gearóid. 2013. Arguing about Geopolitics. In Dodds, Klaus, Kuus, Merje and Sharp, Joanne (eds) *The Ashgate Research Companion to Critical Geopolitics*. Farnham: Ashgate, pp. xix-xxi.

Pain, Rachel and Smith, Susan J. (eds) 2008. *Fear: Critical Geopolitics and Everyday Life*. Aldershot: Ashgate.

Patterson-Markowitz, Rebecca A., Marston, Sallie and Oglesby Elizabeth. 2012. *The Gendered Geographies of Justice in Transition: A Feminist Geopolitics Perspective*, available at http://arizona.openrepository.com/arizona/bitstream/10150/244487/1/azu_etd_mr_2012_0138_sip1_m.pdf. Last accessed 3 December 2014.

Petto, Christine M. 2007. *When France was King of Cartography: The Patronage and Production of Maps in Early Modern France*. Lanham, MD: Lexington Books.

Phelan, Shane. 1999. Bodies, Passions and Citizenship, *Critical Review of International Social* and *Political Philosophy* 2.1: 56-79.

Ratzel, Friedrich [1901] 1966. *Der Lebensraum: Eine Biogeographische Studie*. Darmstadt: Reihe Libelli.

Rief, Michelle. 2004. Thinking Locally, Acting Globally: The International Agenda of African American Clubwomen, 1880-1940, *The Journal of African American History* 89.3: 203-22.

Routledge, Paul. 2003. Anti-Geopolitics. In Agnew, John, Mitchell, Katharyne and Ó Tuathail, Gearóid (eds) *A Companion to Political Geography*. Oxford: Blackwell, pp. 236-48.

Runyan, Anne Sisson and V. Spike Peterson. 1991. The Radical Future of Realism: Feminist Subversions of IR Theory, *Alternatives* 16.1: 67-106.

Rupp, Leila J. 1997. *Worlds of Women: The Making of an International Women's Movement*. Princeton, NJ: Princeton University Press.

Rupp, Leila J. 1994. Constructing Internationalism: The Case of Transnational Women's Organizations, 1888-1945, *The American Historical Review* 99.5: 1571-600.

Schreiner, Olive. 1911. *Woman and Labour*. London: Fisher Unwin.

Secor, Anna J. 2001. Toward a Feminist Counter-Geopolitics: Gender, Space and Islamist Politics in Istanbul, *Space and Polity* 5.3: 191-211.

Smith, Fiona M. 2001. Refiguring the Geopolitical Landscape: Nation, 'Transition' and Gendered Subjects in Post-Cold War Germany, *Space and Polity* 5.3: 213-35.

Smith, Neil. 1984. Political Geographers of the Past. Isaiah Bowman: Political Geography and Geopolitics, *Political Geography Quarterly* 3.1: 69-76.

Smith, Neil. 1986. Bowman's New World and the Council on Foreign Relations, *Geographical Review* 76.4: 438-60.

Smith, Neil. 2003. *American Empire: Roosevelt's Geographer and the Prelude to Globalization*. Berkeley, CA: University of California Press.

Spary, Emma C. 2010. *Utopia's Garden: French Natural History from Old Regime to Revolution*. Chicago, IL: University of Chicago Press.

Spencer, Herbery. 1857. Progress: Its Law and Causes, *Westminster Review* 67: 445-85.

Spivak, Gayatri C. 1993. *Outside in the Teaching Machine*. New York: Routledge.

Spykman, Nicholas. 1942. *America's Strategy in World Politics*. New York: Harcourt, Brace and Company.

Spykman, Nicholas. 1944. *Geography of the Peace*. New York: Harcourt, Brace and Company.

Stengers, Isabelle. 2010. *Cosmopolitics 1*. Minneapolis, MN: University of Minnesota Press.

Sylvester, Christine. 1994. Empathetic Cooperation: A Feminist Method for IR, *Millennium-Journal of International Studies* 23.2: 315-34.

Taylor, Verta and Rupp, Leila J. 2002. Loving Internationalism: The Emotion Culture of Transnational Women's Organizations, 1888-1945, *Mobilization: An International Quarterly* 7.2: 141-58.

Tickner, Ann J. 1997. You Just Don't Understand: Troubled Engagements between Feminists and IR Theorists, *International Studies Quarterly* 41.4: 611-32.

Weber, Charlotte. 2001. Unveiling Scheherazade: Feminist Orientalism in the International Alliance of Women, 1911-1950, *Feminist Studies* 27.1: 125-57.

Yountae, A. 2014. Beginning in the Middle: Deleuze, Glissant and Colonial Difference, *Culture, Theory and Critique*, 55.3: 286-301.

Yusoff, Kathryn. 2012. Geopower: A Panel on Elizabeth Grosz's "Chaos, Territory, Art: Deleuze and the Framing of the Earth", *Environment and Planning D: Society and Space* 30.6: 971-88.

Yusoff, Kathryn. 2013. Geologic Life: Prehistory, Climate, Futures in the Anthropocene, *Environment and Planning D: Society and Space* 31.5: 779-95.

Zimmermann, Susan. 2005. The Challenge of Multinational Empire for the International Women's Movement: The Habsburg Monarchy and the Development of Feminist Inter/National Politics, *Journal of Women's History* 17.2: 87-117.

Chapter 3
Flesh

Introduction

The location and crossing of borders, and the associated rules and regulations as to how, when and whose movement across these will take place, are the very stuff of geopolitics as both a practical series of encounters, and the academic field that critically engages these. Borders cleave and bind. They express both a Cartesian promise as to where voluminous national territories and their contents begin and end, and a topological potentiality as to how things and people can be brought into propinquity. They are where sovereign reach and access are confirmed, thwarted, negotiated and practised, where processes of identification and documentation are intensified, and emotions and affects pertaining to belonging and expulsion are mobilised. Thus the body of the 'traveller,' for example, makes visible a series of geopolitical apparatus,' from the 'securing' of those volumes of space claimed by nation-states, and the protections and obligations granted by these, to the carving out of legal and illegal passages of transit (the flight-space, the tunnel, the diplomat's bag and so on) and the possibilities and constraints upon a corporeal mobility that emerge in their traversal. The posted package does similar work: here, transport geographies composed of logistics and carriers, export/import agreements, wrapping, tracking and guarantees, both allow for and mark the passage of a thing from one place to another.

Bearing in mind the import of a feminist materialism for geopolitics, as outlined in Chapter 2, I want to delve into the strangeness of these borders. I do so by turning in the following sections to *Flesh on the Move*, and *The Becoming of Flesh*. To be sure, geographers have noted the increasing 'commodification' and 'codification' of the traveller, the refugee and the migrant as security measures, alongside the increasing pace of international traffic, usher in an increasingly complex yet ever standardised experience of cross-border movement wherein the flesh is encoded and uploaded into diverse data banks for cross-referencing (Amoore and Hall 2009). On occasion, the manner in which such procedures examine and treat fleshiness – as when, for example, bodies are rendered visible to inspection via x-rays, or overflow seat capacities – become intense points of media interest (Brown and Narain 2012). And, medical interventions such as inoculations, as well as quarantine procedures, have long been concerned with the mutable flesh of people, animals and food on the move, insofar as these may harbour or become exposed to 'alien' pathogens (Budd et al. 2011).

What tends to be obscured in such public as well as scholarly discussions, however, is the rapidly increasing mass of 'corporeally disassociated' flesh on the move, by which I mean living material that has been removed from the body, stored and modified to serve diverse experimental, commercial or therapeutic purposes, transported across international borders, and held in reserve in banks or processing centres for use in the laboratory, the hospital, the factory, and even the art studio. Why look to this flesh? There is a certain 'shock factor,' to be sure, that makes the familiar notion of a bodily movement across borders unfamiliar. It prompts questions around what geopolitical apparatus' and agreements (as well as disagreements) hove into view as being responsible for the emergence and circulation of such materials, and how these work to transform them. What technologies, for example, allow for these material movements? How does this living matter attain a particular identity, or 'subject formation,' when entering such travel arrangements? And, what happens to concepts of belonging and expulsion when posed in this context?

But more importantly for my purposes, designating flesh as an object of analysis at the very outset invites a feminist geopolitics to concern itself with the matter, or the 'what,' of such movement, and how this speaks in turn to the matter of gendered and sexed bodies. The great majority of tissue on the move across international borders is derived – or 'harvested' – from the bodies of women by transnational companies taking advantage of a highly differential regulatory geography, whilst the emergent products, such as stem cell facials, are more often than not targeted to women engaging in stem cell beauty as well as medical tourism. Certainly, the rapid development of both *in vitro* fertilisation (IVF) technologies and stem cell banking have been predicated on the cultivation of maternal anxieties. In terms of substantive content alone, then, this chapter would appear to fall firmly within the remit of a feminist geopolitics concerned with how cross-border relations, political, economic, regulatory, impact upon the lives of women.

In the section *Flesh on the Move*, however, I want to outline something of the life of the tissues 'themselves,' as they proceed to emerge into and occupy times and spaces outside of variously gendered and sexed bodies, and as they proceed to (sometimes, but largely not) become part and parcel of the same. Of course, this process does not mean that gender and sex somehow become irrelevant issues; the processes by which this disassociation occurs, and the various scientific, economic and political imperatives that animate them, are differentially inflected by a wealth of social relations and biological capacities, and the manner in which these become enmeshed. One can think, for example, of the 2005 scandal at the then world's foremost stem cell cloning laboratory in South Korea led by 'national hero' Professor Hwang Woo-Suk. Ethical irregularities would appear to have encompassed not only paying women for eggs and not informing them fully of the medical risks, but also pressuring junior, female members of the research team to donate eggs (Baylis 2009). One can also reflect upon the biological nomenclature given stem cells themselves. In terms of their biological capacity, stem cells are characterised by a self-renewability, dividing themselves rapidly, but also a capacity to create 'daughters' (via an asymmetric mitosis that differentially locates cell material) that are materially and functionally distinct from the 'mother' cells.

This process can be applied in transplantations, wherein injected stem cells encounter, engage with, and transform the patient's flesh.

To posit flesh in this manner is to eschew the use of 'gender' as a particular giving of form to matter, one that revolves around the individual as complete and whole. Instead, one can think of matter as always and already having a form, and a series of capacities, that can, under particular circumstances, lend itself not only to a corporeality, but to a diversity of reproductive possibilities. In short, my line of argument in this chapter is premised on the belief that engendering precedes gendering. And, such a line of inquiry poses questions as to how such tissues proceed to animate new speeds and intensities between various bodies – including but not limited to, the mother, the father, the child, the sibling, the surgeon and the patient, certainly, but also the tumourous excess and the spoiled sample – and both enrol and prompt diverse technologies and procedures in the process. And, further, how such engendering can be considered not only as "a difference engine," as Adams et al. (2009: 252) put it, but "a futures generator in regimes of anticipation."

I outline some answers to these questions by focusing upon a particular kind of flesh on the move, namely mesenchymal stem cells that can be harvested from the abdominal fat of all human bodies, processed, and developed into therapeutic treatments. What such a non-corporeal focus allows for are renewed geopolitical narratives of sequestration and surveillance, encounter and mingling, purge and scourge, and the quest for order over and against the excessive and unpredictable. On the one hand, the travels and travails of such materials lend themselves to the denotation of such flesh as our 'dark twin,' its parallel movements allowing for sustained experimentation into the fundamental, but also malleable, nature of humanity. On the other hand, however, the unravelling and remaking of flesh becomes an example, as well as emblematic, of a continuous dissolution of the human, which is itself predicated on the notion of a biological 'original.' As such, they lend new resonance to our visions of a future human condition not only grounded in the body, but also in the biotechnologies that assemble and disassemble that body.

It is with this sense of futurity in mind that I turn, in the section *The Becoming of Flesh*, to the work achieved by flesh on the move in reanimating geopolitical discussions around a global distribution of reproduction. There is a deep tradition of feminist work that examines the role of Biology in shaping societal beliefs on the 'sexed' character of human beings, using various species such as fruit flies as analogues, and vice versa, as well as the demarcation of biological criteria used to identify the human from the non-human (see Hull 2006). And, there is more specific work on how rapidly developing IVF technologies have allowed for tissues and cells associated with reproduction, such as eggs, sperm, ova and oöcytes, to be mobilised for trade and exchange alongside more sizeable, 'solid' organs such as hearts, livers and kidneys via the agency of infertility specialists, IVF brokers, and desiring parents (for example, Almeling 2011; Kimbrell 1993; Scheper-Hughes 2012; Pfeffer 2011; Shalev 2012). This 'global distribution of regenerative labour' complicates an already intensive biopolitics of human sexual reproduction, and especially the crucial role played by various state apparatus' in shaping women's reproductive choices and possibilities.

In this latter section, I sketch out how a global redistribution of tissues – flesh on the move inside and outside of the corporeal body – lends itself to a particular becoming of flesh; that is, a reproductive effort enabled via various IVF treatments and centred on the female body. Specifically, I want to draw out how a redistribution of what become designated as reproductive materials is enmeshed with a redistribution of the maternal, and in particular the promulgation of a 'maternal anxiety' as to the future well-being of children, family and even the nation. In recent years, the generation, presence and capacity of these tissues has become closely tied to a mother's responsibility to secure the future of the body politic by locating and insuring against risk; a coming together that reworks, once more, the mythos of the birth of a nation.

Flesh on the Move

On 1st July, 2011, Presidential-hopeful Governor Rick Perry (Republican-Texas) underwent a medical procedure for a recurring back injury that involved his surgeon injecting into his spine and blood stream mesenchymal stem cells derived weeks earlier from his own abdominal fat tissue and multiplied (from a count of around 100,000 to 8 million) in a processing laboratory, or 'bank,' owned and operated by *Celltex Therapeutics*. *Celltex* has rapidly grown to become the largest stem cell bank in the US; housed in Sugar Land, Texas, it deploys licensed technology from *RNL Bio*, based in Seoul, South Korea.

Whilst one can only speculate as to the manner in which either this treatment, or its placebo effect, encouraged Perry to make the formal decision to run for US President on 13th August 2011, there is little doubt that his use of therapeutic stem cells was to become a politically sensitive affair (Ramshaw 2011a). Abortions are a 'flashpoint' issue for right-wing movements in the US, and public debates are very much taken up with fate of foetal materials, such as the harvesting of 'waste' human embryos produced via IVF treatment, particularly in the aftermath of then President George Bush's 2001 ban on federal funding for the same. For Perry, it was important to mark a difference between this, and the harvesting of materials from the adult body in the name of good health and economic development, such that a moral choice could then be signified in regard to avoiding the exploitation of the 'unborn.' He has tapped into a reproductive morality, in other words, centred on the biological materiality of the foetus and its well-being, a theme expanded upon in Chapter 4. As one of Perry's campaign speeches, critiquing President Obama's overturning of Bush's legislation, went on to note, state funding of embryonic stem cell research was,

> turning the remains of unborn children into nothing more than raw material. ...
> [The Obama administration is ignoring] the overriding responsibility of every

government—that is to protect citizens at every stage of their lives, especially those who cannot protect themselves. (*The Political Guide*, 2011)

The fact that Perry, running for the Republican Presidential nomination, invested the 'matter' of biotechnology with profound religious and moral significance is unsurprising. But nor is his decision to undergo this experimental therapy, given his long-standing support of the adult stem cell sector in Texas. His 2009 State of the State address included a call to state leaders to invest in adult stem cell companies to ensure both regional economic competitiveness, better health for its population, and a continued ban on embryonic stem cell harvesting, arguing that,

> This rapidly-growing field is of particular interest to Texans, both economically and in terms of discoveries that improve and save lives.... For example, the folks at the Texas A&M Health Science Center will begin trials on diabetes treatments later this year in Waco. Let's get Texas in on the ground floor and invest in adult stem cell research, the one area of that field that is actually proven to expedite cures. Expertise in this emerging and increasingly promising field will not only bring healing to the suffering and create jobs for Texans, it will also establish an appropriate firewall protecting the unborn from exploitation. (ibid.)

Perry's Emerging Technology Fund went on to award a $5 million grant to the 'folks' at Texas A&M Health Science Center Institute of Regenerative Medicine, as well as a $2.5 million grant to *America Stem Cell* to develop its enzyme technology enhancing the homing and engraftment of umbilical cord blood stem cells (Office of the Governor Rick Perry, Texas Emerging Technology Fund). Perry's treatment, and his support for a Texas-based stem cell industry, can tell us much about the geopolitics of flesh.

First, such international licensing agreements are indicative of the international reach of companies such as *RNL Bio*, certainly, but also the complex geographies of regulation that enable particular minglings of the flesh to occur. As *The Texas Tribune* reporter Emily Ramshaw observes, *Celltex* is, "the Texas branch of a South Korean company that has made international headlines for commercialized dog cloning, 'regenerative' beauty products and allegations of so-called 'stem cell tourism'" (2011b, n.p.). Indeed, the corporate geography of *RNL Bio* is a prime example of the tendency of stem cell companies to operate between and betwixt national regulatory environments. The parent company is able to take advantage of world-leading expertise in stem cell isolation, screening, and multiplication in South Korea itself, but because stem cell injections are currently banned here must needs send both cells and patients to affiliated clinics in Japan and China for treatment to occur (Cyranoski 2012). In similar vein, a Los Angeles affiliate, *RNL Life Science*, which opened in 2009 in a shopping mall, arranges for plastic surgeons to remove around five grammes of fatty tissue from patients in a nearby clinic before sending the sample to a Maryland processing centre. From here, mesenchymal cells are isolated and sent on to Seoul to be cultured. According to a 2010 *Nature* news piece, around 10,000 patients, including 130 from the US, have subsequently been given injections by RNL affiliates; about half of these treatments take the form of stem cell facials, the remainder being for Parkinson's disease, kidney failure, and diabetes (Cyranoski 2010).

Small wonder, then, that stem cell treatment so often requires an intricate array of mobilities, with materials crossing a series of sub and inter-national borders. Small wonder also that the differential possibilities for action so produced have become a profitable financial opportunity, as investment becomes concentrated in regions such as the American 'wild west' wherein regulatory supervision of stem cell therapies is relatively lax. This highly diverse regularity geography in regard to stem cell harvesting, processing, storing and medical deployment has emerged as nation-states struggle to keep pace with a rapidly evolving biotechnology knowledge and practice base, whilst at the same time bring to bear cultural sensibilities on the nature of various human-derived tissues and the ethics of their manipulation and engineering.

What has become clear over the past few years is that investment capital is highly responsive to this geography, such that an extensive, international corporate structure rapidly accommodates the 'placing' of various practices, technologies and knowledges. And, in doing so, throws up a dynamic topological geography of affiliated clinics, hospitals and banks that depends upon a series of financial, knowledge, and fleshy transfers. *Cryo-Cell*, for example, founded in 1989, has over 240,000 clients from 87 countries (see *Cyro-Save* website). *Cryo-Save Group N.V.* is a holding company under Dutch law, whilst *Cryo-Save AG*, the working company, has offices in Pfäffikon, Switzerland. Affiliates are present in 40 countries, from Colombia to Pakistan, and are composed of 'daughter companies' and business partners representing the *Cryo-Save Group* through licensing agreements. Stem cells from both daughter companies and business partners are stored centrally in Belgium, excepting those from Dubai, India and Germany.

Such topologies are very much tempered, however, by a more traditional politics of territorial protectionism by both national and sub-national state apparatus's. Texas, for example, because of its substantial biotechnology knowledge base in universities and hospitals, combined, as noted above, with a relatively lax set of regulations on providing stem cell injections, is very much in competition with the Shenzhen Province of China, where the market dominance of *Celltex* is matched by *Beike Biotech*. *Beike*, since its founding in 2005, has grown to house the largest stem cell collection in Asia. Here, a similar combination of state finance (from Jiangsu Government and Shenzhen City Hall) and university/hospital funding and expertise (from Peking University, the Hong Kong University of Science and Technology, and Jiangsu Provincial People's Hospital, amongst others) has allowed for the rapid take-off of China's regenerative medicine and bio-medical industry. Future plans include processing and storage banks in the provinces of Guizhou, Liaoning and Henan, as well as in India and Hong Kong, housing cells derived from umbilical cord, fat, bone marrow, placenta and amnion membrane. Whilst careful to note that the centre will follow a, "stringent implementation of international quality benchmarks," *Beike*'s Vice President for Medical, Scientific and Regulatory affairs, Dr. Ying Song, also observes that this is an opportunity for China as a nation-state to achieve world leadership, insofar as, "Stem cells are the crown jewel of medical research" (*Bieke Biotech* Press Release). Such grandiose plans may well be curtailed, however, by future regulatory action: whilst China has recently passed a requirement that all stem cell therapies should be clinically trialled, there is continuing debate over how these should be implemented, resulting in a legal limbo.

Second, underlying many such legal ambiguities is an intense debate over the ontological status of these corporeally disassociated tissues – does their 'place' lie within an organism, for example, or as an industrial end-product and a legal proof of innovation? Regional competitiveness in the US, for example, is complicated by regulatory disputes between the federal Food and Drug Association (FDA) and state entities such as the Texas Medical Board. The FDA has sought to ban untrialled stem cell therapies on the basis of their failure to attain Good Manufacturing Practice, rather than Good Tissue Practice as found in the blood and human tissue transplantation sectors (Koleva 2012). Arguing that cells have been 'manipulated' before injection, such that they now constitute an engineered drug, the FDA has successfully stopped *Regenerative Sciences* of Broomfield Colorado from administering mesenchymal cells as 'Regenexx' to patients for the treatment of orthopaedic injuries. Regardless, the Texas Medical Board has approved draft rules that require physicians to receive approval from what it calls an 'independent review committee' before treating patients, thus paving the way for a substantive federal-state wrangle over the legality, as well as the status, of therapeutic mesenchymal stem cells. The South Korean FDA looks set to follow suit in regard to classifying manipulated stem cells as a drug, ushering in the likelihood of yet another global round of industry investment.

According to Jin Han Hong, president of *RNL Life Science* in LA, "The government wants to define[the therapeutic mesenchymal stem cell] as a drug and make it illegal. From our viewpoint it is just part of the patient's body" (cited in Cyranoski 2010). Certainly, defining the legal ownership of these is complex and at times paradoxical, and depends a great deal on the forms of consent under which tissues were removed and the guarantees of individual clinics, but also the requirements of various national and international regulatory bodies. The storage of an individual's mesenchymal stem cells in a bank, with the accompanying expectation that these can be withdrawn for future medical use by that individual for themselves or family members, does indeed denote these as 'belonging' to a particular body. And, as we shall see below, there is a careful tracking of samples, as well as a variety of data protection policies, with the aim of ensuring a potential, future re-encounter between patient and cells. Yet, US rules concerning the ineligibility of patenting 'life itself' have undergone several key changes since 1980, with the result that stem cells not banked under these guarantees but otherwise donated to or bought by these same clinics and banks and modified, can be claimed under patent by virtue of the specialist, technological know-how required for their production. Moreover, because words alone cannot express this knowledge and its product, a physical example is required to be placed in a collection, such as a national stem cell bank. It remains a legal point of debate as to whether these can be accessed for research from such collections without license from the 'owner' (Isasi and Knoppers 2009; Graff et al. 2011). In practice, what this means is that stem cell companies based in countries across the globe can, under US law, and within the territorial reach of the US nation-state, 'protect' their modified stem cell lines from competitors, at least for the duration of the patent, thereby exerting a high degree of legal ownership. To make matters more complex, patent law itself has a highly diverse international geography. In October 2011 the European Court of Justice, for example, ruled that procedures involving human embryonic stem cells cannot be patented insofar as this would violate current European law banning the industrial use of human embryos, as well as being 'contrary' to both ethics and public policy (Moran 2011).

In regard to stem cell marketing, we subsequently see an interesting tension between claims to special expertise, as denoted by references to patented or trademarked collection kits, screening and multiplication techniques and mediums only available at certain clinics at the leading edge of science, and a text and image-based rhetoric of the 'naturalness' of these techniques when compared with other forms of treatment. A prime example is provided by *Future Health Bio*, a firm established in the UK in 2002, but with offices in over 23 countries, and samples collected from 50 countries. A key selling point for their services is that treatment involves cells taken from the patient's own body, thereby allowing for a perfect match if need be. According to the company's revelatory text:

> When a liposuction procedure takes place, the fat removed from your body is disposed of as medical waste. But what if this 'waste' held a secret that could one day help you if you became ill? ... Recently, scientists discovered that this tissue contained special mesenchymal stem cells, also known as lipo stem cells. Lipo stem cells have an ability to transform into lots of other cells in the body... So, for instance, if you were to develop a heart disease or multiple sclerosis in later life, lipo stem cells may be able to help you recover. Another reason for their growing popularity is that, because they are your own cells used to treat you, they would be a perfect match, with no problems of rejection. So, before you have your liposuction procedure, remember to plan ahead, to save and store some of those valuable stem cells. Discarding some of them may help to improve your present shape, but banking some could help to improve your future health. (*Future Health Bio* website)

Such 'natural' rhetorics are both confirmed and complicated by the intensive processing of samples. At the heart of this series of processes is a tension between the 'purification' of the sample via intensive screening measures, and its still-like 'preservation' as a natural resource for specific bodies, ready and waiting to be shipped. The sample of fatty tissue is removed from the patient by a medical technician, most often than not after a liposuction procedure, and placed in a pre-ordered adipose collection kit produced by a medical supply company, such as *Incell* or *Blue Lion Biotech*. This contains, generally speaking, instructions for collection, a sterile aspiration container, a media bag with some form of transport medium to keep the sample 'alive,' biohazard transport bags, cooling packs, return shipping documents, Styrofoam packaging and a cardboard shipping box. This ensemble has a short life span, and must be couriered to a processing clinic, often located close to an airport to save on transport time, where a series of separation, purification, marking, expansion and differentiation procedures are carried out. *Life Technologies*, a company that sells human-adipose derived stem cells kits for research, reports the process in suitably scientific, third-person, process-orientated language as follows,

> ADSCs are extracted from human adipose tissue by mechanical and enzymatic digestion... [Cells] are assayed for purity using flow cytometric analysis of cell-surface antigen expression at passage 2 or 3. Cells are immunofluorescently stained with labeled antibodies specific to cellsurface antigens, and sorted by flow cytometry ...Cells are expanded using MesenPRO RS™ Medium, which supports a much shorter cell doubling time (36 ± 4 hr) compared with expansion in traditional medium (DMEM + 10% FBS), which results in cell doubling time of 54 ± 4 hr.... [Cells] can be expanded to 4-5 passages before they lose their ability to grow or differentiate into all potential phenotypes. (*Life Technologies* website)

Once 'purified,' cells can be cryogenically stored. For those firms selling the processing and banking of cells, a guarantee of the cleanliness of their facilities, the rigour of their sterilisation and cryogenic procedures, and the expertly trained, machine-like operation of their staff, is essential insofar as this protection against contamination and unwanted growth maintains the 'naturalness' of these same cells. In addition, a series of identification procedures are also carried out, such that these now corporeally disassociated cells retain some form of connection to the larger biomass of their donor. And so *Future Health Bio*, for example, promises that,

> Lipo stem cell separation and preservation are carried out by specialised Scientific laboratory personnel, in accordance with strict guidelines, in the GMP clean room facility at our purpose-built sterile laboratory... Once your lipo stem cells are separated, they're placed in cryovials, with a unique bar code to ensure that they are never misplaced and can always be identified as yours. Then they're placed in a cryobox for extra protection. The cryobox is also bar coded and placed in a storage tank containing liquid nitrogen where it will sit, safe and secure, in the nitrogen vapour. Waiting for the day when your lipo stem cells may be needed. (*Future Health Bio* website)

The harvesting of mesenchymal stem cells from patients in most countries wherein this procedure is available is accompanied by a legal requirement that a contemporaneous sample of blood also be collected, such that the presence of particular viruses and pathogens in the donor body can be located. These would signal the problematic nature of the acquired stem cells, which would not go on to storage. Importantly, they also signal a capacity of these cells that is rarely otherwise noted in such advertising websites. That is, it is not simply a number of stem cells that are collected in an otherwise passive sample. Rather, these cells are part and parcel of a unique ecosystem (the sample) that can contain, amongst other elements, infectious microorganisms such as human immunodeficiency virus, hepatitis B virus, hepatitis C virus and human T cell lymphotrophic virus. To be sure, screening procedures can identify these, but some newer pathogens, such as transmissible spongiform encephalopathies and severe acute respiratory syndrome, are almost certainly missed (Cobo et al. 2005). In addition, screening can itself bring new 'contaminating' elements into play, as can the use of bovine serum and mouse fibroblasts as a feeder layer for the development of cell lines. These samples, then, are singular collections of vital matter, with a host of expected, and unexpected, capacities. As Caulfield and Zarzeczny (2012: 366) caution,

> Contrary to the claims made on some websites, the fact that cells originally come from a person's body (eg, blood or bone marrow) does not mean they are safe to reintroduce after they have been manipulated outside the body. For example, cell characteristics can change during expansion, with the result that they lose the ability to differentiate into specialized cell types or to control their own growth ... The fact that cell-based transplants might survive in a patient for many years and might in fact be irreversible makes the potential risks all the more salient.

Third, in order for treatment to take place, not only do cells undergo international travel, as outlined above, but more often than not the patient also must engage in what has been termed 'medical tourism' in order to become reacquainted with their (ideally) purged, scourged, manipulated, and preserved cells. And, as noted above, such movement is adapted to a highly differentiated and dynamic regulatory geography concerning what can be injected. Those countries with relatively lax regulations regarding the introduction of stem cell therapies not yet clinically-trialled have received substantial investment but also, it might be added, adverse publicity, a factor that itself appears to have reshaped such medical tourist geographies.

In 2010, for example, National Public Radio in the US aired a story called, *Offshore Stem Cell Clinics Sell Hope, Not Science*, whilst the International Society for Stem Cell Research (ISSCR) posted an open letter on its site noting the potential for legitimate, 'ethical' research to be unfairly stigmatised. A white paper produced under the auspices of the ISSCR has also been published in *Cytotherapy*, wherein the unpredictable excess over unknown time-frames of stem cell treatments becomes cause for concern. "One example," the authors Gunter et al. (2010: 956) observe, "is a boy with ataxia telangiectasia treated with repeated intracerebellar and intrathecal injections of human fetal neural stem cells at a clinic in Moscow. Four years later, he was diagnosed with a glioneuronal tumour, not of host origin and containing cells from two or more donors." In the same year, China's *Beike Biotech*, mentioned earlier, was singled out for criticism by an expert panel on stem cell tourism convened in London, alongside the *XCell-centre*, based in Dusseldorf, Germany. Subject to a follow up investigation by *The Telegraph*, *XCell* was reported as 'exploiting' a legal loophole in offering stem cell injections for cerebral palsy, multiple sclerosis, autism, Parkinson's, Alzheimer's, heart disease, diabetes and spinal cord injuries (Mendick and Hall 2011a). *XCell* shut down in 2011 as Germany moved to close this particular loophole. Its founder has since, however, established a new clinic in Beirut, *Cells4Health*, where treatments are once more available. Observing the intricate geopolitics of this venture, *The Telegraph* notes that, after a bone marrow sample is removed from a patient in Beirut,

> For a fee [it] is flown to Heathrow then driven the short distance to Precious Cells' base on the campus of Brunel University in Uxbridge, west London. There in a laboratory, visited by *The Sunday Telegraph*, the stem cells are extracted from the bone marrow and sent back to Lebanon for re-injection into the patient. "We can have the stem cells back there [in Beirut] within 36 hours," explained Dr Salem as he showed off his premises. Precious Cells rents the space from Brunel while employing about 45 people worldwide.... Precious Cells is not involved in treating any of the patients and it would be illegal for any clinic to do so in Britain. But there is nothing to stop the company facilitating Cells4health's practices.... (Mendick and Hall 2011b, n.p.)

In their 2009 policy review in *Science*, Kiatpongsan and Sipp note that several stem cell clinics have been closed by law enforcement or regulatory agencies in the US, the Netherlands, and Ireland, whilst others have been forced out of business by negative publicity. Nonetheless, they continue, "Successful clinics that remain in business are sometimes supported by local medical associations, governments, and regulatory agencies" (2009: 1564). One of these is *Theravitae*, which sells adult stem cell therapy for coronary heart disease, congestive heart failure, and cardiomyopathy. Founded in 2003, *Theravitae* is based in Toronto, Canada, with locations in Israel, Thailand, and Hong Kong. It has on its staff, Kiatpongsan and Sipp observe, the current presidents of the Thai Heart Association and the Thai Atherosclerosis Society, and recognition from the Davos-based World Economic Forum as a 2006 Technology Pioneer. "Given the current limits of international law and scientific diplomacy," they conclude, "a global ban on unapproved treatments seems unlikely to succeed, so for now, each government must take great care when granting funds and recognition to programs that fall short of ethical or professional standards" (2009: 1565).

The Becoming of Flesh

In the preceding section, the 'becoming of flesh' implied revolves around the material formation of the donor/patient, as exemplified by Rick Perry, but also the excessive and unpredictable growth of samples undergoing screening and processing, and the multiplication and modification of cells as part and parcel of scientific research projects, both commercial and university-led. In this section, I want to explicitly address how the becoming of flesh speaks to the issue of reproduction. Here, I sketch out a global redistribution of tissues founded, first, on the movement of materials that become part and parcel of a reproductive effort enabled via various IVF treatments and centred on the female body. Some of these are disassociated from the corporeal body in one country, and made ready to encounter new corporeal bodies elsewhere. Other tissues, however, travel as part of the female corporeal body under the rubric of 'reproductive tourism,' and become subject to various forms of encounter, reduction or manipulation within this context. Second, I want to focus on how this geography becomes enmeshed in a redistribution of the maternal, as 'mothering' capacities and emotions are differentially enabled and curtailed. These mobile materials become infused with a 'maternal anxiety' as to the future well-being of children and family, but also, in recent years, part and parcel of a biopolitics of the flesh that seeks to educate women as to their duty in locating and insuring against risks to the larger community, and even the nation itself.

Whilst the stem cell sector deploys materials harvested from diverse biological contexts, including mesenchymal cells as noted above, the bulk of these are drawn from particular corporeal bodies that are able to offer umbilical cord blood, menstrual blood, embryonic tissues, foetal tissue and oöcytes, and that have emerged from or become enrolled in various IVF treatments, or have been sourced in the aftermath of birth. IVF has, over the past few decades, become an ensemble of knowledges and techniques that deal with all manner of tissues in a series of treatments, including embryonic stem cell research for the purposes of therapeutic intervention, but also, as Marcia Inhorn (2012: 238) describes: intracytoplasmic injection (ICSI) to overcome male infertility; third-party gamete donation (of eggs, sperm, embryos, and uteruses, as in surrogacy) to overcome absolute sterility; multifoetal pregnancy reduction to selectively abort high-order IVF pregnancies; ooplasm transfer (OT) to improve egg quality in perimenopausal women; cryopreservation, storage, and disposal of unused gametes and embryos; preimplantation genetic diagnosis (PGD) to select 'against' embryos with genetic defects and to select 'for' embryos of a specific sex; and the future possibility of asexual autonomous reproduction through human cloning. Small wonder that tissues associated with female reproduction have become a valuable commodity.

There is a significant regulatory geography as to if and under what conditions this material may be harvested, ensuing in what Waldby and Cooper (2008: 3) term a global distribution of regenerative labour. "Such material," they note, is generally given for free in the advanced industrial democracies, constituted as a surplus ('spare' embryos) or waste (umbilical cord 'afterbirth,' cadaveric foetuses, poor quality oöcytes) whose generative powers should not be withheld from others. At the same time, among impoverished female populations in developing nations, such biological material is now often procured through frankly transactional relations, where women undertake risky procedures for small fees.

One of the key procedures in IVF treatment, for example, is hyperovulation, wherein hormonal treatment induces the artificial maturation of more than one egg cell, and stimulates the release of a large number of eggs in any one menstrual cycle. This treatment can have serious side-effects, including the potentially fatal ovarian hyper-stimulation syndrome. In addition, the egg retrieval procedure is intrusive, requiring a local or general anaesthesia. The ensuing 'surplus,' as Jyotsna Gupta (2006: 32) observes, can be donated or sold for reproduction or for research, such that, "Within global capitalism women's cheap labour is not only used to produce for the world market, but also to 'reproduce' for the world."

The growing international market in what can become 'human reproductive material' is attributable to an intricate, and dynamic, series of push and pull factors (see Crozier 2010). On the one hand, for example, the domestic policies of those countries that seek to combat a perceived 'economic vulnerability' of poor women – a prime example being Canada, which requires altruistic gifting as opposed to monetary compensation (Spar 2007) – have been noted as contributing to the overseas travel of those desiring, and capable of affording, particular IVF treatments, and a subsequent displacement of such exploitation (Storrow 2006). On the other hand, Shalev and Werner-Felmay (2012: 4) point to the import of a religious *cum* nationalistic commitment: in Israel, they argue, "Jewish tradition places high value on the religious commandment to be fruitful and multiply, and the family is a central institution in social life. Israeli individuals and society have a general propensity to accept and consume technological novelties. Demographic policy is pro-natal against the historic backdrop of the Holocaust and in the context of the Israeli-Palestinian conflict." This context, they go on to suggest, helps to explain why the Israeli Supreme Court has struck down restrictions on access to reproductive technologies, on the grounds of a constitutional right to parenthood.

In similar vein, Inhorn and Shrivastav (2010: 698-708) detail a flourishing 'reproscape' in the Middle East, with the emergence of, "hundreds of [IVF] clinics in countries ranging from the relatively small Arabian Gulf countries to the larger but less prosperous nations of North Africa … This fluorescence of a mostly private Middle Eastern ART industry is not surprising," they suggest, insofar as, "Islam encourages the use of science and medicine as solutions to human suffering, and it is a religion that can be described as 'pronatalist,' encouraging the growth of an Islamic 'multitude.'" *Conceive*, for example, a clinic that is located between the adjacent emirates of Dubai and Sharjah, and is owned by a United Arab Emirates (UAE) businessman, serves a growing number of reproductive tourists including Indian, Lebanese, British, Pakistanis, Sudanese, Filipinos, and Palestinians, most entering on a multi-month visitor's visa. Because the UAE bans third-party tissue involvement, however, "those needing donor eggs may travel to Lebanon and Cyprus. Those needing foetal reduction (abortion) may travel to London or India. And those with financial constraints may undertake diagnostic laparoscopy in India to save on costs" (Inhorn and Shrivastav 2010: 738). To add to the complexity of this reproscape, cryopreservation and embryo couriers have been outlawed in the UAE since 2010, such that Emiritis must needs travel abroad for such services.

These movements certainly help to enact a global distribution of regenerative labour, insofar as there is a continual transfer of materials across borders, some corporeally disassociated, some not, and largely orchestrated by a series of companies that operate between and betwixt a differential regulatory geography. But, it is also important to note how these movements are both enabled by, and allow for, a 'distribution of the maternal' as a particular biological capacity is infused with particular expectations around the subject-formation of a dyadic mother-child relationship. To be sure, for those selling or donating eggs and oöcytes, the capacity for reproduction becomes dis-placed, and this has led to extensive and critical media commentary on the impacts of 'baby farms,' wherein wealthy women are able to gain an emotional as well as biological motherhood at the expense of donors.

An article in the *Daily Mail*, for example, outlines what is perceived to be the warped geography of designer baby factories, wherein the reporter David Jones (2012, n.p.) finds, "eggs from beautiful Eastern Europeans, sperm from wealthy westerners and embryos implanted in desperate women," whom he describes as, "uneducated, bare-footed, dirt-poor Indian women from outlying villages." These women "are so desperate to feed, clothe and educate their own families that they are prepared to risk being shunned by their husbands and communities" by 'hosting' the developing foetus, "often delivered prematurely by Caesarean section to minimise the risk of perinatal complications without so much as one, brief departing cuddle – to ensure there is no risk of them bonding." Follow up reports in the equally conservative *The Telegraph*, filed on 26th May from Delhi by reporter Shekhar Bhatia (2012) are less interested in beautiful European women. Instead, the first notes how "babies are being created" close to New Delhi's colonial capital "on a scale far greater than anywhere in Britain," an approach that magnifies the reference to wombs for rent. A second article comments on the loose state governance of this booming industry. Both interpret womb surrogacy as the paradoxical abnegation of future children by a desperate cohort of women who want to support as best they can their extant family members.

Whilst the sensationalism of the above is eschewed in academic analyses of this redistribution of the maternal (or a 'transnational surrogacy' as it has come to be called), there is yet a pronounced emphasis on the proliferation of a physical and emotional vulnerability through such a process. For some, a pervasive commodification of the capacities of the body is manifest here, such that reproduction becomes 'outsourced' in much the same way as a north-south manufacturing was, and with similar outcomes in the form of a gender, class and race-based exploitation (Bailey 2011; Mohapatra 2012; Twine 2012). We can also discern, however, a rights-based line of argument, wherein it is a sovereign control over the corporeal body – as expressed in the freedom to participate in surrogacy – that is denoted as empowering from a feminist perspective (Parks 2010; Spar 2007).

What has been relatively absent from such discussions, however, and is usefully brought to bear upon a geopolitics of the flesh, is the weight of maternal anxiety placed upon the provision of stem cells, both as a private therapeutic resource for family use, and as a service to community and the nation. In surveying the advertising literatures from stem cell banks across the globe, a recurring thematic is indeed the responsibility and duty of the mother to locate and insure against the risk of ill health. *LifeCell International*, for example, which is comprised of a network of over 50 centres in India, Sri Lanka and Dubai with plans for future offices in Bangladesh, offers the wondrously-named 'Femme' programme, by which is meant the harvesting of mesenchymal cells from menstrual blood. Under the banner, 'Celebrate the power of Womanhood!,' *LifeCell* suggests that,

> As women, we face multiple challenges in maintaining our good health. Childbirth, age, nutrition, domestic pressures, periods…there are so many factors which affect our body. Today, however, research shows us that those very same things are giving us a biological advantage like never before. **Only we women have the power to take care of our health in the future and that of our genetically related family members (our precious children, siblings & parents).** Yes! Our periods (those hated things) are a rich source of Mesenchymal stem cells. These self renewing cells are being researched the world over, with new and exciting possibilities for therapeutic use looming large. **These amazing cells are found month on month, in your periods. So 'those 4 days' are actually more of a monthly miracle than a monthly curse.**
> (*LifeCell* website, emphasis in original)

LifeCell is also India's first collector of umbilical cord blood (UCB), and this remains the largest single source of stem cell harvesting. Research into UCB therapies emerged in the 1970s, and is focused on how blood-forming stem cells, hitherto taken from closely matched bone marrow donors, could develop into red and white blood cells, as well as platelets, thus proving effective in the childhood treatment of certain cancers, blood diseases and immune deficiency disorders. The quantities acquired from the umbilical cord are not sufficient for adult treatments; yet, UCB banking, which began in the US, is now a multi-million dollar industry with over 15,000 transplants worldwide by in the treatment of 45 different blood disorders by 2009 (Rao et al. 2012).

Interestingly, the purported ownership of the UCB sample – that is, what kind of subject can appropriately lay claim to possessing it – not only wavers between company websites but within an individual company's literature. *Cells4Life*, for example, with laboratory headquarters in Sussex, and an affiliate *Cells4Life Middle East*, refers to the post-birth collection of the "maternal sample" via a special collection kit, which not only firmly places responsibility for this in the hands of women as donors, but also negates any perceived confusion between these and embryonic or foetal stem cells. In outlining the rationale for banking, however, they note that,

> ... the real reason to store stem cells is to take advantage of the increasing evidence that they will be one of the cornerstones of future medical treatments. It is likely that the chances of using your child's stem cells will increase as the number of clinical uses of stem cells increases. (*Cells4Life* website)

Here, in a discussion of possible future treatments, the emphasis is on the natural, perfect match between child and modified and stored stem cell.

US firm *CorCell* ('saving baby's cord blood'), by contrast, refers to "baby's umbilical cord blood," And the doubly possessive "your baby's cord blood," which, they promise, will receive expedited shipping to their processing and storage facility, which operates under the FDA's Good Manufacturing Practices regulations:

> Due to time and temperature sensitivity, it is vital that the cord blood is shipped by a medical courier who understands the need to preserve the integrity of the shipment by reducing the transit time between destinations and protecting the umbilical cord blood collection from extreme temperatures. That's why CorCell uses AirNet. AirNet provides prompt pickup from the hospital room and delivery to the cord blood bank, carefully following AABB temperature guidelines during ground and air transit. Airnet has 10 years of experience in shipping cord blood. Our courier team members – drivers, pilots and customer support staff – are specially trained in the intricacies associated with handling these types of medical shipments... In addition, our in-house lab is located only minutes from Las Vegas McCarran International Airport. (ibid.)

Intensive surveillance measures, alongside cryogenic storage in liquid nitrogen, provide the promise that baby's stem cells will continue to reside in a safe, protected environment. These include: a security lock-down system that is monitored 24 hours seven days a week; hourly reports of freezer temperatures and activity; the presence of stand-by 'at temperature' cryogenic tanks; intrusion detection systems; fire prevention systems; security cameras at all entry doors to the facility; security access to all labs; security 24/7 cameras in the Cryogenic Storage Lab itself; LN_2 cryo monitors for each tank; LN_2 bulk storage to ensure an uninterrupted supply to the tanks; and automatic shut off in the event of decreased O_2 levels in the Cryotank Room.

The advertising tag lines produced by companies such as *LifeCell International* ('possibilities, well protected'), similarly emphasise the safeguarding of the future.

And, the accompanying visual rhetorics emphasise where the responsibility for providing such possibilities, and for safeguarding them, lies: with the mother. The banking of stem cells is here sold as part of a natural birth process; it is a practice that sits alongside the antenatal classes for expectant mothers that *LifeCell* also provides, which stress, "many ways to work with the labour process to reduce the pain associated with childbirth, and to promote normal birth and the first moments after birth" (*LifeCell* website).

In *LifeCell*'s literature, the mother and child take centre stage; at *Cryoviva Thailand* ('lifeline for a lifetime'), close-up shots of smiling and surprised babies, as well as baby and child shots, abound, each framed in a circular bubble. At *Swiss Stem Cell Banks*, an expectant woman gazes pensively at her tummy, whilst the accompany text asks earnestly,

> Are you pregnant? A once-in-a-lifetime opportunity to safeguard your child's future. If you are, you know how important your child's future is, and that his future will depend on the choices you make today. Stem cells found in the umbilical cord at the moment of delivery are a unique and irreplaceable genetic inheritance: storing them is a responsible choice, storing them in Switzerland is the best choice.

An implicit reference to Switzerland's other, iconic, banking industry is also made, with the rhetorical question,

> **Why rely on a Swiss Bank?** Because a structure that commits itself in storing your baby's stem cells for at least twenty years, must offer serious and solid guarantees. (ibid., emphasis in original)

In an interesting, and rare, example of men appearing with babies that speaks to the financial aspects of such a practice, *ViaCord*, headquartered in Massachusetts, promotes UCB banking to grandparents, noting that they can help emotionally and financially with raising children and, moreover, help parents 'understand' the importance of this decision. In the following, this rhetoric is matched by a reference to the 'mother'-like naturalness of stem cells, and their preservation rather than waste:

> **It's natural for some** of those parental instincts to be reawakened when a grandchild enters into the picture. The instinct to protect is just one of many that may kick into high gear. The good news is that there is something you can do to help protect and prepare your grandchild for his or her future. By understanding the power of cord blood stem cells you may be able to help the expecting parents decide if cord blood banking is the right choice for their family.... Unlike conventional medicines that just treat symptoms, cord blood contains stem cells known as 'mother cells.' Mother cells can 'become' other cells, like tissue and other organ cells, to help repair a condition permanently.

> As the building blocks of blood and the immune system, they can correct and/or replace damaged cells ... While there is a lot of public debate about stem cells, cord blood stem cells are *non-controversial* and therefore are free from political and ethical debate. Banking a child's cord blood simply preserves what would otherwise be discarded. (*ViaCord* online magazine *Grandlife*, emphasis in original)

The latter point made by *ViaCord* – that is, the procedure's freedom from ethical and political controversies – echoes Rick Perry's distinction between the 'bad' use of embryonic stem cells, and the 'good' use of adult stem cells, though in this case such a distinction is rewritten as a means of preserving and safeguarding part of the embryonic flesh. As Loane Skene (2012: 491) points out, whilst there "is understandably an emotional appeal for a woman giving birth to be offered a chance to store the child's cord blood later as 'insurance' for the child if the child should later need a transfusion of stem cells matched to that child, or perhaps a sibling," nevertheless, there are issues here around the communication of physical risk, access to and use of materials collected, and a potentially compromised patient care as attention is directed away from the mother towards the collection procedure.

ViaCord also provides a Gift Registry and Baby Shower Planning, making banal the notion of UCB banking as part and parcel of a pregnancy lifestyle. In similar vein, *Cordlife Singapore* and *Hong Kong* ('one chance, one choice') presents the Cordlife Circle Membership Card, in partnership with an array of businesses dealing in maternity and infant products, but also "food and beverage health and wellness" and "enrichment programmes," all geared towards giving "you and your family more reasons to enjoy family life" (*Cordlife* website). Inspiration can also be taken from 'Cordlife Celebrity Moms' (ibid.).

Certainly, in these and similar rhetorics on 'private' banking, maternal anxieties and responsibilities are tied to the future well-being of the child, their siblings, parents and grandparents, an unit held together by close DNA matching overlain by a series of expectations as to familial care and duty. But, recent years have also witnessed the emergence of a rhetoric of civic responsibility, as 'community' banking has become increasingly advertised, and 'national stem cell banks' have sought to increase their stocks. Trading on its reputation as a more socially aware business corporation, the Virgin Group, for example, has opened the *Virgin Health Bank* ('with you for life'), which offers a service wherein,

> you keep a small amount of your baby's stem cells for your own family, but at the same time support your community and potentially contribute to saving someone else's life in the future. This service uses the same high quality processing, testing and storage procedures as our Family Banking service, and includes 25 years of storage.... Importantly, using this service means that your family will only retain the stem cells from the first 5ml of cord blood collected. All the remaining cells will be donated to the public through our cell donation programme. These donated units are made available to other families who

require them for lifesaving transplants. Virgin Health Bank does not make a charge to the recipient of the cells or to the transplant centre beyond recovering the costs of preparing and transporting the unit. (*Virgin Health Bank* website)

Virgin Health advises that the small amount retained for family use is not enough to provide treatment, but, "over the next five to ten years cell expansion and regenerative medicine technologies are expected to become available, which may allow this unit to be utilised as a treatment on its own" (ibid.). Clearly, this community-orientated service is regarded as a promising business model more globally, as Rajan Jewtha, head of the *Virgin Health Bank Qatar*, opened in 2009, observes that, "social enterprises can make a profit and do good. I like to think we are the architects of Arab stem cell banks" (cited in Wadvalla 2012, n.p.).

To a degree, this service has emerged in response to medical and paediatric criticisms of the selfishness and waste of 'family,' or 'private' banking, insofar as the likelihood of these cells being used is extremely rare. The American Academy of Pediatrics (AAP), for example, observed in 2007 that many companies exploited new parent fears, particularly around 'minority' and adopted children, and presented misleading statistics on the potential need for what was essentially a stem cell insurance policy. In contrast, the AAP strongly advocated public banking by expectant mothers either through the American Red Cross, or their local university hospital. Here, again, there is the weight of maternal anxiety, this time in regard to the future well-being of communities at large. What appears to be a fast emerging 'biopolitics of the flesh' iterates the importance of educating expectant mothers as to their duties and responsibilities therein, as 20 US states, for example, have now enacted legislation (based on the Institute of Medicine guidelines) that either directs or recommends doctors to educate such women as to the benefits of therapies based on stem cells derived from umbilical cord blood. These include the effective treatment of children and adults with haematologic malignancies, marrow failure, immunodeficiency, haemoglobinopathy, and inherited metabolic diseases, all without the need for a full donor match, alongside an explanation of the differences between private and public banking (Cord Blood Awareness website). In May 2007, Governor Perry signed in House Bill 709, requiring the Texas Health and Human Services Commission (THHSC) to produce a brochure on what was termed 'family banking' and 'public donation,' to be given to pregnant women before the third trimester (Texas Department of Health State Services 2007).

What is more, national Stem Cell Banks have burgeoned in recent years as governments seek to advance medical stem cell research, and to build up a diverse stock of modified stem cells for therapeutic treatment. Few so far, however, have tied this effort quite so firmly into a nationalistic imperative to 'territorialise' these tissues as the Greece-based *Stem-Health Hellas* ('the Best Stem Cell Bank in Europe'), which helpfully advises potential donors, with emphases in bold, that,

> The units that are currently stored in public banks in Greece are about **2,500**, which is well below the minimum necessary of between **10,000 and 20,000 selected** units to cover the needs of compatible transplants for the Greek population. **Certainly a donated unit could be made available** and, **therefore, save the life of a patient that is not Greek**, although the probability is much less. (*Stem-Health Hellas* website, emphasis in original)

This explicit marking of the flesh as Greek or Other is all the more poignant in the face of economic meltdown, EU-driven austerity measures, an increasingly visible far-right movement, and an uncertain future for many.

Concluding Remarks

At one level, it is possible to can draw out an interesting tension in the above between the felt needs of the familial unit, so often taken as a necessary foundation for a modern nation, and the posited obligations of a responsible mother to community and populace. What this indicates is a complex biopolitics that interweaves all manner of subjectivities and the power relations within which these are embedded; subjectivities that speak to the notion of how singular bodily capacities allow for particular forms of good citizenship. It is also possible to map out something of the distributed character of borders, registered here as a material assemblage that incorporates all that is involved in the interactions between its elements, compounds, energy sources and organisms from the molecular to the molar levels. These borders are a matter of paperwork, permits and contacts; they are also blood-rich, sticky, frozen and thawed. Composed in part from the flesh, they help to form a unity of composition of Self and country that binds and cleaves insides and outsides.

This flesh on the move, and its differential becoming, can tell us something more, however, about how the human is being reasserted and reconceptualised in light of the shifting morphologies and anatomies facilitated by a rapidly advancing biotechnologies, to be sure, but also deeply embedded concerns over the material, emotional and psychic constitution of the Self and Other. That is, the human body in Western culture is generally depicted as sovereign; it is physically cut off from others, and provides the biochemical and neurological substrate for an individual free will. The implications of this rendering of the flesh as an enveloping material are two-fold. First, it is the threat of an intermingling of flesh that helps drive a xenophobic Gothic politics, a theme developed further in Chapter 5. And second, the possibility of a cut or penetrated flesh helps to drive an anxiety around the reach of an externalised, profligate Nature; a theme taken up in Chapter 6. This imaginary is, however, very much destabilised through the kinds of medical procedures outlined above. Indeed, stem cell research, alongside cybernetics and transgenic engineering, has been rendered legible time and again though its monstrosity; these technologies are afforded the demonic power to invade, subvert or even erase an essential humanness. Biotechnology in particular, Hillel Schwartz (1996: 357) avers, has introduced us to the "blade and the claw." The blade is there to cut away the signs of excessive diversity (the extra finger, the extra chromosome), while the claw of the chimera hovers overhead, dreadful in its implication that in the drive for progress we lose a sense of definition, becoming instead a mere collage. In such a context, the procedures by which a leaking and bloody flesh becomes treated as a fragment, and stored in preparation for a potential, future re-engagement with the corporeal body, pose a profound challenge to the easy biological framings that underpin so much of the discussion around the nature of geopolitical subjects.

Seen in this vein, the concerted efforts by businesses to 'naturalise' the procedures and their products are more than mere advertising rhetoric; they speak to the integrity of the corporeal form. And yet, these concerns at a looming 'posthuman' condition, mobilised through a range of emotions from a maternal anxiety to the fostering of a xenophobia, also point up what Margrit Shildrick (2008: 31-2) calls a "plasticity," or "amenability to reconstruction" of the flesh. This is very much a fluid material, she argues, capable of being grafted into new forms and reconstituting itself anew; and, it is this same fluidity that is, paradoxically, welcomed precisely because it offers the promise of a reassembled corporate identity that, "sidesteps the ever-present threat of excessive proliferation, and of disintegration and decay." The same biomedical science that offers to rid the body of monstrous anomalies such as cancer, eradicating a biological difference in the process, is able to enhance the individual body's longevity; what is more, it provides some assurance of the successful reproduction of future, healthy generations. The biomedical *cut*, then, which has become such a feature of the birth process, also helps to cut away possible, unwelcome futurities for the family, community and nation.

References

American Academy of Pediatrics. 2007. Cord Blood Banking for Potential Future Transplantation, *Pediatrics* 119.1: 165-70.
Adams, Vincanne, Murphy, Michelle and Clarke, Adele E. 2009. Anticipation: Technoscience, Life, Affect and Temporality, *Subjectivities* 28: 246-65.
Almeling, Rene. 2011. *Sex Cells: The Medical Market for Eggs and Sperm*. Berkeley, CA: University of California Press.
Baylis, Françoise. 2009. For Love or Money? The Saga of Korean Women who Provided Eggs for Embryonic Stem Cell Research, *Theoretical Medicine and Bioethics* 30.5: 385-96.
Bhatia, Shekhar. 2012. They Queue to Donate their Eggs and Rent out their Wombs. One Payment Can Transform their Lives, *The Telegraph* 26 May, available at http://www.telegraph.co.uk/health/healthnews/9291913/They-

queue-to-donate-their-eggs-and-rent-out-their-wombs.-One-payment-can-transform-their-lives.html. Last accessed 24 September 2014.

Bieke Biotech Press Release, available at http://biekebiotech.com. Last accessed 24 September 2014.

Brown, Larisa and Narain, Jaya. 2012. Controversial 'Naked' Airport Body Scanners to be Scrapped after Failing to Receive European Approval,' *Daily Mail* 18th September, available at http://www.dailymail.co.uk/news/article-2204422/Controversial-naked-airport-body-scanners-scrapped-failing-receive-European-approval.html. Last accessed 24 September 2014.

Budd, Lucy, Bell, Morag and Warren, Adam. 2011. Maintaining the Sanitary Border: Air Transport Liberalisation and Health Security Practices at UK Regional Airports, *Transactions of the Institute of British Geographers* 36.2: 268-79.

Caulfield, Timothy and Zarzeczny, Amy. 2012. Stem Cell Tourism and Canadian Family Physicians, *Canadian Family Physician* 58.4: 365-8.

Cells4Life website, available at http://www.cells4life.co.uk/stem-cell-storage. Last accessed 24 September 2014.

Cobo, Fernando et al. 2005. Microbiological Control in Stem Cell Banks: Approaches to Standardisation, *Applied Microbiology and Biotechnology* 68.4: 456-66.

Cord Blood Awareness website, available at http://cordbloodawareness.org/popups/print_cord_blood_legislation.htm. Last accessed 24 September 2014.

Cordlife website, available at http://www.cordlife.com/sg/en/faq-cordlife-circle. Last accessed 24 September 2014.

Crozier, Gillian K.D. 2010. Protecting Cross-border Providers of Ova and Surrogacy Services? *Global Social Policy* 10.3: 299-303.

Cyranoski, David. 2010. Korean Deaths Spark Inquiry, *Nature* 468: 485.

Cyranoski, David. 2012. Stem-cell Therapy takes off in Texas, *Nature* 483: 13-14.

Cyro-Save Website, company web-pages, available at http://www.cryo-save.com/. Last accessed 24 September 2014.

Future Health Bio website, available at http://www.futurehealthbiobank.com/services/lipo-stem-cells?v=pricelist. Last accessed 24 September 2014.

Gunter, Kurt et al. 2010. Cell Therapy Medical Tourism: Time for Action, *Cytotherapy* 12.8: 965-8.

Gupta, Jyotsna A. 2006. Towards Transnational Feminisms Some Reflections and Concerns in Relation to the Globalization of Reproductive Technologies, *European Journal of Women's Studies* 13.1: 23-38.

Hull, Carrie. 2006. *Ontology of Sex: A Critical Inquiry into the Construction and Deconstruction of Categories*. London: Routledge.

Inhorn, Marcia C. 2012. Globalization and Gametes: Reproductive Tourism, Islamic Bioethics, and Middle Eastern Modernity. In Knecht, Michi, Beck, Stefan and Klotz, Maren (eds) *Reproductive Technologies as Global Form: Ethnographies of Knowledge, Practices, and Transnational Encounters*. Frankfurt: Campus Verlag, pp. 229-54.

Inhorn, Marcia C. and Shrivastav, Pankaj. 2010. Globalization and Reproductive tourism in the United Arab Emirates, *Asia-Pacific Journal of Public Health* 22.3: 68S-74S.

Isasi, Rosario M. and Knoppers, Bartha M. 2009. Governing Stem Cell Banks and Registries: Emerging issues, *Stem Cell Research* 3.2: 96-105.

Jones, David. 2012. The Designer Baby Factory: Eggs from Beautiful Eastern Europeans, Sperm from Wealthy Westerners and Embryos Implanted in Desperate Women, *Daily Mail* 12 May, available at http://www.dailymail.co.uk/news/article-2139708/The-designer-baby-factory-Eggs-beautiful-Eastern-Europeans-Sperm-wealthy-Westerners-And-embryos-implanted-desperate-women.html#ixzz2DbaXMtcO. Last accessed 24 September 2014.

Kiatpongsan, Sorapop and Sipp, Douglas. 2009. Monitoring and Regulating Offshore Stem Cell Clinics, *Science* 323.5921: 1564-5.

Kimbrell, Andrew. 1993. *The Human Body Shop*. New York: Harper Collins.

Koleva, Gergana. 2012. Stem Cells, FDA, and the Edge of Science: Three Expert Viewpoints, *Forbes* 19 February, available at http://www.forbes.com/sites/gerganakoleva/2012/02/19/stem-cells-fda-and-the-edge-of-science-three-expert-viewpoints/. Last accessed 24 September 2014.

LifeCell website, available at http://www.lifecellfemme.com/what_is_femme.aspx. Last accessed 24 September 2014.

Life Technologies website, available at http://www.invitrogen.com/etc/medialib/en/filelibrary/pdf.Par.6278.File.dat/StemPro-ADSC-Kit.pdf. Last accessed 24 September 2014.

Mathews, Debra et al. 2011. Access to Stem Cells and Data: Persons, Property Rights, and Scientific Progress, *Science (Washington)* 331.6018: 725-7.

Marey, Etienne-Jules, Amoore, Louise and Hall, Alexandra. 2009. Taking People Apart: Digitised Dissection and the Body at the Border, *Environment and Planning D: Society and Space* 27: 444-64.

Mendick, Robert. 2011. Stem Cell Clinic that 'preyed on the vulnerable, *The Telegraph* 8 April, available at http://www.telegraph.co.uk/health/healthnews/9192157/Stem-cell-clinic-that-preyed-on-the-vulnerable.html. Last accessed 24 September 2014.

Mendick, Robert and Hall, Allan. 2011. Europe's Largest Stem Cell Clinic Shut Down after Death of Baby, *The Telegraph* 8 May, available at http://www.telegraph.co.uk/news/worldnews/europe/germany/8500233/Europes-largest-stem-cell-clinic-shut-down-after-death-of-baby.html. Last accessed 24 September 2014.

Mohapatra, Seema. 2012. Achieving Reproductive Justice in the International Surrogacy Market, *Annals of Health Law* 21: 191-200.

Moran, Nuala. 2011. European Court Bans Embryonic Stem Cell Patents, *Nature Biotechnology* 29.12: 1057-9.

Office of the Governor Rick Perry, Texas Emerging Technology Fund. Available at http://governor.state.tx.us/ecodev/etf/etf_awards/. Last accessed 10 October 2014.

Parks, Jennifer A. 2010. Care Ethics and the Global Practice of Commercial Surrogacy, *Bioethics* 24.7: 333-40.

Pfeffer, Naomi. 2011. Eggs-ploiting Women: A Critical Feminist Analysis of the Different Principles in Transplant and Fertility Tourism, *Reproductive BioMedicine Online* 23.5: 634-41.

Political Guide, the, available at http://www.thepoliticalguide.com/Profiles/Governor/Texas/Rick_Perry/Views/Stem_Cell_Research/. Last accessed 24 September 2014.

Ramshaw, Emily. 2011a. Perry's Surgery Included Experimental Stem Cell Therapy, *Texas Tribune* 3 August, available at http://www.texastribune.org/texas-people/rick-perry/perrys-surgery-included-experimental-stem-cell-the/. Last accessed 24 September 2014.

Ramshaw, Emily. 2011b. Perry's Adult Stem Cell Treatment Was Doctor's First Attempt, *Texas Tribune* 4 August, available at http://www.texastribune.org/texas-people/rick-perry/perrys-stem-cell-treatment-was-doctors-first-attem/. Last accessed 24 September 2014.

Rao, Mahendra, Ahrlund-Richter, Lars and Kaufman, Dan. 2012. Concise Review: Cord Blood Banking, Transplantation and Induced Pluripotent Stem Cell: Success and Opportunities, *Stem Cells* 30.1: 55-60.

Shalev, Carmel. 2012. An Ethic of Care and Responsibility: Reflections on Third-Party Reproduction, *Medicine Studies* 3.3: 147-56.

Shalev, Carmel and Werner-Felmayer, Gabriele. 2012. Patterns of Globalized reproduction: Egg Cells Regulation in Israel and Austria, *Israel Journal of Health Policy Research* 1: 1-15.

Scheper-Hughes, Nancy. 2012. Bodies, Biotechnologies, and Moral Economies, *Current Anthropology* 53.4: 514-18.

Schwartz, Hillel. 1996. *The Culture of the Copy: Striking Likenesses, Unreasonable Facsimiles*. New York: Zone Books.

Shildrick, Margrit. 2008. Corporeal Cuts: Surgery and the Psycho-social, *Body and Society* 14.1: 31-46.

Skene, Loane. 2012. Development of Stem Cells from Umbilical Cord Blood and Blood Banking: "Non-controversial" and "Free of Political and Ethical Debate"? *Journal of Law and Medicine* 19.3: 490-96.

Spar, Debora. 2007. The Egg Trade—Making Sense of the Market for Human Oocytes, *New England Journal of Medicine* 356.13: 1289-91.

Stem-Health Hellas website available at http://stem-health.eu/public/. Last accessed 24 September 2014.

Storrow, Richard F. 2006. Quests for Conception: Fertility Tourists, Globalization and Feminist Legal Theory, *Hastings Law Journal* 57: 295-330.

Swiss Stem Cells website available at http://www.stembank.ch/home.aspx?ln=ENG.

Texas Department of Health State Services, 80th Legislative Session Summary Legislation Affecting the Department of State Health Services (DSHS), available at https://www.dshs.state.tx.us/legislative/80thSessionSummary-052307.pdf. Last accessed 24 September 2014.

Twine, France Winddance. 2012. *Outsourcing the Womb: Race, Class and Gestational Surrogacy in a Global Market*. London: Routledge.

ViaCord, Grandlife Magazine, available at http://www.google.co.uk/url?sa=t&rct=j&q=&esrc=s&source=web&cd=2&ved=0CDUQFjAB&url=http%3A%2F%2Fwww.viacord.com%2Fbfac6ce5-e674-468a-9e98-dd856ff1f5f0%2FLink.pdf&ei=xTy3UJf5LMGi0QWikICoDg&usg=AFQjCNFYW9mqcsuonYhUON9ZxfG4X29WHA. Last accessed 24 September 2014.

Virgin Health Bank, available at http://www.virginhealthbank.com/our-services/community-banking/community-banking?t=98&. Last accessed 24 September 2014.

Wadvalla, Bibi-Aisha. 2012. Business of Stem Cell Banks Questioned, *Nature Middle East*, 9 April, available at http://www.nature.com/nmiddleeast/2012/120409/full/nmiddleeast.2012.51.html. Last accessed 24 September 2014.

Waldby, Catherine and Cooper, Melinda. 2010. From Reproductive Work to Regenerative Labour: The Female Body and the Stem Cell Industries, *Feminist Theory* 11.1: 3-22.

Chapter 4
Bones

Introduction

The formation, warping, fracturing, knitting and dispersal of human bones has remained a largely unremarked upon, 'background' element of geopolitics. They are readily denoted as collateral damage; one of the many the end-products of violent conflict. Yet, as with flesh, bones have a considerable cross-border movement shaped once again by a fluid distribution of capital, and animate a series of therapeutic and cosmetic becomings. Cadaveric bones and splinters are used to repair damage to the living body, to ameliorate 'deformity,' and to replace bone destroyed or removed because of cancer. Human bone is also ground for cement in orthopaedic operations and as a dental filler. On occasion, we gain glimpses of the extended geography of this market, as when bones stripped from the corpse of journalist Alistair Cooke in a New Jersey funeral home, for example, were discovered to have been shipped to a series of medical tissue companies before being implanted in orthopaedic patients throughout the US, Canada and Europe (Kittredge 2006). In this chapter, though, I want to take a different route in regard to bones, and that is to focus not so much upon their geopolitical 'life' as corporeally disassociated parts – a life underwritten by their diverse physio-chemical and biological capacities – but rather the manner in which these obdurate yet breakable fragments are afforded an 'afterlife.' That is, how they come to be understood, valorised, ignored, and recovered as tangible expressions of a lived experience of suffering and trauma – understandings that play upon the bleeding of time as well as space – but also as touchstones for the creation of gendered knowledges concerning what is appropriate (and not) to the world of war, conflict and international relations.

In this chapter, I want to address how the afterlife of bones helps animate some expected, and unexpected, geopolitical contexts, thereby shedding light on how particular kinds of knowledges and practices, but also a wealth of emotions, are mobilised in the process. And in keeping with my broader argument on the importance of imagining a world outside of a classical geopolitical discourse and its biological underpinnings, I want to start with an estranged way of knowing bones that precedes and pervades the medical-scientific discourses we take so much for granted today. In the next section, *Knowing in our Bones*, I trace something of how our current, intimate knowledge of bones has indeed emerged in concert with the technologies of warfare, such that it is their particular vulnerabilities that became an object of concern. Such knowledges helped constitute a burgeoning European Enlightenment, predicated upon centres of collection, calculation and examination, and their purported margins. I want to stress, however, how this very productive afterlife has also proceeded alongside a knowledge of 'supplemental' female bones, not associated with warfare, but with reproduction, such that two sets of anatomical expertise, highly gendered and understood to exist in counterpart to each other, emerged.

Using as a case study the development of Edinburgh, Scotland, as a medical centre of excellence, I look to the Enlightened pursuit of empirically-grounded, 'useful' knowledge predicated on a detailed, interior knowledge of the military male anatomy, and a reproductive female anatomy, each increasingly disassembled into component parts that could be used as the object of analysis for a particular problematic. On the one hand, for example, male military bones both grounded and prompted ideas on physiological suffering; on the other hand, female bones associated with reproduction allowed for the location and evidencing of the supernatural, a topic very much set apart from the more traditional geopolitical fare of territorial acquisition and battles, despite the violences and terrors it engendered, as well as the critical role played by the suppression of superstition in the making of a modern citizenry for modern nations. Underpinning this section is an emphasis on how this 'coming alive' of bones helps to flesh out the notion of an Enlightenment world composed of rigidly heterosexual, gendered subjects, 'placed' according to their biological taxonomies. Indeed, the representation of parts of the human body in 'anatomical atlases' – images that splayed the body ready for a visual consumption of its interior spaces – were matched by the hatchures and contours, horizons and vistas, of a mapping of territory (Sawchuk 2013), an association that emerged not so much from the translation of cartographic practices into another realm, but from a shared rendering of purported wholes – the body and the country – into their ever more detailed constituent parts, each of which, like the mythological Atlas, supports the larger ensemble.

To refer to an afterlife brings with it an attentiveness to time as lived and embodied, as opposed to abstract and standardised. And, in Chapter 3, such a temporality emerged from the 'becoming' of flesh, and the generation of an anticipatory maternal anxiety. Here, however, I want to focus on how particular temporalities, such as 'remembering,' are capacities of the living body that emerge in association with, and indeed are shaped by, the materialities to hand, and, one might add, the materialities that escape the grasp. Certainly, the physical obduracy of bones as the last readily identifiable remainders of the human body has been pivotal in the mobilisation of all manner of emotions as well as investigations into human anatomy. To paraphrase Sommer (2007: 7), bones possess a physical reality, to be sure, but 'come alive' in the hands, minds and eyes of their manipulators and contemplators. The excavation of bones, for example, allows for their, "entering into spaces and networks of representation, investigation, accumulation, distribution and exhibition [and is] accompanied by a decontextualisation and subsequent recontextualisations, by a disappropriation from their time and place and a translation into ... new times and places" (ibid.). Such bones come alive as, for example: material reminders and touchstones of religious allegiances that work to another global imaginary than that provided by the nation-state; portentous objects that see order and revolution inscribed into the anatomy; evidence and symptom of a brutal colonialism; tokens of reconciliation, remembrance and forgetting; and, of course, stark symbols of the death of the family, community and nation. As with the flesh of Chapter 3, there is also the promise of a future reconciliation offered by bones. This reconciliation lies not so much with the living body, however, than with an individualised, deceased forensic identity that can be confirmed via reference to medical and dental records, or a DNA match with other samples.

Given that so many geopolitical relations and experiences revolve around violence and death, it is unsurprising to find that bones, as the last, relatively large, physically obdurate evidence of a particular human life cut short, have become so politicised as proofs of repression and holocaust, and as a spur to further conflict, but also as a means of reconciliation and peace-making. In the section *The Bones Will Tell*, I outline something of the fraught, visceral politics that centre on bones by reference to the twentieth century's Spanish Civil War and the manner in which a leaving in the ground of the bones of the dead became central to a 'Pact of Oblivion'. Such a leaving was very much out of step with the growing clamour for the unearthing of bones located in mass graves across South America and Africa as well as Asia in the late twentieth and early twenty-first century, and can certainly be viewed as an effort to forestall further civil division that might emerge through a victim identification process. It can also be seen, however, as part of a longer term struggle over the placement of the dead within a state-sanctioned 'public memory,' somewhat akin to General MacArthur's attempt to de-link the defeated Japanese state from the memorialisation of those Japanese soldiers killed in World War II at the Yasukuni Shrine, which houses the souls of people and animals killed in the service of the Emperor. Visits to this site by senior officials, including Japanese Prime Ministers, still generate international controversy, whilst the furore over who was allowed to memorialise what in the aftermath of the Battle of Okinawa, Figal (2007) writes, was a diplomatic imbroglio. What I want to emphasise in the context of the Spanish Civil War, and an ensuing policy of oblivion that centres on the leaving of bones in the ground, is a politics that frames remembrance not so much as an exploration of the past, but as a spectacularised backdrop against which the reanimated dead play out a drama of good and evil. This a politics that both acknowledges and responds to (amongst other things) a hyper-masculine, Fascist fetishisation of the dead and, in turn, the feminisation of a beleaguered populace that must live on. What this emphasis allows me to draw out is how bones come to provide a material reference point not only for executed family members, but the fate of the family under Fascist regimes.

In closing the chapter, I want to bring this attentiveness to memory back into a discussion of the role of bones in a burgeoning Enlightenment world of male and female bodies, and the kinds of knowledges predicated on these. What I want to emphasise is how the fraught politics of remembering, so often carried out as a form of 'public memory,' can serve to destabilise the very notion of a modern nation. That is, rhetorics of familial belonging and loss also animate debates around the fate of bones collected as part of a US government initiative to evidence the racial inferiority of Native American Indians. Here, I want to use recent efforts to reappropriate these bones to shed light on how the centres of collection outlined in section two themselves do not 'rest in peace,' but can become embedded in debates that query not only their authoritative status as research sites, but also their geopolitical import as the intellectual and political centrepieces of a modern day, progressive community of nation-states.

Knowing in our Bones

As Charles Withers (2008) illustrates, the Enlightenment was not simply a network of correspondence among European érudits, *savants* and *philosophes*, and the swapping of curious and interesting objects acquired from the furthest reaches of empire. Enlightenment knowledges that took broad stock of the 'Natural' were firmly rooted in 'local' physical and environmental, but also social, geographies. Indeed, it is the 'power of place' to shape scientific inquiry, Withers argues, as well as the movement of ideas, personnel and artefacts over space, that are key to understanding how the Enlightenment was made and what it was. The rarefied, scholarly world of the Parisian salon, for example, was predicated upon places that were not simply collection sites, ordered and categorised through an emerging Natural History; these were also the setting for often intense power plays and emotional registers.

Certainly, the centres of medical excellence associated with the Enlightenment – Paris, London, Edinburgh – were all enabled to a large degree by far-flung fields of military conflict, and the *in situ* development of particular forms of anatomical knowledge that, over the course of the Enlightenment, became both an empirical grounding for new theorisations of the body, and testament to the brutalism of modern warfare. As I go on to outline below, such knowledges were highly gendered, classed and raced in terms of how they were produced, by whom and in what context. And so this particular coming alive of bones provides insight into the shape and efficacy of colonial, and subsequently imperial, power dynamics underpinning this period. But also, I hope to indicate that this scientific interrogation of bones helped to animate broader understandings of the nature of male and female, and offered authoritative comments on how such understandings were indeed to be empirically 'grounded.'

Knowledge of bones, and a practical attention to bone-setting and surgeries, clearly has a long history and, in recent years, feminist scholars have been keen to point out the role of women in these endeavours, as well as their gradual effacement. In twelfth century Europe, it was a church decree forbidding monks from blood-letting, bone-setting or performing operations that confirmed a woman's place in this regard, insofar as they, amongst other less valued folk, such as male 'barber-surgeons,' were charged with such tasks. In the fourteenth and fifteenth centuries, however, we see the gradual erosion of this right by various governmental apparatus'. An edict of 1313, for example, prohibited women from practicing surgery in Paris unless they had been examined by a competent jury, whilst in 1484 all women, except the widows of barber-surgeons, lost their right to practice (see Pastena 1993). In England, Henry VIII, whilst granting a charter for the Company of Barber Surgeons in 1540, effectively barred women from membership with the famous quote, "No carpenter, smith, weaver or women shall practise surgery" (cited in Wirtzfeld 2009: 318). Nevertheless, women such as Elizabeth Bedell continued to practice surgery from their homes, despite the threat of fines and imprisonment.

In 1543, with the publication in Latin of the Flemish surgeon Vesalius' *De Humani Corpius Fabrica*, there is the first 'authoritative' argument for delving into the hidden interior of the human body, via dissection, as a means of coming to grips with the human condition, albeit based on evidence gleaned from mostly male cadavers executed by the state. It is unsurprising to find, then, that whilst this classic text describes foetal life in the amniotic sac, there is almost no information about the female body, the pregnant female body, or the foetus (Erikson 2007). As the Renaissance unfolded, however, we can discern a rapid expansion of anatomical knowledge of male and female bodies, in large part because of continuing military warfare across Europe, which now featured highly destructive firearms, but also by virtue of the emergence of 'lying in' wards in the larger cities. Surgeons – most but not all men by this point – were able to gain practical experience of working with bones in these two very different sites. And, working across this intensely classed as well as gendered geography was to become a dominant feature of Renaissance surgical careers.

A prominent example of this geography is the career of French surgeon Ambroise Paré (1510-90), initially trained in shaving, hairdressing and poulticing but who also, by attending Paris' largest hospital, the Catholic Church-run Hôtel-Dieu, gained a great deal of practical experience in childbirth. Here, poor women, more often than not four to a bed, were kept in the separate St. Joseph's ward before, during and after childbirth (La Motte 1906). It was Paré who, in 1549, reintroduced the literate, academic world to the podalic version, whereby the foetus is turned around *in utero* and delivered feet first, and who recommended a range of instruments to extract a dead child from the birth canal in addition to the midwives' crochet, or hook. Paré's own writings were in French, thereby significantly expanding the practical knowledge of an emerging cohort of surgeons who, unlike physicians, were not deemed worthy of being taught Latin. Such efforts were also, of course, a confirmation of the pedagogic authority now being invested in men looking at the interior of women's bodies, and wielding a number of instruments as a means of manipulating their contents.

As I go on to outline below, this gendering of who did what, as well as what became known about whom, was to become a defining feature of Enlightenment obstetrics. An oft unremarked upon feature of this burgeoning anatomical work, however, was its equally authoritative medico-legal role in demonising same-sex sex, as well as cases of alleged witchcraft and possession, topics that rarely make their way into discussions of prevailing geopolitics. To a large extent, this is because there is a long-standing tendency in writings on a knowledge of bones and surgery to locate these in terms of the 'advance' of medical science, and the leaving behind of superstition. And, feminist scholarship has done much to highlight the gendering of such practices, as well as the exceptional role played by women such as Paré's pupil Louise Bourgeois (1563-1636), who delivered Marie de' Medici, the wife of King Henri IV of France in her six confinements, and wrote of the inducement of premature labour in women with contracted pelves (Pastena 1993).

Yet, this hagiographic treatment can be further queried by looking to the expert role carved out for male surgeons dealing with all manner of reproductive and sexual issues. Paré's *Des Monstres et Prodiges* (1573), for instance, published in English in 1634, warns of the monstrous nature of female genitalia, which mimics that of the male and, when at risk of being used in a homoeroticism, must needs be cut away. In 1609 another of Paré's pupils, Pierre Pigray (c. 1532-1613), published *Epitome des préceptes de médecine et chirurgie*, which provides advice to young surgeons who may be called upon to provide the 'expert testimony' required of French courts. This included, as Yvonne Petry (2012: 52) points out, investigations of infanticide,

> often suspected when unmarried women lost babies and where the social stigma of illegitimacy increased its likelihood. Rape was broadly defined to include what we would call seduction, and was used as a legal category by the French state to declare elopements invalid and enforce parental authority over their children. Impotence also became a legal issue because it was considered grounds for dissolving a marriage. Even cases of hermaphroditism, several of which gained notoriety in early modern France, involved complex medical and legal issues. As expert witnesses, surgeons played an important function in all such cases, which helped to elevate their professional and social status.

Importantly, such courts also became crucial sites wherein decisions were made as to whether particular bodily ailments could be caused by witchcraft or possession. Such experts, "became participants in one of the most fundamental intellectual enterprises of the early modern era, that is, the clarification of boundaries between the natural and supernatural realms" (Petry 2012: 47).

The authority vested in men such as Paré and Pigray reminds us, I want to emphasise, of an often unremarked upon political situation that unfolded across Europe and beyond on a substantial time-scale, one that parallels the battlefield in terms of loss of life and suffering. Since the eighth century, the Church had made a sustained effort to influence civil law within its spiritual domain, urging anti-witchcraft legislation that would subject acts laid out in, for example, the 'List of Superstitions,' drawn up by the Council of Leptinnes in 744 AD, to prosecution. By the thirteenth century, the Church had issued a series of Papal Edicts on the need for 'inquisitions' that linked together heresy, witchcraft, sodomy, promiscuity and obscenity, rendering them indistinguishable from each other. And, it is between 1450 and 1750 that we see the 'Great Witch Hunts,' manifest in the execution of peasants in Switzerland, then Germany and the Lowlands, Spain, the UK and the US. As Sylvia Federici (2004) argues, the identification, demonisation and expulsion of witches, the vast majority of whom were female, was crucial to a political ordering of people and place not only during this period, but in contemporary communities across the globe (Federici 2010), such that a profound reworking of the personhood of women was, and continues to be, wrought.

It is not too surprising to find that Paré's much vaunted reputation as the 'Father of Modern Surgery' was to emerge not from his work on the ward, or his proofs and disproofs of witchcraft, but from his work on the battlefield, a geopolitical site that has a much more respectable lineage by virtue of the well archived actions of elites, and their territorial understandings and desires. Certainly, Europe at this period was plunged into a series of armed conflicts stemming from a dynastic rivalry between Francis I (King of France 1515-1547), in alliance with Suleiman the Magnificent (Sultan of the Ottoman Empire 1520-1566), and Emperor Charles V (1519-1556), which included a series of Italian Wars. Over the course of the sixteenth century, these were to embroil most of the Italian city-states, the Papal states, and England and Scotland, as well as France, Spain, the Holy Roman Empire and the Ottoman Empire. It is in this context that religion more usually becomes part and parcel of a geopolitical canon, as differing belief systems, as well as a desire for territorial acquisition, become a way of explaining this 'clash' of civilisations.

Graduating in 1536, Paré was to work intermittently over the course of 30 years as a military surgeon, observing the impact of gunshot on bones, and the types of wounds and fractures caused (Figure 4.1). The rounded gunshot of the arquebus, for example – a muzzle-loaded, shoulder-fired gun – despite their low velocity, smashed bones by virtue of their large size and irregular motion, and were accompanied by "contusion, dilaceration, distemper, and swelling" (cited in Milburn 1901: 1532). Fired in volleys by squads of soldiers, the arquebus was to play a devastating role in the military revolution of the late sixteenth century. It was also a crucial tool for colonial subjugation by the dominant European powers during this period: in the 1520s the arquebus was used by soldiers of Hernán Cortés in the conquest of Mexico; they were pivotal to Cristóvão da Gama's 1541-42 campaign in Ethiopia; and were used in the 1590 Battle of Tondibi, which saw the defeat of the Songhai Empire. In publications such as *La Méthod de traicter les playes faites par les arquebuses et aultres bastons à feu* (1545), Paré, "always tended to apply his own commonsense and acute faculty of observation to any practical problem," Page (1952: 336) writes, and remained a pacifist, "freely [expressing] his views on the horrors and barbarities of war and the shortcomings of the soldiery."

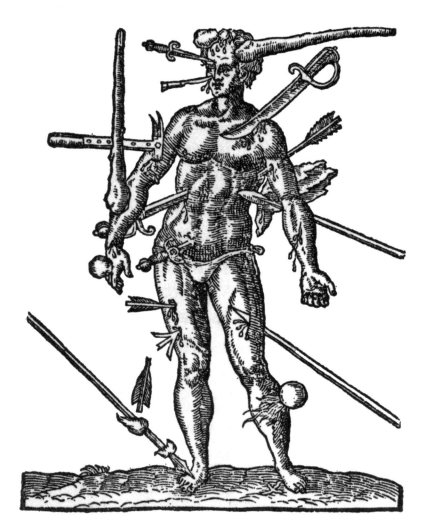

Figure 4.1   Wounds Man, reprinted in Ambroise Paré's *Opera Chirurgica*, 1594

Source: http://commons.wikimedia.org/wiki/File:Wounds_Man.jpg. The original woodcut was created by Johannes Wechtlin (1480-1529); this and similar images featured in numerous field manuals on the treatment of wounds suffered in battle.

French surgeons, but also those embedded in other European armies, continued to learn in the battlefield over the course of the seventeenth century, nurturing a very particular knowledge of bones concerned with their physical character, which was prone to fracturing when hit by gunshot, and the manner in which bones were related to the tearing of the flesh in entry and exit wounds, as well as the internal cavities produced by shots piercing the body. It is not until the eighteenth century, however, that we see a glut of publications on wound treatment that enabled the proliferation of particular techniques across Europe and their increasing uniformity in practice. There are numerous reasons as to why this network of publications and presentations emerged, but in large part they were both symptomatic of, and enabling of, the development of particular sites of Enlightenment learning, wherein battlefield experience was matched by an increasingly specialised series of courses on anatomy taught by both physicians and surgeons, and bolstered by an empirically driven research programme that sought to produce knowledge of how the body worked in physical and neurological detail, and in comparison with other bodies. The Renaissance Hôtel-Dieu at which Paré studied may well be described as a proto-'clinic,' in Foucault's sense of the term, by virtue of its provision of, "abundant opportunities to learn normal and pathological anatomy and to practise surgical operations on the cadavers of deceased indigent patients," and the search for, "solutions to practical problems, problems which, for the most part, related directly to therapy." Yet, there was, Toby Gelfand (1981: 176-7) advises, no responsive and wide-ranging emphasis here on a more abstract knowledge production outside of therapeutic treatments.

We can track something of the transition of a sited body of knowledge and practice, from treatment to research, by looking at the suite of organisations and institutions that combined to make Edinburgh, Scotland, a world-renowned medical centre of excellence. When the Town of Edinburgh authorised the Incorporation of Surgeon Barbers (or, college) in 1505, it allowed them, once a year, an executed man to perform anatomy on, such that practising and learning surgeons would be able to gain a working knowledge of the skeletal articulation, and various muscles, veins and nerves and so on, of the human body. In 1694 the Incorporation asked the Town Council for, "the dead bodies of foundlings who die betwixt the time they are weaned and their being put to school or trades," as well as suicides, a request the Town granted on condition that the surgeons finance the building of a Surgeon's Hall, "where they shall have once a year ... and publick anatomicall dissection" (Struthers 1867: 154). Here, in 1699, was begun a "Library of Physicall, Anatomicall, Chirurgicall, Botanicall, Pharmaceuticall and other curious books," and a collection of surgical instruments that could be loaned out to members. The appropriation of material from 'marginal' members of society for experimentation into the human form and condition was to be accompanied by textual resources and scholarly practices that legitimised such a voracious consumption as for the greater good.

The Royal College of Physicians of Edinburgh was established in 1681, to be followed by the University of Edinburgh Faculty of Medicine in 1726, when the first Professor of Anatomy was also appointed. In 1729 the Edinburgh Royal Infirmary was built and began to take in paying students. It was in 1804, however, that the College of Surgeons established the post of Professor of Surgery and began a wide-ranging collection of 'morbid preparations' to not only aid surgical teaching, but also to build an anatomical collection that would prove an empirical testing ground for theorisations as to how the nervous system, for example, operated.

And, it must be added, to identify Edinburgh via this display as a modern-day, progressive centre for science. Much of the material for this collection was either donated in 1821 by anatomist John Barclay (1758-1826), who had amassed his own comparative collection of over 2,500 specimens, with some sent as gifts from abroad by his grateful students, or bought in 1825 from Charles Bell (1774-1842), a graduate of Edinburgh's Royal College of Surgeons and then the inaugural Professor of Anatomy and Surgery of the College of Surgeons in London.

For Anand Chitnis (1960: 173), medical knowledge and practice increasingly predicated on new and expanded "didactic techniques based on observation, experimentation and practice" lay at the heart of this centre of Scottish Enlightenment, further manifest in the scholarship of David Hume and Adam Smith, as well as the, "building of the Edinburgh New Town; the foundation of the Royal Society of Edinburgh, the Encyclopaedia Britannica, and the Edinburgh Review." Moreover, he writes, "While neither Edinburgh's university nor her Royal Colleges monopolised the education of the most distinguished nineteenth-century British medical practitioners, they did produce the majority of systematically trained doctors, and an estimated one-third of those serving in the medical departments of the Army, Navy and East India Company" (ibid.: 174). Certainly, the Napoleonic Wars (1803-15), emerging from conflicts already set in motion by the French Revolution of 1789, and having manifold repercussions such as the dissolution of the Holy Roman and Spanish Empires (and the accompanying emergence of nascent nationalisms in Germany and Italy, as well as across Middle and South America), provided a field-based learning environment for these Edinburgh-trained anatomists, many of whom were either military surgeons embedded in units, or voluntary surgeons who arrived in the aftermath of particular battles, standing, one might say, like Lord Byron's childe Harold, upon a field of skulls.

Importantly, these field sites themselves were not simply an opportunity to practice and experiment with therapeutic treatments, but provided occasion for new ideas on a wide range of issues to emerge. Charles Bell, for example, who was to play such a large part in building up the College of Surgeon's collections, used his experiences to think through but also to evidence his evolving ideas on neurology, and in particular the physical expression of emotion. Trained in drawing, painting and engraving, as well as anatomy, Bell had illustrated his brother John's *Engravings Explaining the Anatomy of Bones, Muscles and Joints* (1794), co-authored and illustrated *The Anatomy of the Human Body* (1797-1803), and published in 1806 his *Essays on The Anatomy of Expression in Painting*. In 1809, Charles Bell was assigned to the naval hospital in Portsmouth, where he treated and sketched casualties from the Battle of Corunna. These were later worked into 15 oil paintings, intended to illustrate the gunshot wounds that produced the fractures evident in the (largely amputated) bones he collected from here.

The specimens Bell collected – some with musketballs still embedded, others with sabre cuts – are open to view today at the Surgeon's Museum in Edinburgh. As was standard practice through to the end of World War I, Bell as a military surgeon assumed ownership of the material remains of his deceased patients.

The variously macerated and sliced bones are mounted with wire and tagged according to the nature of the wound and the operation performed. Above them are hung the oil paintings Bell produced, lending a further pedagogic quality insofar as we can see where the shot entered and exited, and how ensuing damage to the limbs and torso impacted upon the soldiers' physiological capacity, and instilled particular kinds of trauma. For Bell the surgeon, these images helped him to think through and convey the nature of suffering, literally carved into the soldier's body. Contemporary visitors to the museum can see here the vulnerability of flesh and bone, a vision that, perhaps, we are less familiar with, not because there are no more suffering soldiers (or civilians), but because many of us have grown used to the hard-bodied masculinism of the war movie, or the grainy footage of bombs dropping. There is not the same immersive affect in these oil paintings; they remain framed, at a remove, held up against the wall. But, the layers of flesh tone, splashed with red and bereft of insignia, do afford some sense of the messy tide of warfare. Even for those not conversant with prevailing military technologies, the paintings, set alongside the bone fragments, convey something of the geography of combat, especially the intimate distances involved between gun and body, sabre and body, and the sweeping velocities required to inflict injury. Such images may well have been shocking, we can speculate, to a nineteenth century audience more used to the nationalist aesthetics of military display performed, for example, by ranks of mounted cavalrymen in pristine uniforms (as discussed by Hoegaerts 2010).

Bell was also to be involved in the Napoleonic Wars (1799-1815), often described as the first modern or 'world war' insofar as large segments of the British population were to be mobilised as part of the nation's war effort (Townsend 2005). This required not only that the soldiers themselves developed an individualised initiative and commitment to fight in these drawn out campaigns, but that citizens become emotionally embroiled in its unfolding through their consumption of a media spectacle that transported them to the battlefield. If the philosopher Hegel, Susan Buck-Morss (1992) observes, writing his *Phenomenology of Mind* whilst the Battle of Jena (1806) waged within earshot, came to the opinion that Napoleon's ascendance signified the realisation of Reason, the effect of war on surgeon Charles Bell was, by contrast, an attentiveness to the visceral. Indeed, the experience of war was a sensory overload that subsumed Reason and the articulation of either sentiment or meaning. Only the sketch – replicating as it did the contours of flesh and bone (Figure 4.2) – could convey something of the horrors of battle. For Bell, reflecting on his work treating enemy combatants in Brussels in the aftermath of Waterloo in 1815,

> All the decencies of performing surgical operations were soon neglected; while I amputated one man's thigh, there lay at one time thirteen, all beseeching to be taken next ... It was a strange thing to feel my clothes stiff with blood, and my arms powerless with the exertion of using the knife; and more extraordinary still, to find my mind calm amidst such a variety of suffering... After being eight

days amongst the wounded, I visited the field of battle. The view of the field, the gallant stories, the charges, the individual instances of enterprise and valour recalled me to the sense the world has of victory and Waterloo. But this was transient. A gloomy, uncomfortable view of human nature, is the inevitable consequence of looking upon the whole as I did – as I am forced to do. It is a misfortune to have our sentiments at variance with the universal sentiment. But there must ever be associated with the honours of Waterloo, in my eyes, the shocking signs of woe: to my ears, accents of intensity, outcry from the manly breast, interrupted, forcible expressions from the dying-and noisome smells. I must show you my note book, for as I took my notes of cases by sketching the object of our remarks, it may convey an excuse for this excess of sentiment. (cited in Pichot 1860: 80-82)

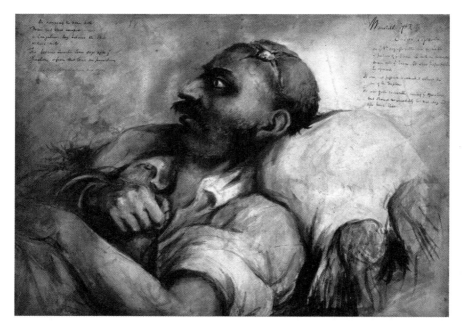

Figure 4.2   Sketch by Charles Bell, 1815, illustrating a gunshot wound to the skull and trepanning

Source: Royal Army Medical Corps Muniment Collection, Wellcome Images.

The muscles of the face – the 'fifth nerve' – particularly intrigued Bell, insofar as they organised expression, which in turn was both a manifestation of the mind and a language to be read by another. The sense of shock, and ensuing trauma, that Bell identifies, Buck-Morss writes, is akin to both Sigmund Freud's analysis of World War I 'shell-shock,' and Walter Benjamin's neurological understanding of the 'excessive' experience of modernity and the capacity of reason to shield us from this. Such a shock is, not a psychological category of sympathy or compassion, of understanding the other's point of view from the perspective of intentional meanings, but, rather, physiological – a sensory mimesis, a response of the nervous system to external stimuli which was 'excessive' because what he apprehended was *un*intentional, in the sense that it resisted intellectual comprehension. It could not be given meaning. The category of rationality could be applied to these physiological perceptions only in the sense of rationalization. (Buck-Morss, 1992: 15, emphasis in original)

Bell's insights into a soldier-centred, visceral geopolitics, one might add, have also been built on by subsequent historians of surgical practice such as Milburn (1901) and Page (1952). Their accounts draw out the impact on bodies of the switch to Minié rifles in the latter half of the nineteenth century, for example, with their large, spinning shot that burst bones in the US civil war battlefields, as well as those of Algerian soldiers facing the French army in North Africa. The introduction of elongated 'pencil bullets,' and, later, nickel-coated bullets, actually lessened bone damage, as these projectiles tended to squeeze between bone and tissue. Dum Dum bullets, however, engineered for the British army in India and the Sudan, were designed to expand on impact. These were eventually banned (by 22 votes to 2) under the 1899 Hague Convention at the behest of the German delegation. As Barbara Tuchman (2011) observes, the unsuccessful British defense of the Dum Dum was that it was required to stop the fanatical advance of the colonial 'savage' who, in contrast to the rational European soldier, would not stop at a mere wound, an argument the US representative apparently concurred with.

Whilst the pictures of splayed flesh and exposed bone fragments accompanying much more recent reports on military injuries still invoke a sense of disgust at what can be done to bodies, the explicit pacifism, and discourse on the horror of warfare, apparent in such early accounts by military surgeons are no longer to be discerned. Instead, bones are now explained by virtue of their mechanical stresses and failures, which are teased out, physically as well as metaphorically, by the relative mass, velocity and spin of various projectiles. The rhetorics deployed in engineering armaments have been extended into the flesh and bone of those on the receiving end, weaving their fragmented bodies into a thoroughly apersonal network composed of energy and stress, force and resistance. Consider, for example, Rozen and Dudkiewikz's (2011: 22) explanation of a high-energy gunshot wound, wherein,

> More rigid tissue such as bone resists deformation, and offers a greater resistance, resulting in greater energy transfer. The energy transfer may cause tissue damage by direct laceration by the projectile. Energy lost due to the resistance of the tissue results in the development of compressive waves that radiate away from the projectile tract and can damage tissues (with the formation of a temporary cavity) by accelerating energy transfer to anything in contact with the projectile

as it passes through the tissue (Cavitation), which is thought to be the most significant factor in tissue injury from high-energy projectiles.

By comparison, military historians and historical geographers provide glimpses of the battlefield as a complex, fraught site of bodily trauma, some of which remains traced in the bones collected by surgeons such as Bell. And these, I want to argue, help to trouble the explanatory language of centres and margins that has haunted literature on the Enlightenment. It is tempting, for example, to note Edinburgh as a centre of calculation and research over and against those 'peripheral' places in India patrolled, for example, by men such as Charles Ballingall, appointed assistant-surgeon of the 2nd battalion in 1806. Ballingall took the opportunity to send his teacher, James Barclay, numerous animal as well as human bones for his collection during his 13 years in India. And, it is telling that when fully articulated human skeletons for teaching and research remained difficult to get a hold of, even after the passage in the UK of the 1832 Anatomy Act, collection efforts shifted to some of the Empire's poorest regions, such as Western Bengal, spawning a series of grave-robbing, cleaning, preparation and export businesses that were to remain in operation until 1985. As Carney (2007: 270) reports,

> In India, members of the *dom* caste, who traditionally performed cremations, were pressed into service processing bones. In the 1850s, Calcutta Medical College processed 900 skeletons a year, mostly for shipment abroad. A century later, a newly independent India dominated the world market for human bones. In 1985, the *Chicago Tribune* reported that India had exported about 60,000 skulls and skeletons the year before. The supply was sufficient for every medical student in the developed world to buy a bone box along with their textbooks. Price: $300.

Stripped of flesh, these bones were cleaned to a pristine whiteness prized by medical students and doctors; a whiteness that has since become the aesthetic norm. A media-led panic over the purported killing of hundreds of children for their much sort after skeletons prompted the Indian Government, in 1985, to outlaw the export of human remains. In consequence, Carney adds,

> the global supply of skeletons collapsed. Western countries turned to China and Eastern Europe, but those regions produce relatively few skeletons. They have little experience producing display-quality specimens, and their products are regarded as inferior. (2007: 271)

Whilst recognising the sustained military intervention that allowed for the presence and activity of men such as Ballingall, it would be misleading to assume, however, that such Enlightenment geographies were either one-way or clear-cut, such that one can summarily refer to centres of calculation as located within Enlightenment Europe. To be sure, as Nair (2005) remarks, from the 1770s onwards the East India Company, with men such as Joseph Banks (1744-1820) as advisors, systematically collected and shipped out a host of 'natural productions' from across the Indian subcontinent. What is more, surgeons such as Frederic Mouat (1816-1897), a graduate of Edinburgh University and member of the military Indian Medical Service in India, took the opportunity to collect specimens whilst in service; indeed, Mouat was to eventually produce his own anatomical atlas in 1849, published by the Bishop's College Press, Calcutta. Small wonder, then, that, "Writings in the history of modern science in India have largely been dominated by the view that scientific practice in late eighteenth and early nineteenth century was wholly shaped by the mercantilist motivations of the Company" (Nair 2005: 280). Yet, during the late eigteenth century, early nineteenth centuries, Nair adds, Raja Serfoji (1777-1832) of the Maratha principality of Tanjore in southern India was inspired by these same ideals concerning individual and social progress to systematically collect and undertake detailed and intimate research into the human body. To do so he financed the construction of new learning and research sites including a pharmacy, a menagerie, libraries, Marathi and Tamil printing presses and educational institutions.

Here, Nair argues, we see not the displacement and awkward juxtaposition of artefacts in a cabinet of curiosity – a mode of collection, I go onto note in Chapter 5, that resonates with a mercantilist philosophy – but rather their careful emplacement within an assemblage of objects and practices, all rendered significant by virtue of their capacity to provoke a reasoned and empirically grounded understanding of the body, and of the human condition *per se*. Central to Serfoji's efforts were surgical instruments, anatomy plates and texts including those produced by John and Charles Bell. The collection also included bones, skeletons, and preserved human bodies, this despite Serfoji belonging to the *kshatriya* caste that forbade the touching of skeletons and dead bodies. Such objects, made knowable via reference to the Bell brothers' large, colourful plates, and their detailed exposition of bones in relation to muscles, nerves, arteries and so on, performed a geography of their own, one that takes the form not so much of a network of objects, but of a series of visceral, as well as cognitive, encounters.

It is worth noting, moreover, that in such encounters there remained a paucity of female representations, though the coveted skeletons of women and children shipped from Western Bengal to places such as Edinburgh somewhat made of for this pedagogic shortfall. In large part, this was because the anatomical atlases that scholars such as Raja Serfoji so admired for their probing and faithful view of the human body were produced prior to the UK's 1832 Anatomy Act, and so were primarily drawn from the more readily accessible male cadavers. In terms of what *was* available, Susan Erikson (2007: 67) notes, "It was as if anatomy sought to dispel fantasies about the power that mothers have over life. Instead, in the minds of the anatomists, and in their books of instruction, mothers were already in pieces, already symbolically dead." Both Glasgow-trained surgeon (or, 'man midwife' as the profession became known) William Smellie's *A Sett of Anatomical Tables, with Explanations,* and *an Abridgment, of the Practice of Midwifery* (1754), and London-based William Hunter's *The Anatomy of the Human Gravid Uterus Exhibited in Figures* (1774), Erikson argues, emphasised an aesthetic as well as physical cutting off of the 'unnecessary' bits of the female body, leaving as a remainder meat-like objects. Their presentation of hard-edged anatomical specimens, she observes – with Smellie using life-size line drawings, and Hunter using rounded engravings – contrasts with the French-trained Charles Jenty's 1757 atlas, *The Demonstrations of a Pregnant Uterus*, where mezzotint engravings printed on soft paper reveal, under a raised gown, glimpses of breast and thigh, as well as a pregnant body peeled of its skin.

Together, such representations, Erikson concludes, were part and parcel of a widespread, male professional struggle against female midwives, wherein bones and associated muscles and organs identified as reproductive became understood as mechanical machines prone to obstruct birth, and which could be manipulated via the speculum, forceps and perforator, and demonstrated via reference to a womb-like contraction. In mid-eigteenth century Edinburgh, William Smellie, for example, used a wooden statue with leather belly, in which resided a wax doll. In Germany, a wood and canvas adult female torso with peel-away abdominal wall was used. In Italy, by contrast, reproductive anatomical demonstrations were being carried out by women such as Anna Morandi, skilled in making anatomical waxworks, a medium that, observes Lucia Dacome (2007), afforded a domestic, intimate and 'polite' ambiance to the encounter. Nevertheless, the hard-edged mechanics of male midwives were to become a standardised technique: while the use of obstetric forceps, for example, was initially modest during the nineteenth century, it had become *de rigeur* for difficult deliveries by the mid-twentieth century. Significantly, this particular medicalisation of pregnancy and birth had repercussions not only as to who is given authority to pronounce upon and oversee them, but also where that authority is to be invested. The modern-day obstetric hospital or ward becomes the product of socio-political relations that privilege biomedical constructions of childbirth, and also of the pregnant body; this is a densely constructed space, moreover, that does not encourage or easily accommodate itself to alternate understandings of birth. "[I]t is not that birth is 'managed' the way it is because of what we know about birth," Barbara Rothman (1989: 178) concludes, "Rather, what we know about birth has been determined by the way it is managed."

Paralleling the collection of broken and shattered military bones, the acquisition of bones now firmly located as significant by virtue of their reproductive role, alongside associated tissues, organs, and muscle, was to proceed apace across Europe and the US. In Germany, for example, Erikson (2007) details how the anatomical collection of embryos, twins, newborn babies, and infants with malformations became the norm at obstetrical teaching hospitals in Berlin, Göttingen, and Jena, insofar as their physician-directors had rights of acquisition over unclaimed corpses. Even Goethe, she adds, established an anatomical collection in Jena, comprising children's skeletons and skulls. In the US, embryos and foetus's tended to form the basis of teratological collections, a topic that I take up in depth in Chapter 5. With the establishment of the Department of Embryology, based at Johns Hopkins Medical School in 1913, a systematic collection was initiated, with doctors across the country urged to provide material. By the 1940s, the collection had grown to over 9,000 human embryo and foetal specimens (Morgan 2006).

Taken together, the emphasis in these collections upon parts over and against the whole female cadaver not only speaks to the pervasiveness of a mechanical understanding of (distinct) male and female anatomies, wherein the body becomes decomposed into specific functioning systems, but also, again, the increasingly specialised nature of a progressive education, wherein each system was to be addressed by a particular expert cohort. Having said that, there yet remained one collection of bone and flesh that was taken as a whole unto itself: the foetus. In large part this ensued from a long-lasting debate between anatomists as to whether or not the foetus was already present as a miniature, fully functioning human being *in utero*, or developed into one via the differentiation of parts over the course of pregnancy (see Lupton 2013). The foetus, then, was a particularly challenging object of analysis, best understood by observing its changing form and character at particular stages. And, such discussions had a profound import insofar as they promised to shed light on the correct versus the incorrect unfolding of lifeforms.

For the moment, though, I want to conclude this section by noting that this anatomical investigation made increasingly visible the image of the free-floating foetus, divorced from the female, pregnant body. Such imagery has proliferated far and wide, not only in political debates on the moral weight of the foetus as unborn child, as manifest in the discourse of Governor of Texas Rick Perry (noted in Chapter 3), but also in ecological, cultural and economic frames of reference. We can discern the lingering impacts of such authoritative work, for example, in the relatively recent coming together of a free-floating foetal imagery with the spectacle of a globe floating in space: combined, Sarah Franklin et al. (2000) argue, they buttress a 'small world, one earth' philosophy that transcends political borders. Certainly, in *2001: A Space Odyssey*, the iconic cosmic foetus appearing at the film's closing seems to signify a new phase in humanity's development, but also that of Earth. No wonder, Lynn Morgan (2009) observes, the free-floating foetus has been used to sell cars, amongst other commodities, as both wondrous and family-friendly. Significantly, at the same time that this foetal imagery has become viral, we see the almost wholesale disappearance from view of the physical object itself. Whole sets of specimens have been disposed of, some quietly buried, some incinerated. Foetal bones and tissues are deliberately 'disappeared,' Morgan (2006: 438) writes, "to be replaced by sanitized, beautified, supposedly lifelike models and images of human development."

The Bones Will Tell

Further along from Charles Bell's paintings in the Surgeon's Museum lie another grouping, this time bone fragments collected by Rutherford Alcock (1809-1897), Deputy Inspector General of Hospitals to the British Auxiliary Legion, sent to Spain in 1835 to fight alongside French and Portuguese troops on behalf of the more 'liberal' Queen Isabella, and against the absolute monarchism of the Infante Carlos, whose supporters rallied under the charge of 'God, Country and King!' Alcock, who was later to become a consul in China, consul-general in Japan, and President of the Royal Geographical Society, took the opportunity to amass a sizeable collection of osteological specimens illustrating the effects of gunshot injuries, and later published a detailed account of the medical history and injury/illness statistics of the British volunteers (see Kaufman 2001). Through to 1876, the Carlist Wars were to unfurl time and again across Spain, though the British government abandoned a military presence after 1837.

The spaces and times into which these bones, collected by Alcock and currently displayed to tourists in Edinburgh, have emerged stand in sharp contrast with other bones emerging from the Spanish Civil War of 1936-39. In some ways, this war was an ideological continuation of the Carlist conflict, now pitting a Republican government, supported by the USSR and Mexico and augmented by the International Brigades, against the Carlists in alliance with the Fascist Falange, and supported by Portugal, Nazi Germany and the Kingdom of Italy. Leaving aside the issue of how 'purely' Fascist the victorious Franco regime indeed was, it undertook to produce a Spain predicated on military and economic autarky, as well as a state-run capitalism, and nurtured a Spanish nationalism founded on 'traditional,' apparently iconic cultural elements including folklore, as well as the physical and figurative execution and 'expulsion' of Republicans, Jews and Freemasons (Ortiz 1999).

Spanish Civil War bones also display evidence of the military technologies of the day, and reference a chain of decision-making as to where and against whom they would be directed; technologies that now included a cohort of armoured tanks, as well as aerial bombardment. As Derek Gregory (2006) observes, aerial bombing was by no means a revolutionary technology by this point. Bombs had been dropped on Turkish sites during the Italian-Ottoman War (1911-12), and the First Balkan War (1912-13), and bombing raids had been carried out by the British against Afghan tribes in the 1920s as part of their 'aerial policing' strategy. Somewhat akin to the earlier Dum Dum bullet, the efficacy of these bombs was considered to lie in their capacity for 'taking out' the 'natives.' According to the 1924 directive given to pilots, "In warfare against savage tribes who do not conform to codes of civilized warfare[,] aerial bombardment is not necessarily limited in its methods or objectives by rules agreed upon in international law" (cited in Chandler 2011, n.p.). Hence, Gregory writes, the blitz bombing by Franco's Luftwaffe allies of the Basque town of Guernica, as painted by Picasso, was, "a sort of imaginative counter-geography that wrenchingly displaced the Euro-American complacency that aerial warfare was always waged in 'their' space and that its horror could remain unregistered" (2006, n.p.).

In sharp contrast to the bones of the Carlist Wars, however, those lying in and emerging from their civil war graves are located within a highly contentious and emotive series of debates as to the motives behind their collective exhumation, and their signification of past and current political strife, but also their individual importance as the physical touchstone of deceased family members. As I go on to illustrate, there is a fraught politics of amnesia and remembrance here; one, moreover, wherein the bones unearthed, and the bones that remain underground, become symbolic of a wounded nation-state.

As numerous commentators have noted, atrocities such as mass executions and burials were carried out on both sides during the civil war; the majority, however, were carried out by the Franco forces, with some estimates reaching 70,000–100,000 during and after the conflict (see Neocleous 2005). Many of these victims were unionists, the liberal middle class, and urban workers. On the death of General Franco in 1975, and in an attempt to broker a reconciliation of sorts, the transitional government tacitly introduced a politics of forgetting – a 'Pact of Oblivion' – manifest in an amnesty law that freed imprisoned Franco opponents, allowed the return of those in exile, and absolved the military and previous regime's senior officials of any responsibility for atrocities. And, which left the dead of both sides in the ground.

Until 2000, Francisco Ferrándiz (2006: 8) notes, "apart from a few exhumations that had mostly regional, local or just family impact, a wall of silence surrounded Spain's Civil War mass graves." To an extent, such a politics can be seen as an effort to side-step the reanimation of the dead – the coming alive of bones – that proved so effective for Fascism itself. As Walter Benjamin (1969) famously observed, Fascism nurtures a very particular aestheticisation of politics, culminating in the glorification of war, destruction and a heroic death. Such spectacles give expression to the masses, but preserve a fundamental social inequity. Certainly, the *Valle de los Caídos* (Valley of the Fallen), built in part by political prisoners and consisting in part of the largest memorial cross in the world, as well as the interred remains of over 40,000 Catholic dead, was intended to stamp upon the landscape an homage to the fallen of the 'crusade' (Fernández 2002: 75). The bones of Franco himself lie in a basilica here, alongside Nationalist forces, but also the bones of Republicans, brought to help flesh out the crypt's cavernous spaces. In Germany, the death of two million German soldiers in World War I was to become the fulcrum of a death cult manifest in numerous reburials and memorials. 'Long Live Death!' became a rallying call here as well as Italy and Spain, between the wars, and referred to the heroic sacrifice of one's life in the cause of Fascism. Each regime introduced a range of death images – the *squadristi* black shirts, for example, as well as the *totenkopfring*, or 'skull ring,' of Himmler's SS – that were portable for everyday use, and spoke reams about the allegiances and commitment of their wearer. Working in German schools in the run up to 1938, Gregor Ziemer (1941) concluded that children were being 'educated for death,' while Deleuze and

Guattari (1987: 230) suggest that a suicidal longing (and glorious resurrection) underpinned Nazi ambitions. "It is curious," they write,

> that from the very beginning the Nazis announced to Germany what they were bringing: at once wedding bells and death, including their own death, and the death of the Germans. They thought that they would perish but that their undertaking would be resumed, all across Europe, all over the world, throughout the solar system. And the people cheered, not because they did not understand, but because they wanted that death through the death of others... Suicide is presented not as a punishment but as the crowning glory of the death of others.

There is suggested here a hyper-masculinism in such Fascist rhetoric and imagery so excessive that it warps and finally destroys the Romanticised family unit, and which becomes overlain onto the union of state and populace. This is a hyper-masculinity (so gloriously spoofed in Mel Brooks' faux musical 'Springtime for Hitler' in the 1968 hit *The Producers*) I want to suggest, that finds its opposite not only in a feminised German populace, but also a wounded and traumatised Spain, more usually described as suffering from a 'fraternal antagonism' (Denevy 1993).

These impulses can certainly be seen in recent, popular and acclaimed films dealing with the Spanish Civil War. Whilst Hollywood had critically commented on the early years of the regime – as manifest in the 1943 film adaptation of Hemingway's *For Whom the Bell Tolls* – by the 1960s Cold War politics had turned Spain into a US ally. Meanwhile, an internal censorship meant that artists in all mediums could make but indirect, heavily symbolic allusions to the recent past. The release of Victor Erice's *The Spirit of the Beehive* (1973), which centres on the physical and emotional isolation of a young girl in the closing years of the war, and her fascination with Frankenstein's monster, signalled an easing of this political pressure (Miles 2011). It was not until the release of Mexican director Guillermo Del Toro's *El Laberinto Del Fauno* (*Pan's Labyrinth*, 2006), however, which won Academy Awards in 2007 for cinematography, art direction and make-up, that the Spanish Civil War and its aftermath regained a globe-wide public.

The widespread visibility of such films, Iosif Kovras (2008) argues, has in turn re-enthused efforts to unearth the bones of the civil war dead. Whilst such efforts had been an intermittent feature of the Franco regime, particularly under the aegis of expatriates, and public debate in Spain had been galvanised by the arrest in London in 1998 of ex-Chilean dictator General Pinochet at the behest of a Spanish judge (Baltasar Garzón), it was not until January 2000 that Emilio Silva, a journalist, began to organise the exhumation of a mass grave containing his grandfather. The presence of archaeologists and forensic anthropologists at the graveside was to become a feature of future exhumations carried out by the *Asociación para la Recuperación de la Memoria Histórica* (Association for the Recovery of Historical Memory, or ARMH), which Silva helped to found, and which began a dialogue with the UN Task Force for Forced Disappearances.

Other organisations, many associated with ARMH, were set up across Spain, whilst the Communist Party helped establish the *Foro por la Memoria* (Forum for Memory). Both organisations rely on the authoritative voice of forensic evidence to recreate how the killings took place, but there are also crucial differences, writes Ferrándiz (2006: 9) in how they proceed to afford these bones an afterlife, in that,

> ARMH identifies itself as an association of relatives of victims and sympathizers with no direct affiliation to any political party, and considers the relatives of victims to be autonomous and decisive in the organization of mourning. Foro por la Memoria works from within the Communist Party and supports the politicization of the exhumation and handling of the bones. In their ceremonies exhumations are often carried out under a Republican flag, and at times incorporate other elements of the traditional left-wing commemoration protocol, such as speeches by Communist Party leaders, references to the heroism of the victims, raised fists and singing hymns over the remains, etc.

The familial encounters that bones engender, so intimate and yet so removed, exceed the expert dialogues that locate them, whether forensic, anthropological, psychological or historical. Thus, it is no small matter that the unearthing of bones from mass graves, and their identification as family members, becomes a way of negotiating the trauma of the period: these bones come alive as fragments of an individual who suffered during that time, but they also come alive as testimony in a now wide-ranging debate on how to remember those who died, and those who killed them. They are excavations of memory, as Victoria Sanford (2003) writes in the context of the opening up of Guatemalan mass graves; and such memories, I would add, derive their efficacy precisely because they both invoke and query public and private, state and family, national and local, the factual and the imaginative.

Concluding Comments

The fraught negotiation around the unearthing of bones noted above can certainly be seen in other contexts, such as the repatriation of bones, for example, from the Korean and Vietnam Wars (see Cho 2008, and Kwon 2008). For the most part, these are framed within a politics of reconciliation, or with regard to the now well established mechanisms and protocols of Truth Commissions. I would like to conclude this section, though, by reference to the fate of a large tranche of Native American Indian bones. My reason for doing so is that we can see here the 'coming alive' of bones within contexts that do not lend themselves to such formalised international relations between governments. Indeed, this effort to reappropriate bones forms an explicit critique of the terms upon which such geopolitical relations are based. Moreover, this example has telling implications for the current and future geopolitical import of the centres of scientific study that underpinned and propelled the Enlightenment, and which were to become the vanguard of a progressive, reasoned science that sought to describe and explain the diversity of a world revealed by colonialism.

In the fast burgeoning US 'nation' of the nineteenth century, centres of scientific as well as political import were evidence not only of an ability to keep pace with European progress in, for example, anthropology and archaeology, but also of a white, racial 'manifest destiny' over and against indigenous populations (Thomas 2001). In 1839 Samuel George Morton – trained at Edinburgh University, and Professor of Anatomy at the University of Pennsylvania – published his *Crania Americana*, using a vast number of Native American skulls collected from graves, battlefields, prisoner camps and via military contacts to illustrate how, as Elise Juzda (2009: 159) puts it, "their measurements were found wanting in relation to the large-headed Caucasians, but ranked significantly above the darker-coloured races." In Washington DC, the Army Medical Museum (est. 1868) set itself the goal of competing with the Surgeon's Museum in Edinburgh, and made the collection of Native American skulls from diverse tribes a priority, insofar as this would enable empirically-based, craniological research into their varying intellectual capacities, a debate which in turn fed into long-standing ideas concerning the utility of the skull in evidencing an ontological division of humanity into 'races,' as well as emerging evolutionary concerns regarding the progressive, but also the possible regressive, development of such races. According to Bieder (1996), such efforts buttressed the notion of the 'Vanishing Red Man,' whose place could now be taken by the advancing settlers. This was also, he notes, the one known example of a government officially engaged in the unearthing and collection of human crania and, moreover, explicitly using warfare – in this case the so-called 'Indian Wars' – in order to do so. In 1906 this appropriation by the state of Indian bodies was formally recognised under the Antiquities Act, which designated Indian cadavers buried on federal lands as 'archaeological resources.'

Whilst protests against such practices were intermittently visible over the next century, it is not until 1990 that then President George Bush signed into law the Native American Graves Protection and Repatriation Act (NAGPRA), which recognised a fundamental inequality in the civil rights afforded Native American Indians and Native Hawaiians, and requested museums to inventory such specimens, and associated knowledges concerning them such as their geographic and tribal origin, and to liaise with tribes as to their possible return. For one supporter of NAGPRA, Senator Daniel Inouye (Democrat – Hawaii), such collections were clear evidence of racism, insofar as there were, he observed, no similar repositories of the bones of white soldiers or early white settlers (Inouye 1992). For Trope and Eco-Hawk (1992), the rationale for such legislation – to repatriate thousands of dead relatives or ancestors – was firmly predicated on the sanctity of the family and the broader tribe of which such families were a part. Importantly, this bonding was not only framed temporally as existing over generations, but also territorially. In addition to DNA evidence, as well as oral traditions, archaeological indicators, and linguistic commonalities, claimants could provide evidence of a 'cultural affiliation' based on the occupation of a particular locale as part of a case for the return of remains. An attachment to land becomes here the surrogate for an attachment to community.

Such familial and civil rights discourses – and the powerful emotions mobilised as part of these – firmly separate out this body of bones from their Edinburgh counterparts. They have served as leverage points in an effort to not only physically dismantle such collections, but also their status as archaeological remains and, by extension, the authority and rights invested in research centres such as the Smithsonian. The fact that new legislation was required for such an effort is testimony to the political and legal context within which such science was carried out, a fact extensively commented upon by those academics working on the governmental practices of an expanding US government where, as Matt Hannah (2000) observes, national subjects were to be 'rationally manipulable' by virtue, preferably, of some form of quantitative measurement scheme. The craniology undertaken at the Army Medical Centre very much lent itself to contemporaneous, if yet feeble, governmental efforts to bureaucratise a census of population cohorts, though in this case the measured cranium was to become the 'dark twin' of the statistical citizen.

What adds to the complexity of such an example, of course, is that while the living bodies were not legally defined as US citizens, their remains, if found on federal land, were subject to US property laws. With the passage of NAGPRA, their disposition remains subject to US government determinants as to civil rights and general property law, and its interpretation of the relative merits of folklore evidence and so forth. Such complexities serve to query the taken for grantedness of the 'internal integrity' of the US, whose territorial and sovereign claims, for many geopolitical commentators, are of interest only with regard to current conflicts with other recognised states. But more specifically, I want to suggest, they intimate the past, present and future of what Susan Buck-Morss (2002) calls the 'wild zone,' wherein the US state's monopoly over the 'legitimate' use of violence within its territory, proffered as acceptable because of the simultaneous promotion of a 'ubiquitous' rule of law that subsumes the state itself, is exceeded. These excesses of extra-legal violence, such as the breaking of treaties and the forced removel of peoples, are not incidental to the operation of the state, nor are they an extreme reaction. They are, rather, intrinsic to its operation, its post-hoc rationalisation of past activities, and its anticipation of future crises and their resolution. Wild zones are themselves, it might be said, the largely invisible 'dark twin' of state territoriality, achieving a tangible presence when the state moves against a 'common enemy' that threatens its own role as *the* arbiter of legitimate violence. What bones may tell us, then, is not so much a story of warfare between states, but, and somewhat paradoxically, the violences enacted in the defence of the state's right to enact violence.

References

Bell, John. 1794. *Engravings Explaining the Anatomy of Bones, Muscles and Joints.* London: Longman, Hurst, Rees and Orme.

Bell, Charles. 1806. *Essays on The Anatomy of Expression in Painting.* London: Longman, Hurst, Rees and Orme.

Bell, Charles. 1821. On the Nerves; Giving an Account of Some Experiments on their Structure and Functions, which lead to a New Arrangement of the System, *Philosophical Transactions of the Royal Society of London* 111: 398-424.

Bell, John and Bell, Charles. 1797-1803. *The Anatomy of the Human Body, 4 Volumes.* Edinburgh: Mundell and Son.

Benjamin, Walter. 1969. *Illuminations.* Arendt, Hannah (ed.). New York: Schocken Books.

Benjamin, Walter. 1979. Theories of German Fascism: On the Collection of Essays War and the Warrior, *New German Critique* 17: 120-28.

Bieder, Robert E. 1996. The Representations of Indian Bodies in Nineteenth-century American Anthropology, *American Indian Quarterly* 20.2: 165-79.

Brussat, Frederic and Brussat, Mary Ann. 2007. *Spirituality and Practice: Film Review*, available at https://www.spiritualityandpractice.com/films/films.php?id=16154. Last accessed 24 September 2014.

Buck-Morss, Susan. 1992. Aesthetics and Anaesthetics: Walter Benjamin's Artwork Essay Reconsidered, *October* 62: 3-41.

Buck-Morss, Susan. 2002. *Dreamworld* and *Catastrophe: The Passing of Mass Utopia in East and West.* Cambridge, MA: MIT Press.

Carney, Scott. 2007. The Bone Factory: Preparing Skeletons for Med Schools is a Shadowy Business. Inside India's Trade in Human Remains. *WIRED-San Francisco* 15.12: 268-73.

Chandler, G. 2011. The Bombing of Waziristan, *Air and Space Magazine* July, available at http://www.airspacemag.com/military-aviation/The-Bombing-of-Waziristan.html. Last accessed 24 September 2014.

Chitnis, Anand C. 1986. *The Scottish Enlightenment and Early Victorian English Society.* Oxford: Oxford University Press.

Cho, Grace M. 2008. *Haunting the Korean Diaspora: Shame, Secrecy, and the Forgotten War.* Minneapolis, MN: University of Minnesota Press.

Copeman, William S.C. 1963. The Evolution of Anatomy and Surgery under the Tudors: Thomas Vicary Lecture delivered at the Royal College of Surgeons of England on 25th October 1962, *Annals of the Royal College of Surgeons of England* 32.1: 1-21.

Dacome, Lucia. 2007. Women, Wax and Anatomy in the 'Century of Things,' *Renaissance Studies* 21.4: 522-50.

Deleuze, Gilles and Guattari, Felix. 1987. *A Thousand Plateaus: Capitalism and Schizophrenia*, translated by Massumi, Brian. Minneapolis, MN: University of Minnesota Press.

Denevy, Thomas. 1993. *Cain On Screen: Contemporary Spanish Cinema*. Maryland, MD: Scarecrow Press.
Erikson, Susan L. 2007. Fetal Views: Histories and Habits of Looking at the Fetus in Germany, *Journal of Medical Humanities* 28.4: 187-212.
Faulkner, Sally. 2009. Lola Cercas en Soldados de Salamina (David Trueba, 2003), *Historia Actual Online* 15: 165-70.
Federici, Sylvia. 2004. *Caliban and the Witch*. Brooklyn, NY: Autonomedia.
Federici, Sylvia. 2010. Women, Witch-Hunting and Enclosures in Africa Today, *Sozial.Geschichte Online* 3: 10-27.
Fernández, Paloma Aguilar. 2002. *Memory and Amnesia: The Role of the Spanish Civil War in the Transition to Democracy*. London: Berghahn Books.
Ferrándiz, Francisco. 2006. The Return of Civil War Ghosts: The Ethnography of Exhumations in Contemporary Spain. *Anthropology Today* 22.3: 7-12.
Figal, Gerald. 2007. Bones of Contention: The Geopolitics of "Sacred Ground" in Postwar Okinawa, *Diplomatic History* 31.1: 81-109.
Franklin, Sarah, Lury, Celia and Stacey, Jackie. *Global Nature, Global Culture*. Thousand Oaks, CA: Sage Publications.
Gelfand, Toby. 1981. Gestation of the Clinic, *Medical History* 25.2: 169-80.
Gregory, Derek. 2006. Plenary Address to the Arab World Geography Conference in Beirut, December 2006 available at http://geographicalimaginations.files.wordpress.com/2012/07/gregory-in-another-time-zone_illustrated.pdf. Last accessed 24 September 2014.
Hannah, Matthew. 2000. *Governmentality and the Mastery of Territory in Late Nineteenth Century America*. Cambridge: Cambridge University Press.
Hoegaerts, Josephine. 2010. Manoeuvring Men: Masculinity as Spatially Defined Readability at the Grandes Manoeuvres of the Belgian Army, 1882-1883. *Gender, Place and Culture* 17.2: 249-68.
Hunter, William. 1774. *The Anatomy of the Human Gravid Uterus Exhibited in Figures*. Birmingham: John Baskerville.
Inouye, Daniel K. 1992. Repatriation: Forging New. Relationships, *Arizona State Law Journal* 24.1: 1-3.
Jenty, Charles. 1757. *The Demonstrations of a Pregnant Uterus of a Woman at her Full Term in Six Tables, as Large as Nature*. London: Burgess.
Juzda, Elise. 2009. Skulls, Science, and the Spoils of War: Craniological Studies at the United States Army Medical Museum, 1868-1900, *Studies in History and Philosophy of Biological and Biomedical Sciences* 40.3: 156-67.
Kaufman, Matthew H. 2001. Clinical Case Histories and Sketches of Gun-shot Injuries from the Carlist War, *Journal of the Royal College of Surgeons of Edinburgh* 46.5: 279-89.
Kittredge, Susan C. 2006. Black Shrouds and Black Markets, *New York Times* 5 March, available at http://www.nytimes.com/2006/03/05/opinion/05kittredge.html?pagewanted=all. Last accessed 24 September 2014.
Kovras, Iosif. 2008. Unearthing the Truth: the Politics of Exhumations in Cyprus and Spain, *History and Anthropology 19.4: 371-90*.

Kwon, Heonik. 2008. *Ghosts of War in Vietnam*. Cambridge: Cambridge University Press.
Leggott, Sarah. 2009. Memory, Postmemory, Trauma: The Spanish Civil War in Recent Novels by Women, *FULGOR* 4.1: 25-33.
La Motte, Ellen N. 1906. The Hôtel-Dieu of Paris: An Historical Sketch, *Medical Library and Historical Journal* 4.3: 225-40.
Lupton, Deborah. 2013. *The Social Worlds of the Unborn*. Basingstoke: Palgrave Macmillan.
Milburn, C.H. 1901. An Address on Military Surgery of the Time of Ambroise Paré and that of the Present Time: Delivered before the East York and North Lincoln Branch of the British Medical Association, *British Medical Journal* 1.2112: 1532-5.
Miles, Robert J. 2011. Reclaiming Revelation: *Pan's Labyrinth* and *The Spirit of the Beehive*. *Quarterly Review of Film and Video* 28.3: 195-203.
Morgan, Lynn Marie. 2006. The Rise and Demise of a Collection of Human Fetuses at Mount Holyoke College, *Perspectives in Biology and Medicine* 49.3: 435-51.
Morgan, Lynn Marie. 2009. *Icons of Life: A Cultural History of Human Embryos*. Berkeley, CA: University of California Press.
Nair, Savithri Preetha. 2005. Native Collecting and Natural Knowledge (1798-1832): Raja Serfoji II of Tanjore as a 'Centre of Calculation,' *Journal of the Royal Asiatic Society* 15.3: 279-302.
Neocleous, Mark. 2005. *The Monstrous and the Dead: Burke, Marx, Fascism*. Cardiff: University of Wales Press.
Ortiz, Carmen. 1999. The Uses of Folklore by the Franco Regime, *Journal of American Folklore* 112: 479-96.
Page, C. Max. 1935. The Development of Orthopædic Surgery: (Section of Orthopædics), *Proceedings of the Royal Society of Medicine* 29.1: 63-9.
Page, C. Max. 1952. The Effect of War on Surgical Practice: Robert Jones Lecture delivered at the Royal College of Surgeons of England on 1st July, *Annals of the Royal College of Surgeons of England* 11.6: 335-49.
Paré, Ambroise. 1545 [2008]. *La Méthod de traicter les playes faites par les arquebuses et aultres bastons à feu*. Paris: Presses Universitaire de France.
Paré, Ambroise. 1573 [1980]. *Des Monstres et Prodiges*. Translated by Janis L. Pallister. Chicago, IL: University of Chicago Press.
Paré, Ambroise. 1594. *Opera Chirurgica*. Frankfurt A.M. J. Feyerabend for P. Fischer.
Pastena, Janis 1993. Women in Surgery: An Ancient Tradition, *Archives of Surgery* 128.6: 622-6.
Petry, Yvonne. 2012. 'Many Things Surpass Our Knowledge': An Early Modern Surgeon on Magic, Witchcraft and Demonic Possession, *Social History of Medicine* 25.1: 47-64.
Pichot, Amédée. 1860. *The Life and Labours of Sir Charles Bell*. London: Richard Bentley.

Pigray, Pierre. 1609 [1634]. *Epitome des préceptes de médecine et chirurgie*. A Rouen, chez Robert Valentin, tenant la boutique dans la Court du Palais.

Rothman, Barbara K. 1989. *Recreating Motherhood: Ideology and Technology in Patriarchal Society*. New York: W.W. Norton.

Rozen, Nimrod and Israel Dudkiewicz, Israel. 2011. Wound Ballistics and Tissue Damage. In Lerner, Alexander and Soudry, Michael (eds) *Armed Conflict Injuries to the Extremities*. Heidelberg: Springer Berlin, pp. 21-33.

Sanford, Victoria. 2003. *Buried Secrets: Truth and Human Rights in Guatemala*. New York: Palgrave Macmillan.

Sawchuk, Kim. 2013. Biotourism, *Fantastic Voyage*, and Sublime Inner Space. In Marchessault, Janine and Sawchuk, Kim (eds) *Wild Science: Reading Feminism, Medicine and the Media*, pp. 19-23.

Smellie, William. 1754. *A Sett of Anatomical Tables, with Explanations, and an Abridgment, of the Practice of Midwifery*. London: no publisher shown. Digitised online at http://search.lib.virginia.edu/catalog/uva-lib:1002833/page_turner#openLayer/uva-lib:853701/3403/2332/0/1/0. Last accessed 6th December 2014.

Sommer, Marianne. 2007. *Bones and Ochre: The Curious Afterlife of the Red Lady of Paviland*. Cambridge, MA: Harvard University Press.

Struthers, John. 1867. *Historical Sketch of the Edinburgh Anatomical School*. Edinburgh: MacLachlan and Stewart.

Thomas, David H. 2001. *Skull Wars Kennewick Man, Archaeology, and the Battle for Native American Identity*. New York: Basic Books.

Townshend, Charles. 2005. Introduction: The Shape of Modern War. In Townshend, Charles (ed.) *The Oxford History of Modern War*. Oxford: Oxford University Press, pp. 3-19.

Trope, Jack F. and Echo-Hawk, Walter R. 1992. The Native American Graves Protection and Repatriation Act: Background and Legislative History, *Arizona State Law Journal* 24: 35-76.

Tuchman, Barbara W. 2011. *The Proud Tower: A Portrait of the World before the War, 1890-1914*. New York: Random House.

Vesalius, Andreas. 1543. *Andreae Vesalii Bruxellensis, scholae medicorum Patavinae professoris, de Humani corporis fabrica Libri septem*. Digitised online version, available at http://www.e-rara.ch/bau_1/content/titleinfo/6299027. Last accessed 6th December 2014.

Wirtzfeld, Debrah A. 2009. The History of Women in Surgery, *Canadian Journal of Surgery* 52.4: 317-20.

Withers, Charles WJ. 2008. *Placing the Enlightenment: Thinking Geographically about the Age of Reason*. Chicago, IL: University of Chicago Press.

Ziemer, Gregor. 1941. *Education for Death: The Making of the Nazi*. New York: Oxford University Press.

Chapter 5
Abhorrence

Introduction

In the preceding two chapters, on flesh and bone respectively, I have outlined an approach to the embodied, geopolitical body that does not thereby presume an individuated corporeality. There is a diversity of content and capacity apparent here that, at the broad scale, underlines the potentialities of the matter in hand and which, more specifically, opens out the not only the physio-biological capacities that help comprise the subject of a classical geopolitics, but also the making of gendered knowledges pertaining to these. Yet, as Rosi Braidotti (2002) points out, there is a diversity within diversity – a singling out amidst a universal matter-ing, one might say – that must be accounted for, insofar as within particular contexts it is precisely this gendering that matters. In this chapter, I want to take on board this attentiveness to singularity and context, and address particular corporealities that, because of their specific biologies – the twists and whirls of flesh and bone, the textures and pigments of hair and skin, the presence and absence of bodily symmetries and so on – and the visceral as well as interpretive apprehension of these, have become pivotal to a geopolitics driven by abhorrence. That is, I want to dwell on how these whirls and textures, presences and absences, are apprehended as significant in the context of larger ensembles such as a corporeal body, but also of a social body such as a population, and a Natural order pertaining to the world as we know it. Indeed, what is interesting about these fleshy/boney features is how they become configured as synecdoches – that is, representative of and indicating – wider disorderings, which in turn, reveal by their very 'wrongness' what the world *should* look like. Though such a conjuring of 'wrongness' can, of course, be conveyed through words and imagery, and can engender a suite of 'felt' emotions, there is also a profound aesthetic dimension to such engagements that speaks to all manner of learned, embodied responses that, though they may be rationalised, are neither subsumed nor represented by reason.

These corporealities may be summarily termed monsters, or monstrous bodies, though as I hope to show below there is an analytic point to be made in drawing a distinction between these two terms. Monsters evoke manifold responses, from wonder and curiosity, as Lorraine Daston and Katharine Park (1998) amply illustrate, to fear and loathing, responses that exceed containment in rhetoric or discourse. More pertinently, monsters can be understood as locatable in large part because of the mobilisation of abhorrence; an etymology of abhor, from the Latin *abhorrere*, that directs us to shudder, to draw away from, to bristle in the presence of, whilst the Latin *monstrum* reveals an object of dread and portent. It is not too surprising to insist on the fundamentally political character of such monsters. After all, the figure of the classical monster is there to warn of the dangers associated with the transgression of all manner of borders, as well as the ever present threat of that which lies outside of the body politic. Where Cerberus, for example, guards the Gates of the Underworld, the Cyclops, Homer relates, mark the threshold of civilisation itself. These monsters, "have no assemblies for the making of laws, nor any established legal codes, but live in hollow caverns in the mountain heights, where each man is law giver to his own children and women, and nobody has the slightest interest in what his neighbours decide" (2005: 3). As the example of the Cyclops indicates, monsters are often times wrought by a warped gendering that references, even mimics, conventional social and familial expectations, yet confounds the same.

Just as Daston and Park (1998) go on to point out the contextually specific emergence of three 'complexes' – horror, pleasure, and repugnance – I want to draw out something of the specificity of a geopolitics of abhorrence, a term too easily defined as a loathing, or aversion to some-thing. There is a corporeal situatedness (more often than not sexuated and raced) to the monster that is understood to be the singular expression of the Other, the unnatural, and the abnormal, all of which have a substantial role in the fulmination of geopolitical relations. To a large degree, these specificities can be located in the shifting terrains of what are now regarded as religion, superstition and a modern day Enlightened Science. And so Park and Daston (1981) draw attention to a marked epistemic shift in Europe in the sixteenth and seventeenth centuries, as the classical monsters of Aristotle (who advocated the investigation of anomalies), Cicero (who looked to monsters as divine portents), and Pliny (who applauded the mapping of monstrous races), gradually gave way to an effort to explain monstrosity as part and parcel of the Natural order of things, an effort culminating in teratology, from the Greek *teras* this time, meaning 'marvel.' But, such a progressive account tends to gloss over the tangled spaces and times of these, wherein the subject and content of science cannot be sundered from ritual, spectacle and a moral ambition. Nor, as Laura Knoppers and Joan Landes (2004: 6) insist, does it, "wholly account for the wide range of metaphorical and political uses of the monstrous," such as "defining religious, ethnic, and national boundaries; legitimating faith; asserting cultural identity; or reinscribing anomalous, strange and aberrant experiences." For Dixon and Ruddick (2011: 432), certainly, monsters are fickle things. To be sure,

> The monster that patrols the boundaries of unstable discourses is still very much alive, for example, in the maintenance of contemporary hegemonic fictions in such constructs as the 'axis of evil' mythologized under the Bush regime as the presumed confluence of interests between Iran, Iraq and North Korea.

But, there are also a host of 'hopeful' monsters: thus,

> It is, for Deleuze ... a thing 'with paws' that invites the destabilization of prior discourses. We have the 'promising monsters of symbiogenisis' of Donna

Haraway, and the Derridean monster who properly defies domestication. These monsters portend instability and change: but, there is no longer the fear that something is awry with the natural order of things, but rather a hope for a shift in our moral order whatever the outcome may be.

In section one, *Mis-Begotten Bodies*, I tease out something of the historical geography of this geopolitical body through the mobilisation of abhorrence. Here, I dwell on the emergence of teratology, the 'science of monsters.' I begin by noting how an early modern account of monsters as geopolitical portents became contrasted with Enlightened, empirically-grounded explanations of a natural diversity that signalled not the closure of social ruptures, but a discourse on the manifold possibilities inherent in reproduction. Many of the baroque collections of wondrous objects that made manifest their collectors' social standing were transformed into teratological sites, testimony to their owner's commitment to a progressive, modern world, and a suitable spectacle for a middle-class citizenry riven by intellectual curiosity rather than what the satirical magazine *Punch* (1848) contemptuously referred to as a 'deformito-mania' (referenced in Goodall 2002: 19). A useful illustration of this shift from 'Cabinet of Curiosity object' to a 'Natural History exhibit' arises from the fate of two collections acquired in that hub of mercantilism and Westphalian politics, the Low Countries; collections that provoked various forms of 'shudder,' a verb and later noun acquired from the early Dutch *schuderen*.

Teratology, which drew upon reproductive faults and failures evident in women, unborn foetuses and still-born babies, very much helped to nurture an emerging Euro-centric construction of a biological order to the world. In itself, this was a globalising politics that sorted out the Natural from the unnatural, the normal from the deviant, and the healthy from the weak. But, I also want to emphasise the complexities of the relations between this evolving scientific domain and the politics pertaining to nation-building. To be sure, teratology's depiction of an inherited monstrosity was to become enrolled in a pervasive social Darwinism, which, as many academics have noted, served as the scientific basis for a classical geopolitics. Yet, proponents of teratology were also inclined to favour a biological diversity; indeed, to some, this propensity for Nature to be profligate could be usefully understood and augmented in the making of a prosperous and progressive nation. It is only when the reproductive abnormalities identified by teratology, alongside the Others mapped out by physiognomy and animal/plant breeding, were framed in simplistic, evolutionary terms that it became a means of legitimising the 'purification' of populations via immigration controls and eugenics. Bearing this more complex historical geography in mind, and in particular the breadth of opinion available as to how a biological diversity was to be framed and deployed at the state level, that eugenics was to become one of teratology's most enduring legacies is testament to the fact that such a politics did not so much serve a national interest as reflect prevailing inequalities of privilege and resource, pander to particular forms of prejudice, and facilitate certain economic interests.

A pathologising of Nature as profligate and excessive remains a key feature of geopolitics today, as I go on to recount in Chapter 6 on touch. However, the monster as a singular, prodigious wonder is no longer considered capable of fomenting social discontent. Instead, it is the *monstrous* that haunts the geopolitical imagination, as abnormal traits present a threat at the heart of a populace, or hover outside of its borders. It is precisely because the monstrous has a lineage in a series of scientific knowledges and practices, such as teratology, that it has acquired an authority and legitimacy when placed in political discourses on the future health, productivity and competitiveness of a populace. And, whilst it has become something of a free-floating signifier, wherein diverse traits can be called out as deviant, abnormal and so on, the monstrous yet retains the 'aura' of the monster insofar as it implies a shuddering, visceral response to a corporealised some-thing. No wonder, as many commentators have noted, the monstrous has become a crucial means of identifying the Other in opposition to the Self, however incomplete such a process may be. It is in this capacity that the monstrous has been deployed as both proof and symptom of a disruption to the integrity of a state predicated on sameness, thus inserting itself into all manner of geopolitics.

In the section *Gothic Politics*, I draw out how this deployment of the monstrous has helped to re-animate what has been termed the 'Political Gothic,' which articulates a concern with the contagion of social upheaval, as disorder and unruliness in an alien or primitive elsewhere threaten to spill into, or subvert, the here and now. The use of the term monstrous directs us to the complex relations between what we now think of as the relatively autonomous domains of science, religion and political theory – a sorting and winnowing that occurred over the course of a European Enlightenment – and the tracking back and forth of such terminologies, each translation re-energising a particular debate or manifesto. Whilst I do not want to imply a distinct trajectory to the political Gothic such that it 'coincides' with teratology – a paralleling that runs the risk of essentialising both – I do want to outline some of the specificities of this, and in particular the cultivation of a visceral horror that, I want to go on to illustrate, is very much operative in contemporary, vociferous, mass-media campaigns that deploy monstrous Others as a means of bolstering a particular national identity predicated on sameness and, moreover, a view of a world within which this national identity 'makes sense.' What is more, it is within the context of the Gothic that we can discern a preoccupation not so much with a *bio*politics, a calculated disciplining of life, but a *necro*politics, a sovereignty predicated upon a power over the distribution of death (Mbembé and Meintjes 2003).

Mis-Begotten Bodies

For Knoppers and Landes (2004: 6), the term 'early modern Europe' has itself something of a monstrous edge to it, insofar as it blurs periodic thinking by gesturing both forwards and backwards, and confirms an incompleteness. The term, they argue, tracks across territories as well as centuries, encompassing, "colonialism, political centralisation and revolution, transformations in print and communication, religious schism and scientific investigation." In early modern Europe, monsters, whilst awful in form, were nevertheless welcomed as political portents, their bodies providing a series of divinely wrought signs that could be read and applied to contemporary events. As Dixon and Ruddick (2011: 431) relate, the monster of Ravenna, for instance, served to seal off the points of rupture and discontinuity posed to the doctrine of the divine right of Kings when Louis XII and Pope Julius both laid claim to rule over the Italian principality of Ravenna. The victory of Louis over Julius, after a series of protracted skirmishes between 1494 and 1559, was sealed by a portent from God, the birth of a severely deformed child. The child's malformed body became text, a potent symbol warning of the threat that the nascent Italian city-states posed to the rest of Europe. Her/his lack of arms came to signify a lack of generosity of the Italians, her/his wings a sign of fickleness, her/his hermaphrodite sexuality indications of lust and bestiality; the deformed claw like foot a grasping greedy nature; the misplaced eye a love of material things; and the horn an overwhelming hubris. At a time and place when the divine right of kings was the hegemonic explanation for the organisation of rule over states and principalities, this child's body became a kind of bridging device, maintaining divinity firmly at the centre of understanding. Flesh and bone were both sign and 'proof' that victory was not simply attributable to might of arms, but because God willed it so.

In similar vein, the birth of conjoined twins in Worms in 1495 was regarded by many as a call for the strengthening of the Holy Roman Empire, and in particular a coupling of Emperor and Imperial Cities in the face of Ottoman advances in the Balkans. In 1522 the Monster of Freyberg, Saxony, also provided, via his tortured body, a warning: on the eve of the Reformation, Martin Luther interpreted this 'moon-calf' as signalling the depravity of the Church. As Hsia (2004: 80) relates, "his huge ear signifies the tyranny of the sacrament of confession; and his stiff neck the rigidity of the monkish estate." Catholics read the same as a manifestation of the impudence of Martin Luther and his followers, and regarded the monster with a deep repugnance. In 1727, well into the Enlightenment, a Portuguese tract, *Noticia de hum Portentoso Monstro*, described one of the last of these 'classic' portents, a monster emerging from the forests of Anatolia during the reign of the Turks. With a man's face but asexual genitalia, the wings of an eagle and scaly legs, the monster signified to many Western observers the disobedience of the Turks, and the eventual fall of the Ottoman Empire (De Costa 2004).

Monsters drawn from history also served to illuminate the evils of the day. In England, David Cressy (2004: 47) writes, traumatised by the Civil War (1642-51), the regicide of Charles I, and a Cromwellian republic, monstrosity, "was in the air, in the pulpits, on people's slips and in the popular press. More than simply an abomination of tissue, monstrosity pointed to social pathology and religious failing, a disturbance of the natural order." Apocalyptic monstrosities drawn from the Book of Revelation became allegories for both Roundheads and Cavaliers alike. Meanwhile, radical millenarians urged a far-flung Protestant Crusade, beginning with the perfidious Dutch, who deserved punishment for their support of the House of Orange, and ending, they hoped, with the fall of the 'Great Whore of Babylon,' the Papacy in Rome.

More often than not, however, such mis-begotten creatures were couched as the product of silly or headstrong women who, by dint of focusing their mind upon a particular violent image, malformed the foetus in their womb. Such 'maternal impressions' were as much a sign of a gender disorder, Cressy (2004) argues, as they were a religious foment. And, one might add, they speak to an effort to explain monsters in terms of reproductive failure. Such ideas had a long, classical lineage, appearing, for example, in the work of Pliny the Elder. They gained a particular specificity in an era wherein a Renaissance of such classical learning helped to provide a sense of Self that was associated with the mind, spirit and consciousness. Maternal impressions were indicative, Richard Todd (1995) writes, of a 'welling up' of corporeal forces that threatened to drown the Self in a shapeless, fleshy form. Such efforts can also be tracked, I would add, to an emerging body of obstetric knowledge grounded via dissection, as outlined in Chapter 4, that offered insight into the interiority of the body, and a self-knowledge predicated on the triumph of a probing reason over and against the obduracy of the flesh. Maternal impression, bestial and homosexual relations, corruption of the sperm, and 'mechanical' causes such as the pressure of the uterus, for example, were all listed as possible causes of monstrous births by the French surgeon Ambroise Paré in his *Des Monstres et Prodiges* (1573), and repeated in Fortunio Liceti's *Traité des Monstres* (1616). Each type of monster, Paré observed, required a different type of explanation. This sustained interest in the diverse character of the monster served to mitigate, Maria Monti (2000: 8) argues, "the traditionally negative view which saw in monsters signs of disaster … in the past, they had been significant only insofar as they denoted something else, namely what had happened before (the sin) or what would have happened afterwards (the punishment)." The investigation of monstrous births as a medical problematic, "allowed monsters to escape their function of being a sign of disorder in creation and to enter into the natural world without necessarily rendering it less perfect or worthy. If anything, they could now even be seen to enrich and to diversify creation."

Indeed, by the mid-seventeenth century, French learned society was torn between explanations that depended upon Divine cause (whereby God either imprinted monstrosity within the original seed of a species, or intervened in specific organisms) and those who observed that 'accidents' of Nature had occurred, producing various pathologies. The latter was by no means an atheist position, however; rather, it was argued in the Parisian *Académie Royale des Sciences*, for example, that God should be thought of as 'distanced' from the production of such abominations (see Roger 1964). As the eighteenth century progressed, though, *La Querelle des Monstres* was to become much less visible as concerns over the heretical character of Naturalism, as evidenced in the work of the Dutch philosopher Spinoza, for example, led to what Jacques Roger (1964) calls a 'biological theocentrism.' Here, God was to be considered entirely responsible for the wide variety of monstrous forms observed. Monsters were symbolic of the imperfect realm of matter, and hence merely served to emphasise by force of contrast the rightness of most forms and, by extension, the rightness of a world order that contained these.

We can see something of this polarisation of religious and scientific understandings in the shifting geographies of collection, arrangement and apprehension associated with sites such as *Le Jardin du Roi*, Paris, France, founded as a royal 'physic' garden by Louis XIII in 1626. It was here that Jean-Baptiste Colbert, Louis XIV's finance minister, began to collect and catalogue colonial flora in 1660s and 70s, its buildings and internal furnishings very much embodying the Cabinet of Curiosity in both style and symbolism. Over time, *Le Jardin* consisted of extensive gardens and a labyrinth, as well as a collection of living and dead specimens. By the mid-1700s, however, *Le Jardin* had been substantially reorganised under its Director, Le Comte de Buffon (1707-1788): Buffon was the epitome of the Natural Historian, analysing living, dead, and fossilized organisms in an effort to understand their anatomy, reproduction, classification, and distribution. Whilst Buffon continued to purchase numerous objects from the *collections curieuses* of the nobility these were no longer valued for their singularity, Dietz and Nutz (2005) argue; rather, they were harmoniously arranged to present a pleasing sense of wholeness. So ordered, such objects would serve a tangible, pedagogic purpose, helping viewers to make sense of – to explain – the relations between them. As such, they were distinctly different in meaning as well as comportment from the earlier menageries, such as that maintained by Louis XIV at Versailles, whose exotic displays were intended to inspire awe and wonder not only by virtue of their intrinsic rarity, but the power and reach of the monarchy that collected them. These new arrangements still exhibited a royal glory, but their pleasing wholeness now conveyed a connectedness that underlay Nature's diversity, and which could be discerned by the discriminatory eye of the *savant*.

These Natural History experts, Emma Spary (2000) argues, became crucial references for those concerned with social order and the building of nations. Buffon himself was the third most popular author during the latter half of the eighteenth century (Farber 1975: 63), and his *Histoire Naturelle* (1749-67, in 15 volumes) was to become the best-selling publication of the century in France (Hazard 1964: 156). In short, Buffon's work emphasised a descriptive, historical approach to Nature, and the significance of the environment in the differentiation of living organisms. Indeed, it is this attempt to explain diversity via a consideration of the specific placement of organisms that allows for a discussion of him as the founder of modern biogeography. *Contra* the wisdom of Newton and Hume, for Buffon an inductive empiricism allowed for the location of Natural order, and hence the discovery of facts and, hopefully, laws of change. And *contra* Linnaeus' articulation of a logical system of classification, Buffon's (1749) *Histoire Naturelle* dwelt on the physical relations between organisms and their environments, and the distance between the material form of an organism and a concept such as 'species.' For Buffon, complex organisms were actually constituted from simpler *molécules organiques*, such that these could be considered the basic building blocks of life. The implication therein, that life somehow developed without supernatural intervention, as well as Buffon's emphasis upon the place-specific role of the environment, appeared to many theologians to open the door to an 'active' role for Nature – for 'Naturalism' – in producing new animals. Hence, Buffon's appearance for heresy before the Sorbonne, the Theological College of the University of Paris, despite his patronage from King Louis XV, and his subsequent apology.

Buffon was especially curious about hybrids, keeping records of reported cases and attempting to cross-breed on his own estates. As Paul Farber (1975: 68) explains, this was because the biological basis for Buffon's designation of species was provided by reproduction. Hence, "if individuals of different species could breed together successfully and produce fertile offspring then either his breeding definition or his species concept was inadequate." This emphasis upon selective breeding, Spary (2000: 109) notes, rewrote monsters as examples of, "Man's ability to transform Nature from something that was 'brute and dying' to an earthly paradise," and contributed to the garden's advocacy of agricultural innovation as a means of building the strength of the French nation. The cross-breeding of humans, moreover, acquired, for Buffon, an economic as well as moral significance, insofar as the resulting progeny were better equipped to reap the fruits of industry. Such views, it must be noted, did not lead Buffon to propose a separation of humans into distinct races; rather, there existed for Buffon a broad spectrum of human beings, with superficial differences of skin colour, for example, brought about through climatic and other environmental influences.

As Daston and Park (1998: 360) note, monsters, understood as exceptional and prodigious phenomena, were no longer central to the inquiry of men such as Buffon; their continued presence at *Le Jardin* bears witness, "to the fact that marvels still circulated at many levels of Enlightenment culture. But Buffon's uncharacteristic brevity is still louder testimony that they had been banished to the margins of natural history and natural philosophy" insofar as, "The passions of wonder and desire that had singled them out as objects of knowledge had been decoupled and transformed." Monstrous births retained a place in these discussions; they were now, however, examples of what Diderot, inspired by Buffon, called 'disturbed' Nature. Men could learn how, he wrote in the Prospectus of his *Encyclopédie*, to disturb Nature further through art, or to put it back on its rightful path (Diderot 1975: 106). Under the rubric of what is now commonly referred to as Enlightenment science, menageries become zoological specimens, Cabinets of Curiosity become Natural History exhibits, and the emergent discipline of teratology became one of a suite of explanatory modes that sought to empirically ground investigations into the Natural order of living organisms and their environments.

Part and parcel of this Enlightenment, I want to emphasise, was a profound shift in the manner in which an abhorrence of monsters was mobilised as a means of apprehending a world order, and the place of Self and Others within this, as well as, more specifically, the changing nature of international relations. In order to ground this point, I want to draw on collections acquired by Dutch scientists. The first example relates to collections assembled by Albertus Seba (1665-1736), a pharmacist, and Frederik Ruysch (1638-1731), a botanist, anatomist and teacher of midwives. Both collections were sold to Tsar Peter of Russia, who looked to their contents not simply as objects of wonder, but as tangible expressions of his desire to build a modern, scientifically progressive Russia. The second example is a collection of specimens acquired by Professor Gerardus Vrolik (1775-1859), and his son Professor Willem Vrolik (1801-1862), which, on Willem's death, was donated to the Anatomical Laboratories of the *Athenaeum Illustre*, the forerunner of the University of Amsterdam. There are many such cabinets and teratological collections that I could expand upon here, but the Dutch context for these provides an interesting insight into state formation and sovereignty in Europe, issues that are key to prevailing notions of what 'international relations' consists of. The Low Countries, encompassing the current *Benelux* countries but also a large part of what is now understood as northern and eastern France, were the scene of political turmoil, as noted in Chapter 2, and are oft cited as the precursor to a Westphalian international politics. They were also centres of reformist movements, such as Calvinism; exemplars of scientific excellence in a diverse array of fields, from optometrics to anatomy; and the locus of radical philosophies such as Spinozism. These examples, then, provides insight into how the 'global' connectedness of the region, which Nijman (1997) and others remark upon as a condition for political innovation, also enabled a particular form of knowing the world to emerge, grounded in the interrogation of bodies, and discussed in deeply felt metaphysical terms that placed the human in a Natural as well as social order.

Numerous collectors were to take advantage of Amsterdam's trading networks and colonial dominance in the East Indies, India, Sri Lanka, Surinam, the West Coast of Africa, and the Caribbean to acquire interesting objects. Albertus Seba, widely acknowledged to have the broadest collection in the Low Countries, gained many specimens, including monstrous ones, from sailors and ships surgeons, as well as correspondents, travellers and other collectors across Europe and North America (Adler 1989). In 1717 Seba sold his collection to Tsar Peter the Great of Russia; and, it became the basis of Peter's famous *Kunstkamera* ('cabinet of naturalia'), from the Dutch *kunst-kamer*. Some of its constituent parts can still be seen at the Zoological Institute of the Russian Academy of Sciences. Seba was also to play a role in the acquisition by Peter the Great of Frederik Ruysch's collection. Unlike Seba, Ruysch, a *praelector* of Amsterdam Surgeon's Guild, specialised in the monstrous. His collection included zoological specimens, but was dominated by embalmed foetuses and neonates, according to Anemone (2000: 586), "preserved in a secret solution and displayed in glass jars," along with, "individual organs with their vascular systems revealed through injected wax solutions, complete skeletons and examples of skeletal deformities, and various allegorical ensemble constructions composed entirely of organic materials." These were no mere mercantilist collections of the curious and the rare. For Ruysch, a Calvinist who believed in predestination, these specimens became artistic mediums in a baroque display of *vanitas mundi* and *memento mori*. Malformed skeletons would be set against, "'geological' or 'botanical' landscapes composed of hardened veins and arteries, kidneystones, gallstones, bladders, brachial tubes, lung and brain tissue" (Anemone 2000: 586). Irony, as well as a liking for classical proverbs, abounded. In one exhibit, for example,

> With eye sockets turned heavenward the central skeleton – a fetus of about four months – chants a lament on the misery of life. 'Ah Fate, ah Bitter Fate!' it sings, accompanying itself on the violin, an osteomyelitic sequester with a dried artery for a bow. At its right, a tiny skeleton conducts the music with a baton set with minute kidney stones. In the right foreground a stiff little skeleton girdles its hips with injected sheep's intestines, its right hand grasping a spear made of the hardened vas deferens of an adult man, grimly conveying the message that its first hour was also its last ... For the little horizontal skeleton in the foreground with the familiar mayfly on its delicate hand, Ruysch chose a quote from the Roman comic Plautus, one of the favourite authors of this period, to the effect that its lifespan had been as brief as that of young grass felled by the scythe so soon after sprouting. (Luyendijk-Elshout, 1970: 123)

Whilst Ruysch's tiny skeletons functioned as teaching aids for his students, they were also, "actors in a grim and grotesque morality play" (Anemone 2000: 5867) that emphasised the frailty of the flesh (Figure 5.1).

In the hands of Tsar Peter, this collection was to acquire another layer of meaning, however, one that was firmly fixed to the notion of a national advancement within a community of nation-states. And, as such, it was to help mobilise another set of emotions. First and foremost, their presence signalled the princely power of their owner, and a reach that extended well beyond the imagination of his subjects. His specially built *Kunstkamera*, in the new West-facing capital of St. Petersburg, housed both the Ruysch and the Seba collections, to which he himself added malformed, still-born children born in Russia. It also included astronomical and anatomical instruments, mineral and gem collections, more than 15,000 books in diverse languages, almost 1,500 animals, insects, and stuffed birds, and a large number of shells. Collectively, these 'scenarios of power' (Wortman 2006) provided a display of sovereign majesty, but they were also evidence that the Petrine monarchy, and its populace, belonged to a scientifically-orientated, technologically-advanced, modern Europe. Indeed, Tsar Peter had become aware of the work of Seba and Ruysch during his Grand Embassy, wherein he sought to ferret out the best of an Enlightened Europe's economic, cultural and military advances for replication in Russia. Arriving in Amsterdam in 1697 to investigate its mercantile and military fleets, Peter had been drawn to the unrivalled work of its biologists and naturalists.

Abhorrence

Figure 5.1   Engraving by C Huyberts from Frederik Ruysch's
Thesaurus Anatomicus, 1703

Source: Wellcome Library, London.

For visitors to the *Kunstkamera*, Anemone (2000) suggests, it was not the morbid constructs of Ruysch that shocked, but rather the co-presence of living monsters, collected by Peter himself. Such encounters,

> Intended as a vehicle to transform Russia into a modern, civilized, European civilization ... may actually have contributed to Russian alienation from Europe. Indeed, how could the Kunstkamera's display of the diseased, the sexually and grotesquely monstrous have done anything but give rise to ambiguous feelings

of fear, loathing and, perhaps, guilty fascination towards the West among Orthodox Russian viewers in the Petrine period? In this sense, the Kunstkamera may be related to the persistent Russian alienation from Western art, culture, and institutions, one of the reasons why the West appears to many Russians, even today, as a frightening combination of the exotic, the erotic, the forbidden, the fascinating, and the horrifying. (2000: 596)

For Anemone, such monsters were not symbolic of an anxious, suspicious even, bearing towards Western Europe, but were themselves key moments of encounter. That is, the abhorrence mobilised during this face to face encounter was animated by a shuddering away from the presence of the aberrant. It is this feeling that was in turn rationalised as a political disquiet at the sustained Westernisation of Russia under Tsar Peter.

Monsters in the Tsar's collection may well have alienated their Russian visitors. Yet, what is interesting about this argument is that a suspicion of the visceral affect of monsters was registered across Europe during this period, resulting in a multi-pronged effort to control access to their bodies, and to guide interpretations of these. The key issue here, Daston and Park (1998) argue, was the formation of social disorder around the monster's body. These bodies were understood to play upon a febrile imagination, manifest in all manner of disquiet that, moreover, could be channelled into various subversive ends, as evidenced by the proliferation of divine portents during the Reformation. A variety of political but also philosophical discourses on the ascendency of reason over and against such pathological imaginings, then, should be seen in the context of, "broader transformations of intellectual life following the pacification of much of Western Europe after the protracted and devastating civil strife of the sixteenth and seventeenth centuries" (Daston and Park 1998: 331). Small wonder that Immanuel Kant, for example, in his *Critique of Judgement* (1790), was to ponder the sublime as a visceral experience of awe and wonder that prompted thought, thereby evidencing the triumph of a uniquely human judgement.

Whilst teratological collections still placed such monsters on display, these were framed within an explanatory mode that sought to kindle an intellectual curiosity around the comparative physiology of normal and abnormal organisms, and the diversity of Nature these illustrated, rather than shock and awe, or a melancholia. One of the finest of these, acquired by Gerardus and Willem Vrolik is now housed in the Academic Medical Center in Amsterdam. Their collection has been extended over the years, and includes the acquisition of skulls excavated in the 1910s and 1920s from cemeteries in Amsterdam under the direction of Louis Bolk, who sorted the specimens with an eye to anatomical malformations (Stiemens 1929). Both of the Vroliks specialised in cyclopia, with Willem publishing a five-fold classification of the same in his *Handboek der ziektekundige ontleedkunde* (1842-1844) and his *Tabulae ad illustrandam embryogenesin hominis et mammalium* (1844-1849). The collection provided him with five human neonates exhibiting symptoms of cyclopia, as well as 19 animal ones, to ground his research efforts, along with Siamese twins and cases of sirenomelia. It also included, however, the skull of a Sumatran prince and a tusked narwhal, evidence, to some degree, of the continuing aura of prodigious wonder.

In May 2012, a newly refurbished Museum Vrolik presented a thematisised display based around the human body, "with all of its normalities and abnormalities," as well as a contextual history of its collection and the role of anatomy in changing views on the human condition (Vrolik website). Prior to this, however, the layout of the Vrolik maintained something of its nineteenth century character, with labelled specimens arrayed in cabinets, amongst which the public could saunter, taking in the apparently limitless possibilities of human form. As Armand Leroi (2005: 67) describes its effect upon an audience,

> The only visual referent that suggests itself are the demonic creatures that caper across the canvases of Hieronymus Bosch – another Dutchman – that now hang in the Prado. Of course, there is a difference in meaning. Where Bosch's grotesques serve to warn errant humanity of the fate that awaits it in the afterlife, Vrolik's are presented with clinical detachment, cleansed of moral value. And that, perhaps, suggests the best description of the Museum Vrolik. It is a *Last Judgement* for the scientific age.

Nevertheless, for Leroi, a Professor of Evolutionary Developmental Biology, these are frightening figures, signalling just how quickly a foetus can transform in the womb in response to various chemical or temperature changes.

It would be a mistake, however, to assume that with the disappearance of the portent, and the emergence of teratology, that monsters were thereby sundered from geopolitics. To be sure, teratologists were highly condemning of what they saw as a low-brow fascination with the freakish and a moribund superstition. And yet, their own work, whilst admiring of Nature's diversity, was to become imbricated with a broad-based eugenics effort at eliminating the same in the name of the future health and welfare of a population. Scholars such as Buffon, and philosophers such as Diderot, had extolled the many social benefits of hybridity, and applauded scientific efforts at disturbing Nature even further, efforts that were in turn to become deplored as a Faustian will to practice more than Heaven allowed (for example, Shafer 2005). In the nineteenth century, however, the identification of monstrous traits was to become scientific evidence of a degeneracy that lay within a populace, a degeneracy that, moreover, could be rooted out via more vigilant controls over the reproductive process itself. In large part, this imbrication of teratology with a social Darwinism ensued from an insistence upon atavism as one explanation (amongst others) of monstrous births; such atavisms could easily be read as 'evolutionary throwbacks,' and, more insidiously, as proofs of a society in decline.

There are many studies on the emergence of eugenics as a form of biopolitics across the globe, whereby an acknowledgement of the sciences of animal breeding and plant pollination, as well as a racialised reading of Darwin's 'survival of the fittest' and an increasing emphasis within anthropology upon inbred criminal traits – all of these occurring alongside the emergence of teratology – facilitated and legitimised a welter of domestic and international legislation aimed at halting degeneracy, and purifying the population via a policy of racial hygiene. The physical education of boys, for example, became extolled in the 1880s as a means of strengthening national defence, whilst interest in the disciplining of women's reproductive capacities – manifest par excellence in the pelvic area – became a matter of putting them to effective use in the birth of model citizens (Bohuon and Luciani 2009). Meanwhile, the Eugenics Record Office in the United States opened in 1904, the German Society for Racial Hygiene in 1905, and the British Eugenics Society in 1907, all extolling the gathering of 'medical' data to prove hereditary failures, and presenting a series of legislative solutions. Race – conceived here as a mixture of purported biological determining, and inherited, *in situ* cultural traits – was to become a key organising device for a state-sponsored biopolitics in Europe, Asia and North America. For Jennifer Robertson (2002), *fin de siècle* empire-building was thus also a period of 'eugenic modernity,' in which science provided the legitimising concepts for race-based policies that secured control in the colonies, but that also scourged populations at home in the name of the nation. Such a nation-building was very much predicated, then, on establishing the primacy of matrilineal and patrilineal relations over and against other modes of kinship, thoroughly conflating the blood purity of the family with the purity of the national body.

As Foucault observed, the state became preoccupied with another battle, focused not on the defense of its borders, but on the securitisation of its populace. "It is no longer a battle in the sense of a war," he wrote, "but a struggle in a biological sense: differentiation of species, selection of the strongest, survival of the best adapted races" (cited in Elden 2002: 132). In Germany, for example, economic collapse in the 1920s triggered the disintegration of its welfare system; and, (the much cheaper option of) sterilisation of those considered undesirable residents of Germany's social, as well as physical, space became the solution of choice of the increasingly vocal Nazi Party. "The simultaneous growth of racial anthropology was strongly criticised by the left as a cover for right-wing racism," observes Emily Wittmann (2004: 18), "however the massive growth in the right's political power was able to override the opposition. Once Hitler came to power in 1933 the Nazis were able to pass increasingly stringent eugenic laws with little opposition." The German Nazi Party's policy of racial hygiene was to have devastating consequences for those defined by the state by their Jewishness, Slavicness, homosexuality, mental illness and so on, culminating in the Holocaust, which sought to erase even the memory of those purged. These were victims deemed without the right to exist; who, write Clarke, Doel and McDonough (1996: 458) "ought not to exist, and who were therefore *obligated* not to exist" (emphasis in original). Targeted as parasites, such groups were to be cleaved from the body politic. As Elden (2002: 147) concludes, "A break or cut (*coupure*) is fundamental to racism: a division or incision between those who must live and those who must die."

Goth Politics

In efforts to account for and purify a populace, the singular figure of the monster as a prodigious wonder has long been set aside. As Daston and Park (1998: 367) put it, monsters still please and instruct, but, "they no longer buttress regimes, subvert religions, or reform learning." Yet, part and parcel of this decline has been the proliferation of the *monstrous*, wherein deviations from a posited norm are located within that same populace. Escaping their confinement in the exceptional body, monstrous traits appear dispersed across a spectrum, or clumped in a particular section of society formed across generations. Monsters no longer patrol the edges of civilisation, a warning to transgression, but lurk at its very heart. Importantly, then, the monstrous does not mark the limits of knowledge and understanding, but rather exists in a tension-laden complex of ideas and emotions around norms, standards, mimicry and simulation. Accordingly, what I want to draw out in this section is how this distributed notion of monstrosity has helped to re-animate the Gothic, a term usually associated with art theory and as encapsulating a genre, but which is very much founded in political turmoil and a fear of the infectious character of revolution. I want to begin this time with the French Revolution of 1789, and the response to this from the English conservative statesman, political theorist and philosopher of the sublime, Edmund Burke (1729-1797).

Discussions around the nature of the savage and the barbarian had, of course, long preceded and certainly informed Burke's commentaries, with the former tending to be associated, particularly post-Rousseau, with a pre-civilisation innocence, and the latter a chaotic, alien influence, capable of disrupting the civilising process itself. And, the vista of new peoples, as well as animals, plants, and environments, opened up by colonialism, posed a number of profound challenges as to how Europe was to be located over and against these. It is towards the end of the eighteenth century, however, that an intensification and consolidation of ideas around violent, 'sub-human' elements that could erupt within the social body took place, the key trigger here being the French Revolution and its aftermath, a *terrorisme*. The revolution upended long ingrained practices predicated on a combined sovereign and religious authority, and attempted to actualise Enlightenment principles of citizenship, and the equal and inalienable rights of those citizens. The Women's March on Versailles, on 5 October 1789, which forced the King and his family and entourage to return to Paris, had highlighted the political agency of women in such an effort, as had the militancy of the Society of Revolutionary Republican Women, and the writing of Olympe de Gouges, author of the *Declaration on the Rights of Woman and the Female Citizen* (1791).

For Mark Neocleous (2005), Burke's articulation of the threat posed by a 'monstrous multitude,' as manifest in his *Reflections on the Revolution in France* (1790), evidences a horror not so much with the violence underwriting the revolution, but with the political ideology of democracy; or, as Burke had put it earlier in his *Thoughts on the Cause of the Present Discontents* (1770: 115), "that monstrous evil of governing in concurrence with the opinion of the people."

In 1789, with the convocation of the *Estates-General*, and the passage of the *Declaration of the Rights of Man and of the Citizen*, Burke wrote to his son in October 1789 that, "the Elements which compose Human Society seem all to have dissolved, and a world of Monsters to be produced in place of it" (reprinted in Burke 1958, volume 6: 30). Prominent in Burke's writings was the monstrous inversion of Natural order and propriety by 'revolutionary harridans'; hence, Ian Ward (2010: 208) writes, the sanguinary and sexual violence he recounts is accompanied by reference to "shrilling screams, and frantic dances, and infamous contumelies; and all the unutterable abominations of the furies of hell." For Burke, the French Revolution was a global event, insofar as it had the potential to reach far and wide, and to wage war with Heaven itself; and, the prospect of such an unnatural political order reaching across the English Channel was a fearful one. In contrast to the sublime, which was, "that state of the soul, in which all its motions are suspended, with some degree of horror," and which was to be experienced at a distance, the French revolution, he wrote, simply provoked terror, insofar as it "pressed too nearly" (Burke 1958: 58). Deploying an allegory based on plant breeding, Burke advocated that,

> The very idea of the fabrication of a new government, is enough to fill us with disgust and horror. We wished at the period of the Revolution, and do now wish, to derive all we possess as an inheritance from our forefathers. Upon that body and stock of inheritance we have taken care not to inoculate any alien to the nature of the original plant ... Our oldest reformation is that of Magna Carta. (Burke 1790: 44)

Such sentiments, David Morris (1985) argues, are clearly Gothic in character, insofar as they call for the defence of order and tradition against the arbitrary, the irrational and the unreasoning, as well as a longing for a 'golden age' (the medieval period, for example) when such upheaval was deemed to be impossible. The Gothic is, Foucault (2003) argues, a thoroughly political imaginary; and, divers threats to the body of the nation, and national bodies, were to be couched time and again in Gothic tropes.

The artistic mediums though which the Gothic became manifest – architecture, sculpture, poetry and the 'new' romance horror – certainly reiterate the notion of mis-begotten forms, both real and imagined. In many ways Mary Wollstonecraft Shelley's (1818) *Frankenstein* is, of course, a prime example of this, with its intersection of scientific hubris, reanimation, abhuman form and sublime landscapes. For Ellen Moers (1977: 81), however, this is also a reworking of the Gothic, insofar as it emphasises not the events leading up to birth, but the aftermath. It is a tale, she writes,

> of revulsion against newborn life, and the drama of guilt, dread, and flight surrounding birth and its consequences ... Frankenstein seems to be distinctly a woman's mythmaking on the subject of birth precisely because its emphasis is

not upon what precedes birth, not upon birth itself, but upon what follows birth: the trauma of the afterbirth.

In the Gothic we also see, however, another mode of propagation, via the 'contagion of the passions,' as Burke puts it. Whilst 'maternal impression' had suggested one form of gender disorder, insofar as women had allowed their excessive corporeality to overcome their already weak faculties, contagion allowed for men as well as women to become both propagators and victims. A fleshy contagion thus had the potential to blur a heterosexuality as well as gender. In this Gothic mode there is a specificity in the rhetoric used, and the mode of figures deployed, Robert Mighall (1999) argues, that illuminates particular fears and anxieties around the influence and affect of particular Others and the places they both inhabited and emerged from. In the context of an English Gothic, for example, manifest in the classic *Castle of Otranto* (1764) by Horace Walpole, Ann Radcliffe's *The Mysteries of Udolpho* (1794), and Matthew Lewis' *The Monk* (1796), we can trace a geopolitics of abhorrence that places the monstrous in an elsewhere typified by its 'Easterliness,' its relative rurality and its Catholicism. In Germany, the *schauerroman* ('shudder novels') provoked a thrilling sense of horror in response to tales of international conspiracies, secret societies and necromancy.

In France, vampires had long frequented folk tales, and were even manifest in several Natural Histories of the early eighteenth century. The retelling of vampire narratives in Enlightenment Paris signified heightened fears around the abhorrent practice of dissection, as well as the relocation of graves to the outer suburbs (Huet 1977). The geography inscribed into the French theologian Dom Augustine Calmet's (1746) monumentally popular book on vampires, ghosts and revenants (*Dissertations sur les apparitions des anges, des démons et des esprits, et sur les revenants et vampires de Hongrie, de Bohême, de Moravie, et de Silésie*) makes clear the origin point of such creatures, namely a feudal, superstitious, Eastern Europe. Bram Stoker's (1897) iteration, *Dracula*, traces a similar trajectory, adopting the format and tone of English traveller accounts of strange and foreign lands. The setting of events in the 'Old World,' Transylvania, provides a geography close enough to be infectious, yet alien enough to spawn incubi. It is here that our English traveller is tempted by the sensual carnality of the female vampire, before succumbing to the bite of Dracula himself. Through the course of the novel Dracula – the infectious agent of a sanguinary and sexual violence aimed at both men and women – travels first to Whitby, a Gothic landscape of crags and cemeteries, then London, next door to a lunatic asylum, and finally the bedroom of the book's heroine, only to be defeated and driven back by a Dutchman, an Englishman and a Texan. "If the modern world could encounter the primeval merely by journeying to one of the few blank spaces on the map," Mighall (1999: 137) concludes, "then the 'primitive' could reverse the process and crop up in the very center of the civilised world."

A *fin de siècle* Gothicism, shaped by social Darwinism, called up all manner of degenerate, beast-like monstrosities in the very midst of urban slums, their presence in the world provoking a visceral shudder, the physical manifestation of a sickening of the soul. And so for the Victorian writer H.P. Lovecraft (2008: 152), for example, the subterranean 'horror' at Red Hook, in the city of New York, lies in the miscegenation and atavism that lurks outside of the bright lights. Its populace is,

> a hopeless tangle and enigma; Syrian, Spanish, Italian, and Negro elements impinging upon one another ... They must be, [the hero] felt inwardly, the heirs of some shocking and primordial tradition; the sharers of debased and broken scraps from cults and ceremonies older than mankind ... there had certainly survived among peasants and furtive folk a frightful and clandestine system of assemblies and orgies descended from dark religions antedating the Aryan world...

Here, the irruption of the monstrous threatens to pervade the everyday lives and imaginations of an otherwise civil populace, threatening not only a social disorder, but an unnatural reversal of both space and time. Small wonder, argues Scott Poole (1990: n.p.), that the Gothic, which "posited terrors at the very heart of the world and then triumphed over them," so easily intertwined with a conservative politics, "a political philosophy that very much believes that the thing under the bed and the lurker in the shadows is real...".

Small wonder also that contemporary international events are so often couched in this now familiar rhetoric of fear and loathing. For Maria Beville (2009: 23), there is a clear connection between the pervasive atmosphere of terror in post-Revolutionary Europe, and more recent efforts to make sense of geopolitical events, including a mass-media induced terror in the aftermath of 9/11. Indeed, the capacity of the Gothic to provide a rich, highly effective reservoir of visceral affects has been intermittently commented upon by International Relations scholars, and is especially 'present' as both purported object of analysis, and analytic, in the aftermath of the destruction of the Twin Towers in New York City, and the subsequent 'war on terror' carried out by the Bush and Obama administrations. According to Richard Devetak (2005: 621), for example, the Gothic motifs evoked by President Bush, "involve monsters and ghosts in tenebrous atmospheres that generate fear and anxiety, where terror is a pervasive tormentor of the senses ... ineffable and potently violent and cruel forces haunt and terrorise the civilised world." For Devetak (2005), following Shapiro (2003), the Gothic is part and parcel of a 'political somatics' inherited from the Enlightenment, as the sensate and rational nature of human beings became a prime topic in the political philosophies of Hobbes, Spinoza, Mandeville, Hume, Smith and, of course, Burke. Borders are required to keep monsters at bay, Devetak argues, but they also mark a tortuous 'knot' of emotions wherein revulsion and dread are enmeshed with attraction and desire; this is a complex "aesthetic of pleasurable fear" (Sedgwick, 1986: 11).

To hunt monsters, Devetak warns, is to nurture the monstrous within oneself. This is because such monstrous beings are the perverse, excessive double of ourselves; and, it is this, Elizabeth Grosz (1991: 36) argues, which enables and drives a, "horror of submersion in an alien otherness, an incorporation in and by the other." The monstrous being as perverse copy is unable to confirm a unique and singular human subject identity, no matter how many barriers are erected, including that between the living and the dead. Rather, the repeated failure to exorcise these abject figures serves to highlight a series of regulatory principles, not only in regard to human/non-human but also a same-sex intimacy, by which monstrosity has been labelled as such. A series of blurred, inverted, exaggerated figures emerge that do not break conventional categories so much as threaten to subsume them in a tangled sk(e)in of mirrors, each reflective, each warped. The Gothic, then, is not simply the apocalyptic irruption of nightmares, but is a permanent condition of unease and oppression, with the always present expectation of a violent disordering of appropriately gendered, sexed, classed and raced individuals, as well as a national body predicated upon these.

At the outset of the twenty-first century, Gothic monsters continue to populate the geopolitical imagination. For Karen Engle (2007: 408), commenting on internet cartoons of Osama bin Laden that depict him alongside the Empire State Building, the libidinal force of the Gothic is particularly enlightening:

> Imperialism and anal rape (he is penetrated by the Empire State building), effeminization ("You like skyscrapers, huh bitch?"), and the sprouting penis head (dick-head) are consistent themes in modified images of Osama—the official *head* of Terrorism since September 11, 2001. This hypersexualization makes bin Laden into a modern primitive: a being driven by a libidinal, phallic instinct that has overpowered all rational thought. Evoking Bataille's famous solar anus, bin Laden's penis head resembles nothing so much as a giant pineal gland dwarfing all potential for civilization. The caption, "Why He Wears a Turban," suggestively extends the condition to all turban-wearing populations and thereby reinscribes a discrete division already propounded in the media between self (U.S. straight, White male) and other (Middle Eastern violent, queer terrorist). His emasculation by the Empire State building, an appropriate symbol for American imperialism, underscores that the threat bin Laden poses is read not simply as a general threat to the State's safety but rather as a specific threat to the State's sexual purity. (emphasis in original)

Fear of the 'primitive' emerging into the very heart of civilised society has certainly characterised a great deal of far right rhetoric concerning the legitimacy of Barack Obama's first and second US Presidencies. Whilst the Murdoch-owned *Fox News* has often been cited for its nurturing of Donald Trump and Sarah Palin's 'birther' suspicions, amongst other issues, this readily visible medium belies the scope and impact of the far right's carefully orchestrated deployment of new social media as a means of generating grassroots campaigns, from 'blast faxes' to US House and Senate GOP members organised online, to cross-referenced news blogs advertised through Evangelical Church communities. One particularly vocal entity in this regard is the America's Conservative News (ACN), run out of Lorton, Virginia, and dedicated to 'News the Liberal Media Won't or Can't Print.' ACN maintains an online news bulletin, but also offers special email shots to its approximately 195,000 subscribers, as well as a daily email summary often including items culled from other far right news blogs. These are especially effective, with ACN reporting for October 2012 – in the run up to the 7th November US election – 225,463 'newsletter opens,' and 65,552 website hits (ACN website). For this occasion, ACN also hosted a 'Voter Lookout' tool, to be used to check up on one's own, family and friends voting eligibility, sponsored by *Wall Builders* and *United in Purpose Education*.

Such news reports include the 7th June 2012 headline, 'Man Who Says He Had Sex With Obama Vindicated?' followed by the teaser,

> When Larry Sinclair announced that <u>he had sexual relations with Barack Obama years ago in a limo</u>, the Obama attack machine tried to destroy him. Now, it would appear that Sinclair is on the road to vindication. (ACN 7th June 2012 email, emphasis in original)

And, 'Slam-Dunk Proof The Obama Birth Certificate Is Fradulent [sic],' released in a 18 July email shot, with the teaser,

> Sheriff Joe Arpaio, true to his word, released brand new findings from the Cold Case Posse investigation into Barack Obama's alleged birth certificate at a press conference on Tuesday; findings which conclusively prove that the birth certificate Barack Obama released on the Internet last year is, as originally contended, "a computer-generated forgery". (ACN email 17th July 2012)

In the months preceding the 2012 US Presidential election, ACN was joined by groups such as *GrasstopsUSA Action Alert Newsletter*, which warned, for example, that,

> Barack Obama *has just given the United Nations jurisdiction to go after the State of Arizona* and *the 22 other states that are attempting to enforce the immigration laws that he refuses to enforce* ... Not content with simply filing a frivolous federal suit against the people of Arizona, Obama has transformed *his amnesty feud with the American people into an international human rights cause* and *effectively placed the people of Arizona (and the 22 other states that are considering similar border security legislation) under the jurisdiction of a triumvirate of America-hating United Nations bureaucrats*.... His glib words cannot conceal that fact that he is effectively saying to the people of the United States: *The will* and *the safety of the American people be damned... I want amnesty to further my own twisted political agenda...* The sad but unfortunate truth is that *Barack Obama is starting to behave more like a third-world despot* and *less like the president of the greatest nation in the free world.* (email sent out 21st August 2012, emphasis in original)

Frequent references in such missives to President Obama as an out of control emperor, czar, or king (e.g., ACN email 11th October 2012), as well as references to his allegiance to both the US-hating United Nations and the evil forces of Islam and Marxism/Socialism, certainly reiterate the 'Old World' rhetoric of classical Gothic literature. As do the insinuations as to a sexual 'deviancy' present not only in Obama, but his parents also (ACN email 21st August 2012), thereby reinforcing the idea of Obama as mis-begotten. The cumulative image presented is that of a 'foreign' body that has, with malice aforethought, insinuated itself into the political system as *the* representative of the US populace. And, it is this cumulative image that the liberal magazine *The New Yorker* attempted to satirise with its 21 July 2008 cover of both Barack and Michelle Obama drawn as terrorists, entitled 'The Politics of Fear.' According to the editor, David Remnick, "This [cartoon] is saying a particular thing at a particular time, when these imaginings and dark fantasies and misconceptions about Obama exist. And we're putting it all together in one image and holding a mirror up to it and showing it for the absurdity that it is" (cited in Sklar 2008: n.p.). The monstrousness of such a body ensues from its grotesque mimicry of US values and allegiances, and the contagiousness of such an unAmericanness (as in references to an 'Obama cult'), but also anxieties as to an external audience viewing Obama as the titular 'head' of the US. There is no doubting the world view here within which such claims 'make sense,' as the US is declared uniquely worthy by virtue of its founding upon Protestant ideals and a *laissez-faire* capitalism, coupled with extreme immigration controls that safeguard a white, European heritage.

In the context of what are now decades of civil rights and affirmative action initiatives in the US, the absence of explicit references to Obama's foreignness being based on 'colour' is worthy of comment. At one level, it resonates with what has been termed an antiracialism – that is, the active 'suppression' of race as a topic of reasoned debate (see Goldberg 2009). At another revel, this absence draws attention to the emergence of a much more 'spacious' rhetoric that takes on board various 'signs' and 'indicators,' ranging from literacy and poverty to profligacy and deviancy, of unAmericanness, and underscores these via a variety of genres such as the Gothic, and its emphasis upon the visceral, libidinal threat of the grotesque to a heterosexual, civilised populace. It is this wide-ranging discourse, then, which is used to locate and identify particular bodies, such as Obama and those who voted for him, at the same time that a discourse on the histories and geographies of racism is de-legitimised.

Concluding Comments

Much has been made of the re-emergence of such nationalist, xenophobic discourses since the fall of the Iron Curtain. And, in the absence of a polarised east-west ideological axis, the reworking of Self and Other according to other modes of identification that emphasise belonging and alienation. Much has also been made of the re-emergence of religion as a key geopolitical identification, tempering as well as exacerbating such nationalisms, depending on specific context. We can also now factor in economic crises and austerity measures in mobilising abhorrence. In such turbulent times, it is no small surprise to find that the Gothic once more provides a series of well-worn tropes that help make sense of an impending and all-pervasive threat from 'over there' as it reaches across into 'here and now.' In Europe, for example, the Eurozone financial crisis has led to the villification of those states, such as Greece, considered lax and profligate. It has also, writes Catharine Macmillan (2014: 24), enabled the emergence of a popular discourse in newspapers and politician speeches that represent contemporary Germany as, "an uncanny revenant of the Nazi era, often depicted as a 'Fourth Reich.'" In addition to the presence of the Gothic she finds, in the specific, embodied response of audiences, an uncanny mix of the familiar and the unfamiliar – the return of the repressed, to use a Freudian term – that hinges on current day Germany as the duplicitous double of the twentieth century's Nazi Germany.

In the next chapter, I go on to discuss the role of a profligate Nature in such a Gothic imaginary. In closing this chapter, however, I want to raise the issue of the *neo*-Gothic as an aesthetic, geopolitical imaginary that takes on Gothic tropes and reworks them in order to highlight the monstrosities that go into the exclusion of those considered to be Gothic villains, but also to present possible, alternate futures. At one level, such efforts can be read as simply inverting the good/bad dichotomy of the Gothic. According to Eileen Culloty (2014), for example, ongoing critiques of the US' use of torture, and its carceral activities at Abu Ghraib, gain their currency from villifying a shadowy and corrupt neo-Conservative Republicanism over and against a naturally decent American public. There is more to be said, here, however, in regard to exposing the imaginative base of such constructions, their aesthetic affect, and their political import. As Toni Morrison (1992) demonstrates in her examination of blackness as a critical image that, manifest more often than not in passive, bounded and silenced black bodies, evoked something of the terror that sat at the heart of the American dream of freedom, such Gothic stirrings can be worked anew to produce a literature that reflects upon such problematic constructions. Her Pulitzer Prize-winning novel *Beloved* (1987) gives us, literally, the haunting presence of past abhorrences. The beloved of the title is a ghostly presence in the classic Gothic vein, in that she sucks out the life of her runaway slave mother Sethe; what is more, her mother has committed a monstrous act of motherlove, taking an axe to her young daughter's throat. But, as we learn why Sethe has undertaken such an act, that same presence is key to the unveiling of the monstrosity that is slavery and its state-sponsored necropolitics.

In similar vein, the films of Guillermo Del Toro, mentioned in passing in Chapter 4, become mediums for the reworking of Gothic tropes in light of the conservative regimes they serve to prop up. For Del Toro, such horrors are best introduced and experienced through a myth-rich lens before they can be acknowledged and dealt with. Whilst his earlier film, *El Espinazo Del Diablo* (*The Devil's Backbone*, 2001), used the ghost story, set in a Spanish orphanage at the height of the Spanish Civil War, as a vehicle to relay the cruelty of the Francoist regime and the need for a new beginning, his 2006 *El laberinto del fauno* (*Pan's Labyrinth*) has a magical realist style. Here, a young girl must face surreal monsters that lurk beneath and alongside the 'real' horrors of Fascism. Whilst our heroine is shot and killed by a sadistic and misogynist Francoist Captain (her stepfather) in the 'real' realm, she is reborn in this magical world into a new family. Tortured bodies, tortured families and a tortured nation are thoroughly interposed in this allegorical fairytale. For del Toro, there is a great hope in bringing such monstrousness to light;

> I know for a fact that imagination and hope have kept me alive through the roughest times of my life. Reality is brutal and it will kill you, make no mistake about it, but our tales, our creatures and our heroes have a chance to live longer than any of us. Franco suffocated Spain for decades as he tried to fashion it after what he believed to be 'good for her.' Yet, Spain didn't die: she exploded, vibrant and alive, in the 80s. (cited in Brussat and Brussat 2007: n.p.)

For Jack Zipes (2008), it is the particular, affective capacity of the fairy tale, as animated by film, that allows Del Toro to 'penetrate' the 'reality' presented by powerful elites. Here, a medium more usually trounced as providing a spectacularised politics of amnesia in regard to the same, is valorised as providing an immersive experience that makes us empathise with the victims of war, certainly, but that also teaches us something about how what we see is all too often choreographed and narrated for us. The fairytale does not present us with a more truthful account of the world; rather, like the baroque genre that emerged in the midst of the Reformation, it destabilises our notion of what is real and what is fiction. This example of the neo-Gothic has, to be sure, its human and abhuman monsters: yet, Juliet Rohde-Brown (2007: 167) insists, there is no simple reversal of good and evil here. Instead, she speculates,

> The popularity of this film suggests that perhaps we are resonating with that part of ourselves that acknowledges a deep healing must take place in our world, a healing that involves a dying off of the primitive 'us versus them' mentality and rebirth into a healthy and integrated 'we are all in this together' ... If Gore's [*An Inconvenient Truth*] can serve as our guilty conscience ... then Del Toro's film can serve as our unconscious process as we struggle toward individuation, toward maturing into compassionate stewards of our living alchemical vessel, our life-blood and body – this sphere called Earth.

What is more, whilst one may read such representations as simply providing insight into the gendering of geopolitical relations, events and framings, and the impact of geopolitics on family, this misses the point, I think, insofar as there is no ready demarcation to be found here between 'the family' and 'the state,' as well as the 'imaginative' and the 'real.' That is, whilst the fate of the family becomes a narrative device for coming to grips with the everyday, monstrous realities of the Franco regime, these same realities, it must be emphasised, were constitutive of that regime, which was as much a matter of ideological control as it was physical repression. The neo-Gothic is no mere vehicle for uttering a condemnation of the Self/Other dichotomy that has been such a feature of nation-building, but is also a political mode of expression that works, through its rich imagery and its particular style of story-telling, to produce a vision of what is possible.

References

Adler, Kraig. 1989. Herpetologists of the Past. In Adler, Kraig (ed.) *Contributions to the History of Herpetology*. Oxford, OH: Society for the Study of Amphibians and Reptiles, pp. 5-141.

ACN website, available at http://c4strategies.com/AdSpecs.html

ACN email, sent out 7 June 2012, and linked to http://conservativeamericaonline.blogspot.co.uk/2011/12/obamas-drug-and-sex-party-limosine.html. Last accessed 25 September 2014.

ACN email, sent out 17 July 2012, and linked to http://conservativeamericaonline.blogspot.co.uk/2012/07/slam-dunk-proof-obama-birth-certificate.html#more. Last accessed 25 September 2014.

ACN email, sent out 11 October, and linked to the page http://conservativeamericaonline.blogspot.co.uk/2012/10/obama-claimed-his-father-indonesian.html?utm_source=America%27s+Conservative+News&utm_campaign=93f0280a13-RSS_EMAIL_CAMPAIGN&utm_medium=email#more. Last accessed 25 September 2014.

ACN email sent out 21 August 2012, and linked to the page http://conservativeamericaonline.blogspot.co.uk/2011/06/documents-show-marriage-of-obamas.html. Last accessed 25 September 2014.

Anemone, Anthony. 2000. The Monsters of Peter the Great: The Culture of the St. Petersburg Kunstkamera in the eighteenth Century, *Slavic and East European Journal* 44.4: 583-602.

Beville, Maria. 2009. *Gothic-Postmodernism: Voicing the Terrors of Postmodernity*. Amsterdam: Rodopi.

Bohuon, Anaïs and Luciani, Antoine. 2009. Biomedical Discourse on Women's Physical Education and Sport in France (1880-1922), *The International Journal of the History of Sport* 26.5: 573-93.

Braidotti, Rosi. 2002. Difference, Diversity and Nomadic Subjectivity. Available at http://women.ped.kun.nl/cbt/rosilecture.html. Last accessed 19 October 2014.

Brussat, Frederic and Brussat, Mary Ann. 2007. *Spirituality* and *Practice: Film Review*, available at https://www.spiritualityandpractice.com/films/films.php?id=16154. Last accessed 24 September 2014.

Buffon, George-Louise Leclerc, comte de. 1749-67, *Histoire Naturelle, générale et particulière, 15 volumes*. Paris: Imprimerie Royale.

Burke, Edmund. 1770. *A Philosophical Enquiry Into the Origin of The Sublime and Beautiful*. London: J. Dodsley.

Burke, Edmund. 1790. *Reflections on the Revolution in France. Fifth Edition*. London: J. Dodsley.

Burke, Edmund. 1958. *The Correspondence of Edmund Burke*. Copeland, Thomas W. (ed.). Chicago, IL: University of Chicago Press.

Burke, Edmund. 1958. *A Philosophical Inquiry into the Origin of Our Ideas of the Sublime and Beautiful*. London: J.T. Bolton.

Calmet, Dom A. 1746. *Dissertations sur les apparitions des anges, des démons et des esprits, et sur les revenants et vampires de Hongrie, de Bohême, de Moravie, et de Silésie*.

Clarke, David B., Doel, Marcus A. and McDonough, Francis X. 1996. Holocaust Topologies: Singularity, Politics, Space, *Political Geography* 15.6: 457-89.

Cressy, David. 2004. Lamentable, Strange, and Wonderful: Headless Monsters in the English Revolution. In Knoppers, Laura and Landes, Joan (eds). *Monstrous Bodies/Political Monstrosities in Early Modern Europe*. Ithaca, NY: Cornell University Press, pp. 40-63.

Culloty, Eileen. 2014. Rescuing America from Iraq: The Gothic Remorse of Iraq War Documentaries, *Studies in Documentary Film* 8.2: 130-42.

Daston, Lorraine J. and Park, Katherine. 1998. *Wonders and the Order of Nature, 1150-1750*. New York: Zone Books.

De Costa, P. Fontes. 2004. Between Fact and Fiction: Narratives of Monsters in Eighteenth-Century Portugal, *Portuguese Studies* 20: 63-72.

De Gouges, Olympe. 1791 [1996]. The Declaration of the Rights of Woman, September 1791. Reprinted in Hunt, Lynn, editor and translator, *The French Revolution and Human Rights*. Los Angeles, CA: UCLA Press, pp. 125-6.

Devetak, Richard. 2005. The Gothic Scene of International Relations: Ghosts, Monsters, Terror and the Sublime after September 11, *Review of International Studies* 31.4: 621-43.

Diderot, Denis. 1975. *Oeuvres Comlètes*. Dieckmann, E., Proust, J. and Varloot, J. (eds). Paris: Hermann.

Dietz, Bettina and Nutz, Thomas. 2005. *Collections Curieuses*: The Aesthetics of Curiosity and Elite Lifestyle in Eighteenth-Century Paris, *Eighteenth-Century Life* 29.3: 44-75.

Dixon, Deborah P. and Ruddick, Susan M. 2011. Introduction: Monstrous Irruptions, *Cultural Geographies* 18.4: 431-3.

Elden, Stuart. 2002. The War of Races and the Constitution of the State: Foucault's *Il faut défendre la société* and the Politics of Calculation, *Boundary* 2 29.1: 125-51.

Engle, Karen. 2007. The Face of a Terrorist, *Cultural Studies ↔ Critical Methodologies* 7.4: 397-424.

Farber, Paul L. 1975. Buffon and Daubenton: Divergent Traditions within the *Histoire Naturelle*, *Isis* 66.1: 63-74.
Foucault, Michel. 2003. *Society Must Be Defended. Lectures at the Collège de France, 1975-6.* London: St. Martin's Press.
Goldberg, David T. 2009. *The Threat of Race: Reflections on Racial Neoliberalism.* Malden, MA: Wiley-Blackwell.
Goodall, Jane. 2002. *Performance and Evolution in the Age of Darwin: Out of the Natural Order.* London: Routledge.
GrasstopsUSA Action Alert Newsletter email, sent out 21st August 2012.
Grosz, Elizabeth A. 1991. Freaks, *Social Semiotics* 1.2: 22-38.
Hazard, Paul. 1964. *The European Mind, 1680-1715.* Hammondsworth: Penguin.
Hsia, R. Po-Chia. 2004. A Time for Monsters: Monstrous Birth, Propaganda, and the German Reformation. In Knoppers, Laura and Landes, Joan (eds) *Monstrous Bodies/Political Monstrosities in Early Modern Europe.* Ithaca, NY: Cornell University Press, pp. 67-92.
Huet, Marie Hélène. 1997. Deadly Fears: Dom Augustin Calmet's Vampires and the Rule Over Death, *Eighteenth-Century Life* 21.2: 222-32.
Kant, Immanuel. 1790 [1951]. *Critique of Judgement.* Translated by J.H. Bernard, New York: Hafner Publishing.
Knoppers, Laura and Landes, Joan (eds). 2004. *Monstrous Bodies/Political Monstrosities in Early Modern Europe.* Ithaca, NY: Cornell University Press.
Leggott, Sarah. 2009. Memory, Postmemory, Trauma: The Spanish Civil War in Recent Novels by Women. *FULGOR* 4.1: 25-33.
Leroi, Armand M. 2005. *Mutants: On the Form, Varieties and Errors of the Human body.* New York: Penguin.
Lewis, Matthew. 1796 [1973]. *The Monk.* London: Oxford University Press.
Liceti, Fortunio. 1616 [1708]. *Traité des Monstres.* Leiden: Schouten.
Lovecraft, H.P. 2008. The Horror at Red Hook. In Lovecraft, H.P. *Necronomicon: The Best Weird Tales of H.P. Lovecraft.* London: Orion House, pp. 148-65.
Luyendijk-Elshout, Antonie M. 1970. Death Enlightened: A Study of Frederik Ruysch, *Journal of the American Medical Association* 212.1: 121-6.
Macmillan, Catherine. 2014. The Return of the Reich? A Gothic Tale of Germany and the Eurozone Crisis, *Journal of Contemporary European Studies* 22.1: 24-38.
Mbembé, J-A. and Meintjes, Libby. 2003. Necropolitics, *Public Culture* 15.1: 11-40.
Mighall, Robert. 2003. *A Geography of Victorian Gothic Fiction: Mapping History's Nightmares.* Oxford: Oxford University Press.
Moers, Ellen. 1977. *Literary Women.* New York: Anchor Books.
Monti, Maria T. 2000. Epigenesis of the Monstrous Form and Preformistic 'Genetics' (Lemery-Winslow-Haller). *Early Science and Medicine* 5.1: 3-32.
Morris, David B. 1985. Gothic Sublimity, *New Literary History* 16.2: 299-319.

Morrison, Toni. 2014. Romancing the Shadow (1992). In Alsen, Eberhard (ed.) *The New Romanticism: A Collection of Critical Essays*. New York: Garland, pp. 51-67.
Morrison, Toni. 1987. *Beloved: A Novel*. New York: Alfred Knopf.
Neocleous, Mark. 2005. *The Monstrous and the Dead: Burke, Marx, Fascism*. Cardiff: University of Wales Press.
Nijman, Jan. 2007. Place-particularity and 'Deep Analogies': A Comparative Essay on Miami's Rise as a World City, *Urban Geography* 28.1: 92-107.
Paré, Ambroise. 1573 [1980]. *Des Monstres et Prodiges*. Translated by Janis L. Pallister. Chicago, IL: University of Chicago Press.
Park, Katharine and Lorraine J. Daston. 1981. Unnatural Conceptions: The Study of Monsters in Sixteenth-and Seventeenth-century France and England, *Past and Present*: 20-54.
Poole, W. Scott. 2004. Confederates and Vampires: Manly Wade Wellman and the Gothic Sublime, *Studies in Popular Culture* 89-99.
Radcliffe, Ann. 1794 [1980]. *The Mysteries of Udolpho*. USA: Oxford University Press.
Robertson, Jennifer. 2002. Blood Talks: Eugenic Modernity and the Creation of New Japanese, *History and Anthropology* 13.3: 191-216.
Roger, Jacques. 1964. Réflexions sur l'histoire de la biologie (xvne-xvme siècle): problèmes de méthodes, *Revue d'Histoire des Sciences* XVII: 25-30.
Rohde-Brown, Juliet. 2007. A Review of: "Pan's Labyrinth" Written, Directed, and Produced by Guillermo Del Toro, *Psychological Perspectives* 50.1: 167-9.
Sedgwick, Eve Kosofsky. 1986. *The Coherence of Gothic Conventions*. New York and London: Methuen.
Shafer, Ingrid H. 2005. The Faust Challenge: Science as Diabolic or Divine. *Zygon®*, 40.4: 891-916.
Shapiro, Kam. 2003. *Sovereign Nations, Carnal States*. Ithaca, NY: Cornell University Press.
Sklar, Rachel. 2008. David Remnick On That *New Yorker* Cover: It's Satire, Meant To Target "Distortions and Misconceptions and Prejudices" About Obama, *Huffington Post* (21 July), available at http://www.huffingtonpost.com/2008/07/13/david-remnick-on-emnew-yo_n_112456.html. Last accessed 24 November 2014.
Stiemens von M.J. 1929. Uber die concrescentia atlanto-occipitalis, *Verh Kon Akad Wetensch Amst* 24.5: 1-51.
Stoker, Bram. 1897 [1981]. *Dracula*. New York: Bantam.
Spary, Emma. 2000. *Utopia's Garden: French Natural History from Old Regime to Revolution*. Chicago, IL: University of Chicago Press.
Todd, Dennis. 1995. *Imagining Monsters: Miscreations of the Self in Eighteenth-Century England*. Chicago, IL: University of Chicago Press.
Vrolik, Willem. 1842-1844. *Handboek der ziektekundige ontleedkunde, Volumes 1 and 2*. Amsterdam: Sulpke.

Vrolik, Willem. 1844-1849. *Tabulae ad illustrandam embryogenesin hominis et mammalium tam naturalem quam abnormem.* Amsterdam: Londonck.

Vrolik website, available at (http://www.english.uva.nl/about_the_uva/object.cfm/B58ECD73-5617-4B7D-BC5A0833D2B88F6A/BC8DB46F-E230-4800-BF67CDC9454874B8). Last accessed 25 September 2014.

Walpole, Horace. 1764 [2008]. *The Castle of Otranto, A Gothic Story.* Oxford: Oxford Paperbacks.

Ward, Ian. 2010. The Perversions of History: Constitutionalism and Revolution in Burke's Reflections, *Liverpool Law Review* 31.3: 207-32.

Wittmann, Emily. 2004. To What Extent Were Ideas and Beliefs about Eugenics Held in Nazi Germany Shared in Britain and the United States Prior to the Second World War? *Vesalius: Acta Internationales Historiae Medicinae* 10.1: 16-19.

Wollstonecraft, Mary. 1818 [2008] *Frankenstein, Or, The Modern Prometheus.* New York: Engage Books.

Wortman, Richard S. 2006. *Scenarios of Power: Myth and Ceremony in Russian Monarchy from Peter the Great to the abdication of Nicholas II.* Princeton, NJ: Princeton University Press.

Zipes, Jack. 2008. Pan's Labyrinth (El laberinto del fauno) (review), *Journal of American Folklore* 121.480: 236-40.

Chapter 6
Touch

Introduction

What the preceding chapter has both intimated, and pulled away from, is a haptics of the living body. That is, for a body to shudder, and by this bodily performance to thereby mark the monster, is to enact at once an intimacy, whereby one has felt the monster's touch in the viscera of one's own body, and a distancing, that is, a drawing away from that which threatens a sense of Self. The body of the monster is by default unique and non-substitutable, and its touch is thereby unheralded, unprecedented and irreproducible; yet, its presence is a momentous event that can be rendered legible by reference to all manner of geopolitical concerns. The body of the *monstrous*, by contrast, speaks to the notion of a spectrum and deviations from the same; this is a concept that requires a multitude of otherwise equivalent corporealities. A monstrous touch may be unexpected, even irruptive, but is nevertheless subject to anticipation. This is because the monstrous by its very nature is apprehended in the midst of a citizenry; hence, it needs must be understood in terms of the prevailing regulation of affects and the disciplining of bodies. And, as Adams et al. (2009: 248) note, such anticipation enables, "the production of possible futures that are lived and felt as inevitable in the present, rendering hope and fear as important political vectors." Monstrousness, one might say, after Derrida, is a domestication of, or a living with, the monster.

In this chapter, I want to delve more deeply into the import of such a haptics for feminist geopolitics, and in particular the manner in which touch has been, and continues to be, privileged as a site of geopolitical concern because of its unfolding within an environment that, despite all manner of regulatory efforts, is un-curtailed by either the voluminous spaces claimed by territorial states, or the topological relations that twist and fold between bodies and things. This is a geopolitics that invokes elemental excess and microbial multitudes and that, as is well documented, has been manifest in immense efforts to purge and scourge people and place, including the immunisation of a medicalised population from untoward contamination. Such efforts have been recounted, for example, in William McNeill's (1976) epochal *Plague* and *Peoples*, which dwells on the co-organisation of epidemiological threat alongside pivotal geopolitical, social and economic developments; Laurie Garrett's (1994) *The Coming Plague*, which correlates the modern-day resurgence of epidemic disease, as well as the emergence of new forms, with international travel, migration, agricultural and urban development; and Nathan Wolfe's (2011) *Viral Storm*, which posits an increasingly globalised world as a zoonotic disease incubator. All look to the co-mingling of organisms and an ensuing bio-vulnerability amongst ever-more connected, or 'in touch,' populations. Moreover, such works help to form a backdrop for recent interrogations of the manner in which interventions aimed at regulating and responding to this co-mingling have largely taken a hard-bodied, militaristic approach, such that an all-consuming 'biosecurity' not only negates attempts to analyse specific cause-effect or structural relations within an overly complex and over-spilling system, but neatly subsumes all manner of crises, from hurricanes to terrorist attacks, under the banner of a risk-laden environment. As Brian Massumi (2009: 154) comments, using US President George Bush Jr's rhetoric of equivalence between the second Gulf War and Hurricane Katrina as inspiration,

> ... threat is not only indiscriminate, coming anywhere, as out of nowhere, at any time, it is also indiscrimin*able*. Its continual micro-flapping in the background makes it indistinguishable from the general environment, now one with a restless climate of agitation. Between irruptions, it blends in with the chaotic background, subsiding into its own pre-amplified incipience, already active, still imperceptible. The figure of the environment shifts: from the harmony of a natural balance to a churning seed-bed of crisis in the perpetual making. (emphasis in original)

Such a biosecurity works to a distinct framing of the environment, of course, as a vast, difference-generating reservoir of affects, the potentialities of which must be understood if threats are to be prepared for and responded to, as well as a pathological source of vital matter that must be pre-empted via prevailing military surveillance, and diverse logistical and operational apparatus'. These ever-present crises become harbingers of a neoliberal economisation of life and death. But also, I want to stress, they work to a particular framing of touch. For this is a reservoir of *felt* affect.

In section one, *An Infectious World*, I want to acknowledge how this teeming micro-environment has been pathologised as threatening, and even exceeding, more traditionally geopolitical accounts of territory, and introduce efforts to initiate and put into practice a 'health diplomacy' between nations that is regarded as an appropriately 'global' counter to such an epidemiological condition. As I go on to outline below, such efforts were triggered by the presence of epidemic cholera in Europe, but crystallise long-proceeding concerns over the balance between containing disease and allowing a free flow of trade between nations. To be sure, such a health diplomacy can be understood in a realist sense as one more tool among many used by the state to further its own political and economic success against competitors, such that the key question for debate is whether or not such a practice undermines or furthers a Westphalian politics. Yet, I want to demonstrate, in focusing attention on cholera as a 'prompt' for political action there is more to be said concerning its agency in the reformulation of geopolitical subjectivities. That is, we can draw out the bio-physical materialities at work in epidemic disease, and how these were understood to become animated, and to proliferate (or not), in various ways. Indeed, what this example provides is an insight into just how crucial disease was to the pathologising of people and place – the making of an imperial Gothic one might say – and their ensuing medicalisation. In an imperial context, the medicalisation of entire landscapes became a crucial means of demarcating a population; that is, a colonised population. What is more, the modes of knowledge collection, and means of understanding disease, that emerged have very much helped to shape current epidemiological discourse and practice concerning risk, vulnerability and a global health governance.

In looking to the construction of India as a 'deathscape,' for example, we can consider how bodies were differently configured as material hosts for disease largely in accordance with their 'inherited' and place-embedded weaknesses, or, as a secondary cause, their individual propensity for a moral depravity. There is a two-fold articulation of touch here, firstly as a cleaving of particularly 'earthy' bodies to a profligate environment, and, secondly, to an unchecked contact between bodies, that remains at the heart of epidemiological discourse. In today's fight against ebola, swine flu, bird flu and so on, it is the possibility of these two-fold pathic touches that is registered as risky, and, as such, the focus for all manner of regulatory mechanisms that attempt a behavioural modification of otherwise recalcitrant bodies. Just as British officers in India were urged to lead the fight against cholera, so today's epidemiological staff are warned of the 'invasion' of territories by disease, the need to maintain strict surveillance measures, and to lead by example those weaker corporealities that invite infection. In fighting disease, it is a gnostic, knowing touch, guided by a mindful-ness of risk and appropriate security measures, that becomes valued.

It is the capacity for touch to further proliferate difference that animates much of the debate over epidemiological threats. Yet, just as difference has been accorded a revolutionary edge in much of our modern-day social theory, particularly in feminist thought and practice, so this same capacity has been recuperated as a means of generating new modes of citizenship, diplomacy, negotiation and even territory. In the section *Building Worlds* I want to focus on this rebuilding of our political terms of reference via a generosity of touch that not only acknowledges the presence of what has been termed a 'more-than-human' world outside of our explanatory modes, our intent and our desires, but also an ethical stance in regard to the same. Rather than conjure the body as a primarily autonomous or self contained system for sensory data gathering and haptic assimilation – an imaging that poses the body as at risk of being touched by disease through the lax operation of touch itself – emphasis is placed upon the immersed body. That is, attention is given to the myriad interrelations that are understood to exist between and among the 'interiority' of the human body – that which we may refer to as the psyche or even the soul, but also the meat, flesh and bones of the soma – and an 'exterior' world of other people, life forms, elements and objects. Indeed, it is through these same interrelations that a notion of the human is able to emerge; this is a form of *praesentia*, or the emergence of subjectivity through encounter between Self and environment. Importantly, this is not a simple reversal of priorities, wherein a pathic touch becomes valued over and against a gnostic one by virtue of its authenticity or naturalness. Rather, these are understood to accomplish different kinds of work. A diagnostic touch tends to objectify or separate the subject from his or her own body, but also, despite the presence of physical contact, to establish a 'distance' between the one touching and the organism, person or object being touched. Via a pathic touch, the body allows for the generation of all kinds of knowledge, only some of which can be 'captured' through representational forms. It is the question of how these modalities are related that has preoccupied not just philosophy, but psychology also, as well as the creative arts.

What such analyses presage is an avowedly aesthetic geopolitics, as opposed to a geopolitics that simply takes aesthetics as a mode of governance and art as a tool. As Jeffrey Alexander (2008) makes the case, such aesthetic analyses are anti-essentialist insofar as they eschew the notion that an underlying 'depth' is made manifest within surface appearances, as when the Enlightenment philosopher and geographer Immanuel Kant, for example, sought for moral beauty within the modest demeanour and agreeable *mien* of women. Leaving aside the fact that there may well be object-orientated capacities beyond our ken, we experience, "by feeling, by contact, by the 'evidence of the senses' rather than the mind" (Alexander 2008: 782). And, it is this "sensuous surface of stuff" that, through an embodied learning process that 'makes sense' of the contact of body and environment, becomes imbued with shared understandings. According to Alexander, the aesthetic character of phenomena, "allows us to see, hear, and touch their narrative bindings" (2008: 784), and, it can be added, to rework the affective content of such encounters and, thereby, the narrative bindings concerning our own and others' place in the world that these can invoke.

In order to expand upon this line of argument, I want to draw upon a series of feminist art practices and performances predicated on an immersive touch, Earthliness, and the making of connections. To be sure, a pessimistic framing of the character and potential of art as the arbiter of the aesthetic has prevailed within social theory more broadly. For Theodor Adorno (2007[1936]), for example, bourgeois art was a form of counter-revolutionary idealism, a thematic developed by Terry Eagleton who defined aesthetics as a, "social philosophy founded upon egoism and appetite," wherein, "the whole terrain of sensation' is opened up to 'the colonisation of reason" (1990: 15). Art appreciation, particularly in the Kantian, detached form, affords an emerging bourgeoisie more instruments of control over the affective side of human nature. Yet, it must be recognised, it is this same modernist heritage that has become a creative reservoir for the production of new forms of arts practice that query what Jacques Rancière (2007) calls a 'primal aesthetics'. These aesthetics, he writes, are necessarily political insofar as they underwrite a specific sphere of existence for all life, they describe all manner of phenomena held in common for a 'public good,' and, crucially, they denote subjects to whom the capacity is recognised to designate these phenomena and to argue about them (Rancière 2009: 24). These primal aesthetics are key to the maintenance of both a social and natural order (and a posited gap between these), in that they,

> draft maps of the visible, trajectories between the visible and the sayable, relationships between modes of being, modes of saying, and modes of making and doing. They define variations of sensible intensities, perceptions and the abilities of bodies. They thereby take hold of unspecified groups of people, they widen gaps, open up space for deviations, modify the speeds, the trajectories, and the ways in which groups of people adhere to a condition, react to situations, recognise their images. (2007: 39)

A geopolitical struggle is thus an aesthetic one. It occurs when the necessary supplement occupied by those groups who are out of place and sight within a particular 'distribution of the sensible' (that which is sayable, visible and can be felt as such) have their plight metamorphosed into a structural failing of the broad web of relations of which they are a part. Classical geopolitics has given us many such groups – from the subaltern to the refugee – whose subjectivity exceeds their allotted character and role, and whose experiences have become the touchstone for broader debate on the 'march' of civilisation and the myriad inequalities of a globalised society. To these might be added the denizens of a more-than-human world – such as the discarnate flesh of Chapter 3 – wherein a species- and bio-based demarcation of difference is queried on a number of levels, not least in terms of the distribution of practice and affect.

In their choreography of affect, and their critical reflection on such a process, the creative, immersive works I turn to in *Building Worlds*, by Mierle Laderman Ukeles and Lillian Ball, offer insight into how a generosity of touch can foster a more-than-human framing of geopolitical bodies. What they also offer, however, is a response to the question of what 'remains' of the human under such conditions? What these artworks are careful to negotiate, I want to emphasise, is a lurking biological essentialism, wherein in thinking through the aesthetics of touch the 'interiority' of the Self, which has traditionally been associated with matters regarding reflection and memory, has become 'flattened'. As Novas and Rose make the point, "The psy-shaped space that inhabits the human being is losing its depth, that depth that once had to be mined and interpreted. The psyche is becoming flattened out and mapped onto the corporeal space of the brain itself" (2000: 508). In insisting upon the emotive aspects of touch – the feeling of being in touch/ out of touch – and how these interconnect with the 'exterior' work of sensation, these artworks raise a series of tensions around touch as means of signification of the Self, other people, places and things, and a desire to transcend individualism. The geopolitical subjects they proffer are incomplete, torn and conflicted; and, it is these subjectivities that are called upon to participate in geopolitical struggle.

In closing the chapter, I want to use touch to reopen discussions around Anthropocene geographies that have recently surfaced in geopolitics. To date, these have tended to circle around a global environmental governance, and how this is both predicated upon and exacerbates (in)securities, an emergent eco-citizenry, and a post-normal Earth Science that struggles to evidence impact. To be sure, all of these have import for the construction of gendered bodies, from the 'cleaning' work of microbes to the fate of a 'Mother Earth.' What I would like to emphasise, however, is the importance of aesthetics in the apprehension of, and living with, the Anthropocene. To do so, I focus on an avowedly hybrid art *cum* science project in Chicago by Frances Whitehead that takes as its subject and medium the post-industrial ruins of a carbon economy, but also the making sensible of a world order that is no longer, at least for the artist, so readily demarcated as social or natural, human or non-human. The project I turn to is not intended to be exemplary of a new mode of relationality, for its articulation and affects are contingent. What it does offer, however, is an opportunity to reflect upon how an either/or contradiction can be turned into a contrast of differences.

An Infectious World

Bruce Braun (2007: 15) makes the comment that public health has from its inception taken the body to be a geopolitical one. It is concerned with the physical contacts between and amongst people and things that constitute cross-border traffic, and is also undertaken as a primarily spatial strategy of isolation and containment that restricts and slows down the occurrence of such contacts. Such procedures in turn invoke political debate on liberalism versus state interventionism, individual freedoms versus public safety, as well as the need to improve the spatial and temporal 'visibility' of infectious agents and diseased bodies to the proper authorities. With the full onset of imperialism in the nineteenth century, a perceived need to standardise the ways in which cross-border traffic is managed led to calls for a 'health diplomacy' that, from a realist perspective, explicitly enrols discussions of geopolitical rivalries and the fate of state sovereignty.

I want to begin this section by acknowledging the migratory role of cholera in prompting this transformation of political apparatus'. In doing so, however, what I want to draw out is not so much the articulation of new agreements between nation-states, but the construction of particular forms of geopolitical subjectivity, and the underlying presumptions therein concerning bodily differences and their capacity for making and receiving contact that rationalised and legitimised these. In particular, I want to point to how a disorderly, feminised, and raced body became the centre of medicalisation efforts carried out by hard-bodied agents of imperialism in the name of a global health. This is important because, first, and as Bashford and Strange observe (2007: 89), whilst the movement of some bodies – specifically, Muslim pilgrims and a Chinese diaspora – were very much the subject of a health diplomacy to the point of obsession, by contrast, "English-speaking people moving around the globe were never managed in public health terms en masse or *because of* their Englishness" (emphasis in original). Certainly, one of the few areas of agreement amongst delegates involved in a health diplomacy throughout the nineteenth century was the need to map and manage the regular Mecca pilgrimages. Such an international effort, then, had repercussions as to how bodies were made visible to an emerging cohort of global health experts as 'problematic,' and differentially afforded mobility rights as internationally-recognised citizens. But also, and second, such efforts draw our attention to how medicalisation was a means of denoting a population, its history and its environment; in regard to imperialism in India, to be sure, this was a making pathological of a colonised population. A vast effort to control and contain India as a 'deathscape' prompted the British to experiment with new forms of knowledge production predicated on a pervasive bureaucratisation and the measurement of all manner of phenomena that could shed light on the riskiness, resources and potential productivity of this land.

The British, alongside other European colonising powers, had experienced epidemic cholera in India well before the nineteenth century. It was in response to the presence of cholera in Europe in 1831, however, that the first stirrings of health diplomacy in the name of a 'global public good' were to emerge. That is, concerns from merchants as to the diversity of containment procedures (such as quarantine camps and disinfection stations) they had to negotiate, prompted several European governments to investigate the geography of disease. A report commissioned for the Minister of Commerce in France, for example, identified the need for standardised practices to deal with 'exotic' diseases such that commerce could more easily anticipate and negotiate border stoppages. The first International Sanitary Conference was to convene in 1851 in Paris to discuss cooperation not only on cholera, but also plague and yellow fever, diseases that beset colonisation efforts abroad. Subsequent sanitary agreements were to be folded into the operational procedures of the World Health Organisation (WHO) after its founding in 1948, with the articulation of the International Sanitary Conventions (later, the International Health Regulations, or IHRs). These Conventions were thus very much shaped by the interests and anxieties of previous negotiations, insofar as they struggled to coordinate disease control measures while interfering as little as possible in trade relations between its members (Howard-Jones 1975).

Certainly in India, the British East India Company was loath to further augment quarantine procedures, an attitude that, according to Jeremy Isaacs (1998), disposed its medical officers to reject contagion theories of cholera. Yet, it was the global traffic established via colonialism that was to trigger a slew of pandemic outbreaks in the nineteenth and twentieth centuries. As Charles Briggs (2004: 166) points out, the Western treatment of cholera was (and to a large extent still is) a matter of localising blame onto a pathologised people and place by fusing racial difference with a perceived lack of medical modernity. If we return to the deadly pandemic of 1831, for example, and its reception in France, one observer was to write that, "Cholera is an exotic production, its yeast was borne or developed in the uncultivated plains of Asia ... The miasmata enter into and boil in blood already putrid and therefore disposed to receive them" (Sarazin, cited in Delaporte 1986: 56). It also, however, had a profound impact upon populations that considered themselves civilised. On the one hand, it confirmed the pathological air of rapidly urbanising centres such as Paris, a condition made worse here because of its bloody, revolutionary history; a history that commentators such as Edmund Burke, as noted in Chapter 5, already found to be dangerously infectious. On the other hand, the ravages of the disease, which struck rich and poor alike, provided a creative reservoir for a Romantic 'counteraesthetic' that revelled in the transgressive potential of the grotesque and the abject, as manifest in the deathly pallor of cholera victims. Irruptive disease, etched in the fast changing aspect of friends and family alike, was a profoundly visceral experience that shook the confidence of a Parisian *literati* in the triumph of reason, and prompted new forms of imaging the human body. "This defiant plunge," writes Nina Athanassoglou-Kallmyer (2001: 689), "into the lower depths of the (human) and aesthetic imaginary, a regression, so to speak, to a precivilised barbaric condition, proved unexpectedly fertile... Its defiant elevation of the banished to the status of the culturally sanctioned shook, aired and purged the slate clean of pre-existing musty formulas to make way for modernist innovation."

This 'wave,' which reached Europe in 1831 but had emerged in India in 1826 and persisted until 1838, was actually the second cholera outbreak to travel far and wide. Cholera as a disease is produced when the *Vibrio cholerae* bacillus becomes a 'contaminant' in food or water that is ingested; the bacterium attaches to the lining of the bowel and produces enterotoxins that trigger a release of fluid from the blood capillaries. Around one in 20 cases become severe as the individual loses fluids and salts though repeated vomiting and diarrhoea. These fluids can in turn contaminate water sources, foodstuffs and soils, leading to a further round of infection; the bacterium can also maintain itself on moist textiles for up to 14 days, and for a very short time on the hands. Long recognised as an endemic disease of certain riverine locations in the Indian subcontinent, such as the Ganges delta with its saturated subsoils, what the Europeans referred to as an 'Asiatic Cholera' outbreak had spread from Calcutta on the Bay of Bengal across country to Bombay on the west coast through 1817-1818.

It is during this crucial time frame that most of the trade routes, including the lower and middle range of the Ganges river system, and the Great Roads, were under the military protection of the British East India Country. Troops were stationed all over the country to quell resistance from the Mahratthas to the south, the 'Native Kingdoms' in central India, and the Sikhs and Punjabis to the north west. Under this military system, the rapid movement of small groups throughout the subcontinent was initiated; a scheme formalised in 1817 when the annual relief of troops at military stations on an all-India basis became the norm. Meantime, there had been a rapid transformation of the urban ecologies of the port cities from which goods flowed, and through which troops travelled to all areas of the Empire. One of the many physical expressions of the private speculation engendered by the Company, for example, was the building of large public water tanks in Calcutta, replenished by the often faecally contaminated Hooghly River via aqueduct, and which also served as concentrated reservoirs of infection when water levels were low. Of the three Medical Board Committees set up by the Company in 1820 to investigate the rapid increase in cholera cases, only that of Madras seriously entertained the idea of contagion; those of Bengal and Bombay deferred to the idea of miasmic elements in the air infecting victims, such that they meticulously recorded the prevailing atmospheric conditions during cholera outbreaks (Dixon 1991). The higher incidence rate of infection among the lower orders of the British military was more often than not ascribed to their drinking and licentiousness behaviour, moral failings that rendered their physical bodies more vulnerable to such infectious conditions. The emerging discipline of 'Tropical Medicine' was thus to became a matter of understanding the complex aetiology of diseases such as cholera, and the crucial role played not only by the environment, but also cultural behaviours, in its transmission.

Whereas it was the sudden irruption of the primitive in the midst of a 'civilised' Europe that fuelled much of the political Gothic of the Victorian period, in India was to be found the reversal of such a fraught condition. For authors such as Rudyard Kipling, India was the ultimate Imperial Gothic; it was a nightmarish environment full of death and desolation, in which strong men strived to provide a moral example to the natives. Here, Western bodies underwent a martyrdom in the form of a corporeal breakdown, which yet presaged a future regeneration though this same spilling of bodily essences. "What else are we working in the country for?" Kipling wrote in 1885 back home to his family, "For what else do the best men of the Commission die from overwork, and disease, if not keep the people alive in the first place and healthy in the second? We spend our best men on the country like water and if ever a foreign country was made better through the 'blood of martyrs' India is that country" (cited in Gilmour 2004: 76). Whilst such a masculinist, heroic popular culture both Romanticised and pathologised India as a deathscape, international Sanitary Conferences throughout the Victorian produced reams of text that stressed time and again India's geopolitical relevance as a source pandemic disease. Both types of script served to position Europe as central to geopolitical events, certainly, but also as the locus of history around which other places and peoples revolved (see Chakrabarty 1992). This is, as Spivak (1999) points out, a 'worlding' wherein European imperialism creates and thereby subsumes the 'native' as the Other. Though such a formal geopolitics purported to be global in scope, and has certainly underpinned imperialist projects that profoundly impacted peoples across that globe, there was here simply no acknowledgement of or concern with how those peoples not only lived with imperialism on a day to day basis, but also how they envisioned, and enacted, their own place in the world.

By 1821 cholera had become pandemic, travelling along the trade routes maintained by the Company; it moved across the northern mountains to Nepal and Afghanistan via caravans, and along the shipping routes to Africa, Indonesia, China and Japan. Though this wave eventually subsided, cholera was to remain present in the rapidly urbanised landscape of Calcutta as well as the surrounding farmlands. Contemporary British observers such as James Jameson (1820) pointed to the overcrowded market places and 'black' city neighbourhoods as the 'natural' seedbeds of infection. And, in the decades that followed an increasing array of sanitation policing measures were introduced across India, largely predicated on the careful enumeration of births and death, the incidence and type of disease, and the bringing of 'public nuisances,' such as clogged drains and piles of night soil to the magistrates' attention. As Reginald Orton (1831: 268), a graduate of the Edinburgh School of Medicine, wrote,

> The spirit of active inquiry, however it may have slept, appears now to have thoroughly awakened. It has already collected an immense number of data regarding the epidemic; and there is every reason to hope that it will not rest until the causes and pathology of the disease are completely elucidated.

Regardless of what their medical personnel on the ground believed, however, the British government's health diplomacy was to maintain a rigidly anti-contagionist stance. Even by the ninth Sanitary Conference in Paris, 1894, after numerous bacteriologists had identified a cholera bacillus and used this as evidence of contagion, Britain's delegates were still denying not only this disease aetiology, but also the assertion that India itself was the source of serial pandemics, much to the anger of their French and German counterparts.

Certainly, the Sanitary Conferences were noticeable by their inaction and the lack of agreement reached over the course of the nineteenth century. And, subsequent WHO Conventions have also been extensively critiqued for their lack of efficacy in dealing with what are regarded as global-scale threats. As Feldbaum et al. (2010: 5), for example, observe,

> During the final decades of the 20th century, it became clear to many member states that the IHRs were inadequate: The regulations covered only 3 diseases, countries were often noncompliant, and the WHO had limited flexibility to conduct outbreak surveillance and response. Even with recognition of these weaknesses, attempted revisions of the IHRs stalled until the 2002-2003 epidemic of severe acute respiratory syndrome (SARS). SARS demonstrated the direct and continuing threat that transnational disease epidemics pose to health and economic interests and generated the political momentum necessary to complete the IHR revision process.

One of outcomes of this revision process, they add, was a partial hollowing out of state sovereignty, insofar as WHO decision-making and practice could now be informed by the use of reports from non-governmental organisations and electronic surveillance systems. According to Keller et al. (2009), almost all major outbreaks are now first identified through social media. And yet, Davies (2008) reminds us, such surveillance measures are more often than not directed to African and Asian countries considered the 'ground zero' for future outbreaks; thus, "the WHO's authority in infectious disease control has been strengthened partly because it suited the interests of Western states to allow this to happen" (2008: 308). Identified here is the capacity of those states that work with WHO to operate well beyond their own territorial reach, such that threats emerging 'over there' are identified and dealt with before they spread into 'over here.'

The capacity of a state to impose health-related border controls is very much a tangible, everyday manifestation of the more abstract notion of sovereignty, and Feldbuam et al. (2010) are by no means alone in their identification of a disease-vulnerable body with the fate of a Westphalian geopolitics. The increasingly supranational governance of health has been commented upon by scholars in International Law Studies as well as International Relations and political geography. For the legal scholar David Fidler, for example, there has been a clear shift in how the geopolitical subject has been configured between the emergence of international public health directives in the 1850s, and the aftermath of the twentieth century's two world wars. At the height of imperialism, disease control, he argues, was very much considered the domain of individual nation-states who may well have acted in concert when it came to cross-border microbial movement, but nevertheless maintained rights of sovereignty over their populations (see Fidler 2007). This classic Westphalian tradition, however, was to be replaced by a rights-based approach by the WHO, wherein it is the individual as a corporeally vulnerable subject who is identified as the object of concern and action in its disease eradication programmes. Though somewhat sceptical of the sweeping geography implied here – wherein one mode of governance is supplanted by another – Alan Ingram (2005) nevertheless points to a new geopolitical significance afforded disease by particular constituencies in health, foreign policy and security since the end of the Cold War, especially in the US, where a pathologised environment has become linked to the potential role of disease in, "altering military balances and initiating conflict," as well as "undermining the social, economic and political fabric of societies, exacerbating existing problems and creating conditions were instability becomes more likely" (2005: 530).

Tim Brown (2011) adds, in his analysis of WHO reports that emphasise an increasingly 'universal vulnerability' to pandemic infectious disease, that a 'global' health response remains a matter of securing borders against threats from 'over there.' This is yet another iteration of a Goth politics, Priscilla Wald (2008: 42) argues, insofar as these, "accounts of emerging infections turn space into time, threatening to transform a contemporary 'us' into a primitive 'them.'" And, it is no small surprise to find that the threatening 'touch' of pathogens is understood in militaristic terms, as when Keller et al. (2009: 689), for example, urge that,

> International travel and movement of goods increasingly facilitates the spread of pathogens across and among nations, enabling pathogens to *invade* new territories and adapt to new environments and hosts. Officials now need to consider worldwide disease outbreaks when determining what potential threats might affect the health and welfare of their nation. (emphasis added)

Or that Heyman and Rodier, members of the WHO Communicable Disease Programme, writing in *The Lancet* with the 'WHO Operational Support Team to the Global Outbreak Alert and Response Network,' (2001: 345-8) report that,

> when a complacent world *relaxes its vigilance* and *lets down its defences*, the consequences can be rapid as well as dramatic. Microbes are *quick to exploit new opportunities* to spread, adapt, and resist... The universal nature of *the microbial threat*, with agents of disease, including drug resistant forms, *passing undetected* across increasingly porous borders, has placed all nations on an equally vulnerable footing. The world is now interconnected in matters of health as well as economics and trade, with the result that distinctions between domestic and foreign health affairs have been eroded. (emphases added)

In this postmodern battlefield, where conflict is everywhere to hand, there is no rhetorical difference between microbial threats and terroristic ones. In regard to both, states are denoted as strong or weak in their capacity to secure their borders.

It is no surprise either to find that border security in the form of the surveillance and selective slowing down of some people and things (even while others speed through) remains a priority. As Budd et al. (2009: 436) observe, in an era of unprecedented global aeromobility,

> From inoculation certificates to quarantine and the routine 'disinfection' of passenger aircraft with powerful insecticides, modern air travel is replete with a complex set of procedures designed to lessen the risks associated with flying between different climatic and ecological zones.

As noted in regard to the cross-border movement of a non-corporeal flesh, in Chapter 3, the intense surveillance and 'purification' measures brought to bear in such traffic, such that it can safely be brought back to the sovereignty of the patient body, has very much become a selling point. What might be added here, however, is that whilst the sanitary policies of the Victorian era addressed efforts to control the spread of disease, and 'prevention' via extensive vaccination programmes were a marked feature of the twentieth century, current tactics are more a matter of organising what Miller (2002) calls 'response regimes.' These focus upon anticipated epidemics, largely zoological, that are modelled according to their potential spread across as well as through species. As Adams et al. (2009: 252) argue, such future-orientated regimes allow for, "structured responses to crises that are not simply predicted but already made real. Anticipated 'crises' become the model and the 'event' that demands immediate response via health security measures which generate equivalent financial demands in their wake... Anticipation is a mode of both creating markets and responding to projected needs, whether or not such crises are yet born out in the public sphere." Possible futures are not only narrowed down so as to produce a foregone temporality that is very much felt in the present as a series of anxious awaitenings, but the selection of a best possible future becomes aligned with what Adams et al. call a 'ratcheting up' of hopefulness via the use of a diagnostic, body-aware technoscience that can sense the otherwise invisible touch of disease. Importantly, and given the emphasis upon an environment that is fundamentally profligate, response is geared not towards the eradication of pathogens, but the identification and modification of 'risky' behaviours in endemic 'hotspots, such as those regularly mapped by the World Health Organisation, that allow an unconsidered and unchecked contact with such an environment.

The emphasis in Adams et al. on the production of an embodied, viscerally felt anticipation provides an intimation of what happens when we view the 'touch' of disease not from the perspective of topographic space, against which cases are located, but from a materialist perspective. As Braun (2008) observes in regard to the 2003 SARS (severe acute respiratory syndrome) outbreak in Toronto, there is a topology to be discerned in such epidemics that exceeds topographic renderings. That is, if we trace the movement of the infectious agent, then this becomes a matter not of diffusion across an otherwise empty space, but of a co-constitution of objects (such as fomites) and bodies (such as an infected host). Disease, then, can be more usefully thought of as enacting a topology, insofar as it 'stretches' across a widely diffuse materiality, producing more difference in the process. That is, it has the capacity to rework the nature of the object/body it becomes part of, setting in train new topological connections. In an epidemic, a pathogen is stretched, reassembled, and scrumpled, such that it can 'irrupt' literally at the end of one's fingers or tongue. The body of the host is no mere supine container, but is a vibrant engine for the production of further infectious material, even while some of its own cells lie dying; indeed, the body may well 'reassort' the pathogen itself, producing new strains. For Paul Rae (2011), foraging through various rhetorical strains on human–pig relations, the outbreak of H1N1 (a novel strain of swine flu), Chinese modernity, and a dance performance, such topologies not only upend the Cartesian space of diffusion models, they also exceed master narratives. Accordingly, he begins his account own of the 'suddenness' of a disease's proximity thus, "Somewhere in the world, a pig breathed out, a person breathed in, and at the Chinese embassy in Singapore a woman told me my visa was delayed because of new swine flu restrictions" (ibid.: 403).

The topological geographies that Braun, and Hinchliffe et al. (2013), outline do much to flesh out the 'contact' that so much of our global health governance fears and targets, and to reference not only efforts to curtail some forms of life, but to actively enhance others, including those yet to come. What is more, this geography allows practitioners as well as scholars to appreciate the operation of 'power' beyond territorial location and extension, which tend to be the most readily observable practices of, as well as the prerogative of, capital and the state. Specifically, it enables a consideration of how non-governmental organisations and other ostensibly less powerful entities can make their presence felt in ways that circumvent mere distance. There are yet, however, two further issues that a feminist materialism can bring to bear on the intimate geopolitics of disease via a critical attentiveness to touch.

First, a feminist approach can help unpack the aesthetics at work in a biosecurity, such that 'hot spots' are not simply envisaged as sites of discipline and containment, but as part and parcel of a broader ordering of corporeal, sensory engagements that regulation can actually tap into and reinforce. As Elizabeth Harvey (2003) writes, touch, since the early modern period in Europe, has been eclipsed by the emergence of an occularcentrism, with all manner of repercussions for how human-environment, human-human, and human-animal relations, are 'sensed' and made sense of. To be sure a biosecurity, Nicole Shukin (2011) argues, writing on the 2009 outbreak of H1N1, is concerned with the cultivation of some life forms over and against others; this is a *milieu*-based form of 'biopower' in Michel Foucault's sense of the term that spans biotic and elemental strata alike. But, this biosecurity hinges on, amongst other things, a critical distinction being made between a 'diagnostic' touch – that is, guided, attentive and sensible to risk – and a pathic one. The latter is configured as an unreasoning, animalistic capacity that allows for the unreflective co-mingling of vital matter; it, "signifies the very antithesis of semiosis in as much as it represents the fantasy of a culturally unmediated presence of two bodies to one another, or a 'co-immediacy.' This metaphysics of presence construes the sense of touch as 'animal' in its ostensibly sheer givenness" (2011: 486). It is this touch that becomes identified as 'risky' in the name of a national, and global, health. The increasing presence of masks, hand sanitisers and so on at hotspots such as airports and hospitals – sites considered particularly fraught because of the diversity of their vital matter and the heightened potential for the co-mingling of flesh – are, Shukin writes, tactile prompts for the performance of a diagnostic touch.

What is more, there is a valorising of the sensitive hand, working in concert with the brain, as the sovereign location for this humanised touch. To extrapolate from Shukin's argument, such distinctions of the flesh are predicated upon a species- and evolutionary-based hierarchialisation of sense-making. That is, and manifest perhaps most famously in a Kantian tradition of aesthetic thought, sense-making has been aligned with judgement, such that, for example, pleasure unfolds from an appreciation of how the faculties provide for the conditions of a systematic (and hence universally human) judgement of something as beautiful. The sublime apprehension of an overwhelming Nature that Edmund Burke referred to is, in Kantian fashion, yet further evidence of the unique human intellect, insofar as only the human imagination has the power to comprehend and rationalise such a state. By contrast, a lax, pathic deployment of other parts of the body – the absent-minded tonguing of a finger, for example – not only eschews such a humanising touch, it also weakens the body's defences and permits all manner of mingling to take place.

Second, there is an embodied psychology to the fear engendered by touch that can usefully be brought to bear. Touch emerges from a material contiguity, and hence implies an openness to the world that threatens a sense of the self-possessed, physical inviolability of the body that grounds the sovereign subject. As

Margrit Shildrick (2007: 225) points out, a "consequence of seeking to maintain the illusion of the separation and distinction necessary to the sovereign subject is that all encounters between self and other are potentially risky and must be negotiated within a strict set of normative rules and regulations that construct the parameters of safety and danger." The threat of a pathogen that penetrates the body exacerbates an already present 'corporeal anxiety,' insofar as it re-awakens intimations of a corporeal disorganisation and a lack of self-completion. The touch of infectious disease – that which is at once invisible to the eye, yet possibly present in the sticky, viscous fluids that are expelled from other bodies and linger on the surfaces of everyday objects – is all the more disturbing because it escapes those largely scopic regimes by which, Shildrick observes, the Self learns to distinguish itself from its others. One might add, as Elizabeth Grosz (1994) does, that the fear and anxiety that fixates on a viscosity – a material that, having no borders of its own, seeps through the borders of the Self – cannot be separated from a sexuated difference. That is, there is a tendency to apprehend some materialities, such as those associated with a voracious *vagina dentata*, as more destabilising and contaminating than others, such that the reassertion of control becomes a matter of disciplining some (feminised) bodies more than others. Certainly, one could argue that biosecurity can be considered the transplantation of a formerly domestic struggle against 'dirt' – the responsibility of good mothers and wives – into the more 'formal,' public geopolitical domain.

Building Worlds

The previous section very much dwelt on the notion of a vulnerability opened up by touch, wherein a dynamic and profligate Nature is understood to pervade the physical boundedness of an otherwise stable, sovereign subject. And, it explored how geopolitics in the form of a global health governance can be understood as a sustained effort to instil order and containment into zones of otherwise lax, or medically ignorant, 'contact,' whether these be the hotspots of an irruptive zoonotic disease, or the to-handedness of sanitiser gel dispensed to hospital visitors. Whilst a realist response is to worry at the fate of a Westphalian sovereignty under such conditions, a materialist one concerns itself with a topology of touch, a biopolitics that nurtures particular vitalities at the expense of others, and an aesthetic ordering that not only allows us to make sense of infectious disease, but to render distinctions between human and animal. In regard to this last point, one can 'feel,' for example, an abhorrence at the touch of infection manifest as an aversion to some-thing conceived of as dangerous because of its capacity to contaminate by proximity, cutaneous contact or ingestion.

In the case of cholera this disease may well have prompted states to begin the process of a global health governance, but it was also very much implicated in a sustained and systematic colonisation of bodies and minds in the colonies and in Europe. This was a geopolitical project that was experimental, reworking all manner of rural and urban, public and private, 'over here' and 'over there' sites, and, it must be noted, necessarily incomplete, insofar as new modes of 'being' colonial were ever emergent. As Ann Stoler (2008) argues, this geopolitics may well have conflated and elevated reason, race, science and civility to human universals, and found vast swathes of the globe's population wanting, but the fleshy, lived experience of such an epistemology was messy, conflicted, and subject to myriad unintended effects.

Yet, it is possible to view this play of Self and Other as not only part and parcel of the human condition, but as an opportunity for the building of new allegiances and solidarities. That is, in exploring the manner in which touch has become pathologised one can also trace the often marginalised presence of a somatic politics that acknowledges the ways in which bodies 'become,' intersect, and affirm some (but not necessarily all) new modes of being with and alongside others. In this section, I want to pick up on the idea that a biosecurity in the name of a global health can be considered an up-scaling of previously 'domestic' struggles against impurity and dirt, such that an explicitly feminist concern with how such labours are configured comes to the fore. I want to stress, however, that such a concern, from my perspective at least, is not feminist by virtue of its valorisation of such labour, nor even because of its attentiveness to how such labours have been gendered, though such issues are by no means unimportant. Rather, what strikes me as feminist in this context is how such labour has been reworked, practically and allegorically, from a morbid obsession with cleanliness to a progressive mode of geopolitical engagement. That is, I want to contrast efforts to 'defend' the body and home from risky human and non-human Others with an opening up of the same to materialities that are no longer abject as waste or dirt, but understood to be part of a broader web of people and things in need of care and maintenance.

This emphasis upon a connection, sensorally as well as intellectually, with Others in the building of worlds is something that a host of feminist writers have commented upon. Indeed, touch is a key concern for Luce Irigaray, who comments on its political potentialities thus: "The internal and external horizons of my skin interpenetrating with yours wears away their edges, their limits, their solidarity. Creating another space – outside my framework. An opening of openness" (1992: 59). In similar vein, Gibson-Graham (2011: 4), a collaborative entity who, it might be noted, make explicit a vital touch in their research and writing, consider the physical and emotive intimacies of an Anthropocene geography that not only proliferates uncertainties as life continues to 'become' in all manner of unexpected ways, but also asks us to locate ourselves in as well as alongside such a world. They ask how we might bring together an expanded sense of care for others with a recognition of the pluravitality of matter that helps constitutes the human condition itself. Thus, "While we might feel love for other earth creatures and want to accept a responsibility to care for them," they write, "might we also extend our love to parasites, or inorganic matter, or to the unpredictability of technical innovation? And might not an ethics of attunement to vibrant matter produce a more sensitive, experimental mode of assembling within the 'jizz' of our living environments?"

In this section, I want to draw out some of these 'experimental modes' as they have been practised in the field of art. At first blush, such a recourse may seem strange insofar as art has often been described not only as a fundamentally apolitical activity, but as a thoroughly individualistic one that sees art interpretation, for example, as a site of struggle between the will of the artist and his audience. Yet, as Amy Mullin (2003) points out, a feminist arts practice very much works against such rhetorics (and is often deemed to be fatally ideological, and thus 'bad art,' in the process). Such distinctions, between individual and crowd, genius and propaganda, are themselves party to a 'distribution of the sensible,' to use Rancière's term, one that can be made anew by an explicit commitment to collaborative work. As the feminist art critic and curator Lucy Lippard famously argued,

> A developed feminist consciousness brings with it an altered concept of reality and morality that is crucial to the art being made and to the lives lived with that art. We take for granted that making art is not simply 'expressing oneself' but is a far broader and more important task-expressing oneself as a member of a larger unity, or comm/unity .... (1980: 363)

Small wonder that touch has become such an intense vehicle for expression, as well as object of interest, in feminist arts practice (King 2005; Lee and Duncum 2011). The integral strangeness and insurgency of the tactile, lived body, in touching and being touched, destabilises not only the boundaries between Self and Other, but in the process queries a privileging of the gaze as a means of ordering the same. When bodies are initially conceived of as sighted objects, Irigaray (1992) writes, then there is an accompanying tendency to understand these as discrete; what is more, touching becomes a matter of bringing these discrete entities through some form of negative 'gap' and into a proximity. Yet, if we prioritise touch then we must think of the body as actively, already being open to touching and being touched. This is a porous as well as visceral corporeality that operates to mobilise particular emotions. Touch can dissolve boundaries, make proximate that which was far away, and in doing so not only rearrange our metaphysics of intimacy and distance, but pose a danger to any and all systems of order that rely upon distinction and separation.

One of the key works referenced by Lippard in the making of a feminist practice is Mierle Laderman Ukeles' 'maintenance art.' Ukeles has been the artist in residence for the New York City Department of Sanitation (DOS) since 1977. Prior to this, Ukeles had produced her *MANIFESTO FOR MAINTENANCE ART 1969! Proposal for an exhibition 'CARE,'* which distinguished between two types of work: on the one hand, a modernist 'developmental' work (including traditional configurations of art as a high-brow, elite activity) characterised by a linear progress and a sovereign individuality, and, on the other hand, everyday maintenance (the cleaning of dirty objects and spaces, for example), which is ritualistic in rhythm and is both essential to and abjected from the 'real' world of production. As a response to this bifurcation, Ukeles' *Maintenance Art*

Performances (1973) involved washing clean the floors and steps of the Wadsworth Athenaeum in Connecticut, performances that translated the value of otherwise menial and invisible tasks into curated acts. In one sequence, Ukeles washed the steps so vigorously that people began to avoid walking up these; when some did, Ukeles washed behind their steps, asserting a control over the space that, she said, pushed the idea of maintenance to its limit, "to control of the territory" (Ukeles, cited in Akaret, 1984-86). For Patricia Phillips (1995), this emphasis upon the repeated performance of maintenance in a civic domain is a provocation to space as a carefully carved territory of public and private; it makes visible the structural relations between production and reproduction, but also gestures towards the fact that most every civic act is banal and reiterative. For Helen Molesworth (1999: 121), the piece is also a provocation to the separation of a 'productive' time from those temporalities arising from the reproduction of species, heternormative sexual relations, and domestic routines. In prompting the question, 'What if the world worked like this'? Ukeles asks the audience to engage with an environment, "where maintenance has equal value to art – a proposition which would require a radically different organisation of the public and private spheres."

Ukeles' first project with the DOS was *Touch Sanitation Performance* (1977-80), composed of several pieces, during which Ukeles visited DOS facilities, accompanied sanitation workers on their routes, and noted the manner in which these were encountered and treated during their work. Registering how these bodies were abhorred as polluted and polluting, she conceived of *Handshake Ritual*, wherein she set out to shake hands with all of the over 8,500 New York City refuse workers, a piece which took just under a year to complete. The description of the work by Ukeles reiterates not only a sense of solidarity between artist and subject in the effort to 'maintain' the life of the city, but also the critical role of touch in making explicit this interrelation. She writes,

> Touch Sanitation
>
> Description:
>
> "I'm not here to watch you, to study you, to analyze you, to judge you. I'm here to be with you: all the shifts, all the seasons, to walk out the whole City with you." I face each worker, shake hands, and say: "Thank you for keeping NYC alive." / Performance Duration: 11 months, at least 1 to 2 8-hour/per day work shifts. With 8,500 sanitation workers. / Courtesy Ronald Feldman Fine Arts, New York.

As Mark Feldman (2008: 51) recounts, here a pathic touch is recuperated not as a diagnostic one, but as a marker of mutual respect:

> The handshake is, I think, the vitally important central gesture of this work. Not only is it a contemporary, ritualized way of connecting, but the word for hand is

at the etymological root of maintenance. Main is hand in French and just about everything Ukeles sees as maintenance is work that people do with their hands. The handshake is, of course, a foundational moment of U.S. social relations... Instead of denying that we are all touched and partly determined by the lowly things we cast off, Ukeles's work valorizes this connectedness.

He goes on to note the affect of the photographs taken as part of the piece, insofar as these continue the collaborative capacity of 'touch:'

> The photographs of *Handshake Ritual* actively solicit the viewer in constructing the meaning of the artwork and in creating an extended community. This posture towards the viewer is thus very different from that of most modern art. Typically, modern art addresses the viewer with a sort of challenge: understand me if you can. Ukeles's work addresses the viewer not with a challenge, but with an invitation: why don't you come and shake my hand. Ukeles's work seems to invite the viewer in as an equal partner, and, crucially as someone who helps to make the meaning, not merely *decipher* it. (ibid, emphasis in original)

Importantly for Ukeles, the maintenance she describes is by no means limited to the traditionally private sphere of the domestic sphere; it is very much an Earthly maintenance. In her 1969 manifesto, for example, the exhibition she envisages is formed in part from the following:

> Everyday, containers of the following kinds of refuse will be delivered to the Museum:
>
> – the contents of one sanitation truck;
> – a container of polluted air;
> – a container of polluted Hudson River;
> – a container of ravaged land.
>
> Once at the exhibition, each container will be serviced:
>
> purified, de-polluted, rehabilitated, recycled, and conserved by various technical (and/or pseudo-technical) procedures either by myself or scientists.
>
> These servicing procedures are repeated throughout the duration of the exhibition. (reproduced at the Arnolfini website)

The community that Ukeles invokes is not simply synonymous with society; she gestures, rather, to a vast ecological system within which a host of asymmetrical power relations operate, and the materiality of which is in a constant state of transmogrification. Her critique is not only that some of the labour involved in maintaining this system is denigrated or denied, but that some of these materials are also continually and increasingly abjected as mere 'waste.' Indeed, it is a commitment to reworking conceptions of such materials that drives Ukeles' project on New York's vast Fresh Kills waste disposal site – *Fresh Kills Landfill and Sanitation Garage* (1989 onwards) – which, following its closure in March 2001, is being transformed, albeit slowly, into a public park. Conveniently close to New York City itself, Fresh Kills, which opened in 1948, was deposited in an estuary with the idea that a tidal water flow would speed up biodegradation.

Part of the site was reopened as a crime scene in the aftermath of 9/11 to take in and sort material from what was the World Trade Center; material that mingles vast quantities of dust with lumps of concrete, steel, plastic, glass and human remains, and which, though diverse in detail and texture, nevertheless has an immersive, fluid quality that swamps each discrete entity. It is from this liquid solid that many of the items on display at sites such as the Smithsonian, curated as valued, tangible remnants of a geopolitical trauma, have been gleaned, the remainder joining the rest of the site to make up, according to urban myth, the largest human artefact visible from space. The operation involved personnel from the New York Police Department, an FBI evidence recovery team, 25 state and federal agencies, and 14 private contractors, and has since itself become the subject of a travelling exhibition, *Recovery* (2003-2006), put together by the New York State Museum (NY State Museum 2006).

For Ukeles (1991: 24-5), such landfills now operate as ersatz public cathedrals; these, "will be the giant clocks and thermometers of our age that teach us to tell time and the health of the air, the earth and the water." They can also, perhaps, I want to speculate, be understood in geopolitical terms as allegorical *topoi* in a baroque tragedy. As Walter Benjamin (2003) describes the baroque, with reference to state-building in Germany, a long-standing myth of heroism and transcendence is no longer relevant in a secularised world where decision-making has become associated with the need to respond to an ever-present emergency. Now, as authorities stumble and fall, they turn to political spectacles that collapse human time back into a natural environment that promises to make sense of decline, decay and an inevitable rebirth that lies outside of human striving, failure, will or desire. In the blasted landscapes of time past and future present, "history merges into the setting ... like seeds scattered over the ground" (2003: 92). It is in, "the process of decay, and it all alone, [that] the events of history shrivel up and become absorbed in the setting" (2003: 179). Where Benjamin finds the ruin to be the perfect vision of this new, modern phenomenon, such as those twisted and pulverised remnants that formed Ground Zero, we might add the physically proximate Fresh Kills site. In both we find, "the highly significant fragment, the remnant," that "is, in fact, the finest material in baroque creation. For it is common practice in the literature of the baroque to pile up fragments ceaselessly, without any strict idea of a goal, and, in the unremitting expectation of a miracle, to take the repetition of stereotypes for a process of intensification" (2003: 178). Where the rebuilding of Ground Zero both expresses and promises the rebirth of American pride from the very womb of the city itself, the reclamation of Fresh Kills offers a nostalgic pastoralism, as this site becomes yet one more breathing space for an otherside choked and darkened New York.

There is no urge to mastery in Ukeles' art, concludes Feldman (2008), nor we might add, a Romantic longing for a return to a pristine nature, nor indeed a sublime 'ruin porn,' but a desire to act as a 'sharer' in the making of a post-industrial ecological drama. It is these profligate environments, Ukeles (1992: 12) argues, that are 'hot spots,' not because of their pathogenic potential, but because they are, "rich, awesome Zone[s], highly charged and vibrating, awaiting the entry of Art."As such, Ukeles' imagining of a future Fresh Kills site – reclaimed rather than built anew – very much resonates with other art projects that invoke not only the proximities of a plurivitality, but a scanning across of a series of associated human and non-human temporalities. And, that experiment with the marking of materialites as dirty or pure, waste or resource. These projects are very much concerned with the making not of geopolitical subjects *per se* but of geopolitical *relations* within which various subjectivities emerge in the context of formal state apparatus' (and in particular their invocation of what a good citizen is and can be), as well as an increasingly neoliberal capitalism. Crucially, however, these issues are placed within the context of what Mrill Ingram (2014), following Isabelle Stengers, calls a cosmopolitics that enrols not only the diverse expertises of the sciences and the arts, but also the agency of elements and biota, and that takes responsibility for a 'caring' approach to how these are called upon in the making of new worlds.

Lillian Ball's federal and corporate-funded *WATERWASH ABC*, completed in 2011, is situated in the South Bronx, New York City, home to numerous waste treatment plants and waste transfer stations, on the edge of the Bronx River. The installation takes the form of a permeable recycled glass/locally sourced stone pavement, and a sweeping vegetated swale that is connected by pipe to the nearby ABC Carpet and Home warehouse parking lot, as well as signage, a picnic area and grassland. In preparing the site, Ball and her collaborators, including local youth groups and business people, cut back what were regarded as 'invasive' common reeds (phragmites), and planted salt tolerant 'native' species (such as blazing star, pickerelweed, arrow arum, and lizard tail) in the swale: this remade wetland will help to 'wash clean' runoff water from the nearby gravel parking lot by slowing down and filtering it. As Ingram (2014) points out, the project not only implied the maintenance of the site as a healthy ecosystem, this preparation required an everyday, labour-intensive maintenance to keep the plants alive, for example, before and after planting. It can very much be seen as a tangible prompt for an eco-citizenry, but it is also, she argues, illustrative of a cosmopolitical diplomacy. Just as the swale slows down the water, so human beings need to slow down so as to become open to the work of previously overlooked agencies, such as the filtering of plants; agencies that force us to rethink what indeed the human condition is.

Drawing on the work of Stengers, what Ingram is arguing here is that in acknowledging such agencies we must needs consider not the role and interests of 'humans' as unique and distinctive creatures, but of a 'humanity' that emerges as a relational capacity with and alongside the objects we engage sensorally as well as intellectually. "In short," she writes, "once we understand our humanness as an emergent property of our relationships with objects (even technologies and concepts such as neutrinos), those relationships become fair game for political consideration" (2014: 112). In terms of an emergent geopolitical subjectivity, humans can perform as diplomats whose job it is not to bring a collection of individuals into a 'togetherness,' but to voice the fact that decisions made in the 'general interest' – a healthy ecosystem one might say – have singular consequences for various lifeforms. Instead of mobilising for unity, which Stengers (2005) associates with the onset of military conflict, diplomacy offsets this by drawing out the 'ecological practices' within which various parties are embedded, and specifically the particularity of their global imaginaries, and celebrates those ethical moments when parties acknowledge the contingencies of their own and others' existence. "The diplomatic achievement," writes Stengers (2005: 193),

> means the event of the production of a new proposition, articulating what was a contradiction leading to war. Such an achievement, the slight modification in the formulation of some obligations derived from an attachment, does not result in any final convergence overcoming a previous divergence. The articulation is always a local one. There is no general opening of the border; instead a contradiction (either/or) has been turned into a contrast (and, and).

In the context of Ball's project, such a diplomacy is practised through a collaborative place-making that enrols human and non-human alike, and that prompts an awareness of the relations of care that sustain human life. Yet it also, it must be noted, results in a 'care' driven nurturing of some 'native' lives over and against 'invasive' ones. This site-sensitive, pathogenic marking of species is widely used in ecological discourse to describe plants and animals that proliferate 'aggressively' when freed from the constraints found in their more usual environments, a migratory act that, in similar vein to a biosecurity reading of pandemic disease, quickly becomes interpreted as a militarised one. The ecosystem that *WATERWASH ABC* is designed to encourage may well diverge from a rendering of maintenance as a domestic concern, and a purely social one; but, the material difference that it both proliferates and constrains is yet predicated on an 'organismic' connection between lifeforms and the land they inhabit. This naturalised web of relations may well have the appearance of rootedness and immobility, but these time frames are anthropocentric ones. Arguably, such time frames become valued not because they refer to a past reality that an unthinking human occupation has unsettled, but because they offer a future certainty predicated on things remaining as they are for the comfort of future generations.

Concluding Comments

In recent years we have been witness to an increasing number of what might be termed 'art/sci' projects, emanating from the arts and humanities, that seek to worry away at disciplinary boundaries, to be sure, but that also make visible this more Earthly cosmpolitics. As a means of closing this discussion of a geopolitics of touch, I want to draw attention to work that is geared not so much towards the labour of maintenance, however, as accomplished by human and non-human life acting in concert, but the notion of 'touching' the Anthropocene, an epoch and geography that has come to preoccupy academics and practitioners, as well as governments and activists, across the globe. Artist Frances Whitehead's creative works are very much embedded in a cosmopolitics that draws on the capacities of the state, the natural sciences as well as the arts, and which acknowledges the dependencies and proximities of matter. Her 2005 *SuperOrg* project, for example, designed with Lisa Norton, is geared towards the transmogrification of the Steelyard Commons area of the Cuyahoga River Valley, Ohio, exemplified by their 'granulation' of the slag found there so that it became a sellable slag cement. Subsequently, Whitehead became a part of Chicago's Innovation Program, working in the Department of the Environment, where she developed the *SLOW Cleanup* project, begun in 2008, and which relies on the phytoremediating labour of plant roots to transmogrify the elemental, biotic and social *milieu* of several abandoned gas stations in the city into what she calls a 'phyto-scape.' Rather than simply remove toxic substances to a landfill, the project relies on roots transforming the soil to produce a more healthy ecology. "There's no development pressure," at these brownfield sites, says Whitehead, "so the asset we have is time itself" (cited in Hart, 2014: n.p.).

Whitehead was invited to become the Lead Artist on the design team for *The 606* project, named after the first three digits of Chicago's zip code, and which transforms the elevated Bloomingdale rail line into a trail and recreation park system running East/West through four 'gentrifying' neighbourhoods on the city's Northwest side. This now industrial ruin was built in 1873 for the Chicago and Pacific (later the Canadian Pacific) Railroad, and was one of the many arteries used to haul goods in and out of the city, tying Chicago into its hinterland, as well as the East and West coasts. Closed in 2001, it was locally known as the 'Bloomingdale Trail,' described by the *Chicago Sun-Times* as, "almost three miles of broken rock hashed by creosote-coated wooden ties and steel rails" (Steinberg 2013, n.p.), all connected by 38 viaducts. Much of this new space will be devoted to walking and bike paths, a skate park, picnic areas, event spaces and ornamental planted zones. A key part of Whitehead's design scheme, however, lies with the making tangible of other, non-human temporalities.

At the Western trailhead, for example, Whitehead has planned, in concert with the Adler Planetarium, a spiralling earthwork made from recycled materials that works as a seasonal observatory. And, running out from this to the Eastern railhead is what might be termed a 'haptic device' that makes tangible weather and climate change. Working in collaboration with the Chicago Wilderness

Alliance and the USA National Phenologic Network, Whitehead has envisioned 453 Amelanchier trees (which are berry-bearing, deciduous trees with white flowers). Species include the Apple Serviceberry, often recommended in horticultural and forestry circles for screening hedges and for buffering parking lots because of their year round visual interest, and tendency not to be 'invasive' (Gilman and Watson, 1993). The Alemanchier species were chosen for their aesthetic appeal, their ability to withstand difficult conditions, and their early blooming period, but also for their temperature sensitivity. These trees will tend to bloom in a wave from West to East over the course of what is estimated to be a five day period initially (though this will vary), the time lag being a result of the 'lake effect,' which keeps temperatures cooler near Lake Michigan during the early Spring. The resulting pattern indicates an annual event; but, it can also be assessed year to year, such that later blooming periods will intimate a broader climate change. There are mile markers inscribed into the cement of the running

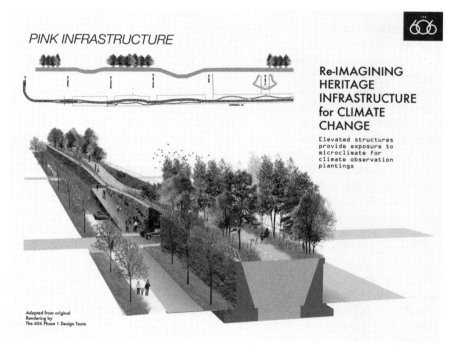

Figure 6.1 Pink Infrastructure for Climate Adaptation

Source: Frances Whitehead, MVVA, Collins Engineers. Courtesy of The Trust for Public Land.

trail, so that the line of trees can be understood as literally constituting a haptic measuring device that registers the touch of weather and climate, while each individual tree will also have a unique QR code so that data can be geo-located (Figure 6.1). As Jeremy Ohmes (2014: n.p.) describes the project,

> The temperature-sensitive plants (what Whitehead calls 'environmental sentinels') will reveal how large bodies of water like Lake Michigan affect local temperature patterns in spring and fall. Modeled after Japanese cherry blossoms whose transient blooming attracts audiences and signifies warmer weather, the concept of this blooming, phenologic spectacle will allow scientists and citizens to study climate change and observe nature's relationship to the Lake Effect.

Phenology is the study of biotic life cycle events, and in this context is used to describe a form of citizen science as visitors are urged to mark the timing and location of shifts in the weather by observing how the flora looks, smell and feels and when. According to Mark Schwartz, who created the climate model for the project, "If it's recorded year-by-year, it will create a climactic centennial for the city" (cited in Rotenberk 2013: n.p.).

The project firmly installs non-human and human bodies alongside each other as the medium through which an experimental art is created. And, it clearly draws inspiration from the Farmers' Almanac type guides to seasonality that have helped 'time' people's relationship with domesticated and 'wild' plants and animals, fostering in the process a sense of stewardship. There is the same emphasis here, as with almanacs, on a sensuous immersion in the environment (undertaken through sight, feel, smell and hearing) that forges a sense of belonging in a now familiar place, but that also intimates a distancing, insofar as it is the gnostic, as opposed to the pathic, touch that is privileged as a way of knowing. What makes this project different to the almanac genre, however, is the recognition that the phenological display in use is itself registering something of the input of human beings over time as the lake effect arrives later each year. This display has been 'upscaled' to the globe, each sensible part of it undergoing to some extent a human-induced environmental change that is the hallmark of the Anthropocene. The project presents us with a touch that facilitates an awareness not so much of the deep time of Earthly processes, but of the material propinquities of global warming. Park visitors and serviceberry trees, warming breezes and well-drained soils, are drawn into a temporal and site-specific collective as elemental *cum* evolutionary beings and instruments of research, albeit differently capable of responding to the same.

As such, I want to suggest, *The 606* provides something of an allegorical counterpoint to Fresh Kills, as described earlier. It also is undergoing a material transmogrification, but this is not a baroque tragedy in the form of a secularised and linear human history writ large and naturalised against a rhythmic Earth time. But nor is it a nostalgic return to myth either, though the park certainly holds to a traditional, picturesque landscaping. The phenological art *cum* science experiment that gives the park its distinctive air splays out what might be termed a melancholic Anthropocenic geography already touched by human hands. Each Spring visitors are witness to the rebirth of a mis-begotten ecological system that, over time, becomes ever more sharply delineated. This is an immersive, reflective art that can neither affirm an autonomous human identity, nor an externalised Nature from which a threat is posed or within which a resolution sought. It cannot even sound out a calamitous event, insofar as the materials that constitute this haptic measuring device are already in motion, from seed to bud, time and again. What visitors can register are degrees of chimerical intimacy, each more disturbing than the last.

As allegory, the phenological display of *The 606* provides an opportunity to reflect upon the question of what is the 'global' that is so often presented as the ultimate geopolitical body, and to which political practices can be upscaled such that they can be termed *geo*political? A materialist approach eschews the notion that the globe can simply be read as a textual construction; it also eschews the primacy of topographic renderings that place phenomena, events and processes within a scalar hierarchy. Clearly, such critiques do much to query the bordered logics of territory, networks and scales. The question that emerges, however, is what, then, remains of a global ontology? To be sure, and following the work of Deleuze and Guattari, Bruno Latour, Michel Serres, Manuel DeLanda and so on, we can point to the sticky work of site-based ontologies, and the assemblage of force-full objects as a means of describing the nature of things. These are both, arguably, tasked with describing a 'matter-processing,' wherein the selection and actualisation of matter's potentials of differentiation, which are both immanent and autonomously self-legislating, are stabilized as 'sites,' only to be dynamically reconfigured and disrupted as part of new differentiations. But, we can also dwell on an Earthly, 'always within reach,' touch that is democratically inclusive. A feminist materialism that explores the constitutive work of affect, or 'elemental passions' as Irigaray (1992) puts it, and material differentiation itself as an ontological force, offers a way forward here. As has been noted elsewhere (for example, Colls 2012; Straughan 2010; Paterson 2007), in dwelling on touch, we can mark the lurking ocularcentism that is all too often uncritically relied upon as theorists further distance their mind's eye to cope with the spatialities of difference (as, variously, Cartesian, 'folded' or 'scrumpled'), as well as an anthropocentrism in which such spatial rearrangements are solely theorised in terms of social (as opposed to non-human) power. In the absence of a Gods-eye, overarching spatial metric for orienting relationalities, we must needs grasp the textured zones of contact that emerge – tangible, permeable, obdurate and friable – between what might be summarily called 'localised' points that have their own, singular spatio-temporalities.

References

Adams, Vincanne, Murphy, Michelle and Clarke, Adele. 2009. Anticipation: Technoscience, Life, Affect and Temporality, *Subjectivities* 28: 246-65.
Adorno, Theodor. 2007 [1936]. Letter to Benjamin. In Adorno, Theodor, Benjamin, Walter, Brecht, Bertolt and Lukács, György. *Aesthetics and Politics*. London: Verso, pp. 120-6.
Akaret, Julie. 1984-1986. *Not Just Garbage: The Maintenance Art of Mierle Ukeles*, 1/2 Hour Video for TV. Available at https://www.youtube.com/watch?v=aJ9GWlFZz1g. Last accessed 25 September 2014.
Alexander, Jeffrey C. 2008. Iconic Consciousness: The Material Feeling of Meaning, *Environment* and *Planning D: Society and Space* 26.5: 782-94.
Athanassoglou-Kallmyer, Nina. 2001. Blemished Physiologies: Delacroix, Paganini, and the Cholera Epidemic of 1832, *The Art Bulletin* 83.4: 686-710.
Bashford, Alison and Strange, Carolyn. 2007. Thinking Historically about Public Health, *Medical Humanities* 33.2: 87-92.
Braun, Bruce. 2007. Biopolitics and the Molecularization of Life, *Cultural Geographies* 14.1: 6-28.
Braun, Bruce. 2008. Thinking the City through SARS: Bodies, topologies, Politics. In Harris, Ali and Roger Keil, Roger (eds) *Networked Disease: Emerging Infections in the Global City*. Oxford: Wiley-Blackwell, pp. 250-66.
Benjamin, Walter. [1963] 2003. *The Origin of German Tragic Drama*. London: Verso Books.
Briggs, Charles L. 2004. Theorizing Modernity Conspiratorially: Science, Scale, and the Political Economy of Public Discourse in Explanations of a Cholera Epidemic, *American Ethnologist* 31.2: 164-87.
Brown, Tim. 2011. 'Vulnerability is Universal': Considering the Place of 'Security' and 'Vulnerability' within Contemporary Global Health Discourse, *Social Science and Medicine* 72.3: 319-26.
Budd, Lucy, Bell, Morag and Brown, Tim. 2009. Of Plagues, Planes and Politics: Controlling the Global Spread of Infectious Diseases by Air, *Political Geography* 28.7: 426-35.
Chakrabarty, Dipesh. 1992. Postcoloniality and the Artifice of History: Who Speaks for 'Indian' Pasts? *Representations* 37: 1-26.
Colls, Rachel. 2012. BodiesTouchingBodies: Jenny Saville's Over-life-sized Paintings and the 'Morpho-logics' of Fat, Female Bodies, *Gender, Place and Culture* 19.2: 175-92.
Davies, Sara E. 2008. Securitizing Infectious Disease, *International Affairs* 84.2: 295-313.
Delaporte, François. 1986. *Disease and Civilization: The Cholera in Paris, 1832*. Translated by Goldhammer, Arthur. Cambridge, MA: Massachusetts Institute of Technology Press.
Dixon, Deborah P. 1991. *Cholera in British East India, 1818-1819*. Master's Thesis, University of Wisconsin-Madison.

Eagleton, Terry. 1990 *The Ideology of the Aesthetic.* Oxford: Blackwell.

Feldbaum, Harley, Lee, Kelley and Michaud, Joshua. 2010. Global Health and Foreign Policy, *Epidemiologic Reviews* 32.1: 82-92.

Feldman, Mark. 2008. Inside the Sanitation System: Mierle Ukeles, Urban Ecology and the Social Circulation of Garbage, *Iowa Journal of Cultural Studies* 10.1: 42-56.

Fidler, David. 2007. Architecture Amidst Anarchy: Global Health's Quest for Governance, *Global Health Governance* 1.1: 1-17.

Garrett, Laurie. 1994. *The Coming Plague: Newly Emerging Diseases in a World Out of Balance.* New York: Farrar, Straus and Giroux.

Gibson-Graham, Julie-Katherine. 2011. A Feminist Project of Belonging for the Anthropocene, *Gender, Place and Culture* 18.1: 1-21.

Gilman, Edward and Watson, Dennis. 1993. *Amelanchier x grandiflora Apple Serviceberry. Forest Service Fact sheet ST-77* (November), available at http://hort.ifas.ufl.edu/database/documents/pdf/tree_fact_sheets/amegraa.pdf. Last accessed 25 September 2014.

Gilmour, David. 2003. *The Long Recessional: The Imperial Life of Rudyard Kipling.* New York: Random House.

Grosz, Elizabeth A. 1994. *Volatile Bodies: Toward a Corporeal Feminism.* Indianapolis, IN: Indiana University Press.

Hart, Joe. 2014. Portrait of the Artist as a Leader, *Public Art Review*, available at http://forecastpublicart.org/public-art-review/2014/08/portrait-artist-leader/3/. Last accessed 25 September 2014.

Harvey, Elizabeth D. (ed). 2003. *Sensible Flesh: On Touch in Early Modern Culture.* Philadelphia, PA: University of Pennsylvania Press.

Heymann, David L. and Rodier, Guénaël. 2001. Hot Spots in a Wired World: WHO Surveillance of Emerging and Re-emerging Infectious Diseases, *The Lancet Infectious Diseases* 1.5: 345-53.

Hinchliffe, Steve, et al. 2013. Biosecurity and the Topologies of Infected Life: From Borderlines to Borderlands, *Transactions of the Institute of British Geographers* 38.4: 531-43.

Howard-Jones, Norman. 1975. *The Scientific Background of the International Sanitary Conferences.* Geneva: WHO.

Ingram, Alan. 2005. The New Geopolitics of Disease: Between Global Health and Global Security, *Geopolitics* 10.3: 522-45.

Ingram, Mrill. 2014. Washing Urban Water: Diplomacy in Environmental Art in the Bronx, New York City, *Gender, Place and Culture* 21.1: 105-22.

Irigaray, Luce. 1992. *Elemental Passions.* Translated by Collie, Joanne and Still, Judith Still. New York: Routledge.

Isaacs, Jeremy D. 1998. DD Cunningham and the Aetiology of Cholera in British India, 1869-1897, *Medical History* 42.03: 279-305.

Jameson, James. 1820. *Report on the Epidemic Cholera Morbus as it Visited the Territories Subject to the ... in the Years 1817, 1818 and 1819.* Calcutta: A.G. Balfour.

Keller, Mikaela, et al. 2009. Use of Unstructured Event-based Reports for Global Infectious Disease Surveillance, *Emerging Infectious Diseases* 15.4: 689-95.

King, Victoria. 2005. *Art of Place and Displacement: Embodied Perception and the Haptic Ground.* College of Fine Arts, University of New South Wales.

Lee, Yujin and Paul Duncum. 2011. Coming to our Senses: Revisiting the Haptic as a Perceptual System, *International Journal of Education through Art* 7.3: 233-44.

Lippard, Lucy R. 1980. Sweeping Exchanges: The Contribution of Feminism to the Art of the 1970s, *Art Journal* 40.1/2: 362-5.

Massumi, Brian. 2009. National Enterprise Emergency: Steps Toward an Ecology of Powers, *Theory, Culture and Society* 26.6: 153-85.

McNeill, William. 1976. *Plagues and Peoples.* Garden City, NY: Doubleday Press.

Miller, Diana. (ed.) 2002. *Terrorism: Are We Ready?* Huntington, NY: Nova Science.

Molesworth, Helen. 1999. Cleaning Up in the 1970s: The Work of Judy Chicago, Mary Kelly and Mierle Laderman Ukeles. In Newman, Michael and Bird, Jon (eds) *Rewriting Conceptual Art.* London: Reaktion Books, pp. 107-22.

Mullin, Amy. 2003. Feminist Art and the Political Imagination, *Hypatia* 18.4: 189-213.

Novas, Carlos and Rose, Nikolas. 2000. Genetic Risk and the Birth of the Somatic Individual, *Economy and Society* 29.4:483-513.

Ohmed, Jeremy, 2014. Trailblazer: How an SAIC Faculty Member is Modeling New Pathways for Artists, *SAIC – Highlights*, available at http://www.saic.edu/highlights/saicstories/fall2013archive/franceswhiteheadandthe606/. Last accessed 25 September 2014.

Orton, Reginald. 1831. *An Essay on the Epidemic Cholera of India.* London: Burgess & Hill.

Paterson, Mark. 2007. *The Senses of Touch: Haptics, Affects and Technologies.* New York: Berg.

Phillips, Patricia C. 1995. Maintenance Activity: Creating a Climate for Change. In Felshin, Nina (ed.) *But Is It Art: The Spirit of Art as Activism.* Seattle, WA: Bay Press, pp. 165-93.

Rae, Paul. 2011. Pigs Might Fly: Dance in the Time of Swine Flu, *Theatre Journal* 63.3: 403-24.

Rancière, Jacques. 2007. *The Politics of Aesthetics: The Distribution of the Sensible.* Translated by Rockhill, Gabriel. London: Continuum.

Rancière, Jacques. 2009. *Aesthetics and its Discontents.* Cambridge: Polity Press.

Recovery Brochure. 2006. Available at http://www.nysm.nysed.gov/exhibits/longterm/documents/recovery.pdf. Last accessed 25 September 2014.

Rotenberk, Lori. 2013. When it Comes to Climate Change, this Artist Lets the Trees Do the Talking, *Grist*, available at http://grist.org/people/when-it-comes-to-climate-change-this-artist-lets-the-trees-do-the-talking/. Last accessed 25 September 2014.

Shildrick, Margrit. 2007. Dangerous Discourses: Anxiety, Desire, and Disability, *Studies in Gender and Sexuality* 8.3: 221-44.

Shukin, Nicole. 2011. Transfections of Animal Touch, Techniques of Biosecurity, *Social Semiotics* 21.4: 483-501.

Spivak, Gayatri Chakravorty. 1999. *Imperatives to Re-imagine the Planet* [Imperative zur Neuerfindung des Planeten]. Vienna: Passagem.

Straughan, Elizabeth R. 2010. The Salon as Clinic: Problematising, Treating, and Caring for Skin, *Social and Cultural Geography* 11.7: 647-61.

Steinberg, Neil. 2013. Bloomingdale Trail to be Chicago Gem, *Chicago Sun-Times* 15 May, available at http://www.suntimes.com/news/steinberg/19149671-452/bloomingdale-trail-to-be-chicago-gem.html#.VADzQMVdUvM. Last accessed 25 September 2014.

Stengers, Isabelle. 2013. Introductory Notes on an Ecology of Practices, *Cultural Studies Review* 11.1: 183-96.

Stoler, Ann Laura. 2008. Epistemic Politics: Ontologies of Colonial Common Sense, *Philosophical Forum* 39.3: 34-69.

Ukeles, Mierle Laderman. 1969. Manifesto, available at http://www.arnolfini.org.uk/blog/manifesto-for-maintenance-art-1969/Ukeles_MANIFESTO.pdf. Last accessed 25 September 2014.

Ukeles, Mierle Laderman. 1979-1980. Touch Sanitation, available at http://www.brooklynmuseum.org/eascfa/feminist_art_base/gallery/mierle_laderman_ukeles.php?i=1111. Last accessed 25 September 2014.

Ukeles, Mierle Laderman. 1991. Stretching the Canvas: Flow City, *Environmental Action* (July/August): 24-5.

Ukeles, Mierle Laderman et al. 1992. A Journey: Earth/City/Flow, *Art Journal* 51.2: 12-25.

Wald, Priscilla. 2008. *Contagious: Cultures, Carriers, and the Outbreak Narrative*. Durham, NC: Duke University Press.

Wolfe, Nathan. 2011. *The Viral Storm: The Dawn of a New Pandemic Age*. New York: Macmillan.

Young, Iris M. 1994. Women Recovering Our Clothes. In Benstock, Shari and Ferriss, Suzanne (eds) *On Fashion*. New Brunswick, NJ: Rutgers University Press, pp. 197-210.

Chapter 7
Inhabiting Feminist Geopolitics

Introduction

In addressing flesh, bone, abhorrence and touch I do not want to intimate that these are somehow a better way of capturing the 'building blocks' not only of geopolitical inquiry, but of any inquiry into an imagining of the global. Such an approach would be needs be predicated upon the notion of academic inquiry as the increasingly accurate observation of a scaled world that organises itself for our apprehension. Nor do I wish to be prescriptive as to what the matter of a geopolitics should be, or how it should matter. Indeed, I take my lead from Judith Butler's double-handed observation from *Bodies that Matter*, wherein she notes, sympathetically, that "On the one hand, any analysis which foregrounds one vector of power over another will doubtless become vulnerable to criticisms that it not only ignores or devalues the others, but that its own constructions depend upon the exclusion of the others in order to proceed" (1993: 18-19). In pursuing flesh, bone and so on as objects of inquiry, there is a vulnerability, to be sure, to the charge that other, more worthwhile, lines of inquiry have been slighted. For me, this is preferable, however to Butler's second possibility. "On the other hand," she writes, "any analysis which pretends to be able to encompass every vector of power runs the risk of a certain epistemological imperialism which consists in the presupposition that any given writer might fully stand for and explain the complexities of contemporary power" (ibid.). There is no sympathy here for such an imperialist 'pretence.'

For me, lines of inquiry that set flesh, bone, abhorrence and touch at the forefront of analysis are useful because they feel for the borders of geopolitical thought and practice and in so doing proliferate certain kinds of difference; that is, they have the potential to invade, infect, and transform geopolitics as an academic field, to eat out the body from within, and produce in turn phantom hosts and viral geographies of contagion. In concluding this book, then, I do not want to simply add up points made earlier, or speculate on forward pathways, but wish instead to take on the question of what kinds of phantom hosts – or conceptual *personae* as Rosi Braidotti (2013) terms these (Chapter 1) – have indeed come to life through this particular articulation of a feminist geopolitics? In the following, I draw on my preceding chapters to outline two such phantom hosts, the *Semi-Living* and *Skeleton Woman*. These are parasitic in the sense that they thrive on the established and the entrenched, consuming these from within, but they are also performative of the future. They embody both an ontological and epistemic divergence from political, capitalist and phallogocentric normative forms and capacities; and, leaving aside the totalising question of what these figures fully contain, they, "construct geometric possibilities in the cracks of the matrices of domination" (Kember 1996: 260). Such figures do not tend to register in geopolitical debates, nor do they sit easily in the pages of geopolitical texts. Nor should they.

What I would also like to point to in this final chapter, however, is the question of what kind of landscape do these figures draw life from and inhabit? In the absence of a scaled and externalised Earth upon which geopolitical subjects tread, what kind of elemental grounding do these draw sustenance from, stand on and traverse? What landmarks emerge as significant, and what kind of sense-making allows us to feel their presence within and without the Self and to navigate our way forward? What kind of history has allowed for such a landscape to unfold, and what traces remain of a past that has shaped possible futures? And, how do we choose to live as and with these figures in the future of past eras, and the present of futures to come? There have been numerous attempts to describe such Earthly formations. As noted in Chapter 3, much has been made of a rapidly developing 'technonature,' for example, whose diverse mediums (from virtual reality to lab-borne species) do not so much mimic a biological original as unravel and construct life as we know it (see Braun, Whatmore and Stengers on the 'matter of politics,' 2010). And, as noted in Chapter 6, we can also reference the Earth as an immersive, 'postmodern battlefield' composed of proliferating and augmented lifeforms, both attuned and contributing to a self-weaponing environment. In recent years, the Anthropocene as a site wherein particular forms of human activity are wielded as a geologic force has also hove into view. All of these have become a means of contextualising a progressively decentred human sovereignty, and in this sense they are conceptual prompts for reimagining ourselves, our Others, and the relationalities between these. But, these formations also capture something of the thresholds of such an effort – of the challenges of thinking and performing the post-human subject and object, one might say – insofar as they are partial, though certainly insightful, truths, and do not claim to exhaust the potentialities of the matter to hand.

In closing out this book, I want to invoke an Earthly formation that helps to animate both the Semi-Living and Skeleton Woman via a sustained attentiveness to the chimerical, the contagious, and the excessive. That is, I want to invoke a monstrous landscape – a ter[r]aformation – that has pervaded all of my chapters, though is most strongly etched in Chapter 5. The term, as conjured by Susan Ruddick (see Dixon and Ruddick 2013) plays upon the Earthliness of 'terra,' as in terrestrial, from the Latin *terrestris* (meaning Earthly), but also the profligacy of 'tera,' from the Greek *teratologia* (meaning the telling of marvels). As noted in Chapter 5, tera became the prefix for teratology, the systematic study of biological abnormalities. Somewhat in the vein of Jacques Derrida's (1993) *telepoiesis*, which is an imaginative grafting of etymologies (from 'tele' meaning at a distance, and 'poiesis,' an imaginative making), for Ruddick, a ter[r]aformation thus invokes a geography of material excess – an immeasurable becoming-ontology – over and against which the taxonomic classifications that sustain family, species, science and state are asserted. It is within this Earthly formation that the following figures 'make sense.'

The Semi-Living

The Semi-Living as a feminist figuration is inspired not by International Relations, or political geography, but by the arts, and in particular a loose genre labelled BioArt that emphasises a post-human reproduction in the context of corporeally disassociated tissues, thereby calling into question the manner in which we consider tissues as engaging in life and death, certainly, but also the manner in which we think the human body and associate capacities, such as a corporeal anxiety and vulnerability. What BioArt provides insight into, as I hope to show below, is the geopolitical potentialities of reimaging the body not as a corporeal container replete with parts, but as tissues that can offer up a sense of wholeness, to be sure, yet which can also be related to a host of other ensembles. Such a reimagining can be regressive, by all means, as when flesh becomes fetishised as one more commodity to be traded and made profitable in a global marketplace. But also, it can be progressive, not only through an ironic mimicry of such fetishising procedures that renders them tangible and open to debate, but in the conjuring of other, care-driven relationalities.

BioArt is a relatively new, necessarily collaborative endeavour between artists and scientists wherein living materials, developed and nurtured within the laboratory, are used as material for art installations. Tissue cultures, but also neuro-physiology, bio-robotics and bio-informatics, artificially produced DNA sequences, Mendelian cross-bred organisms, xeno-transplants, homo-grafts, and medical self-experimentation, have all come under the banner of a critical BioArt. Using the BioArt collective hosted by SymbioticA, in the School of Anatomy and Human Biology, University of Western Australia, to flesh out the 'semi-living' as a working concept, I want to highlight how scientific experiment upon tissues is afforded an explicit aesthetic: part and parcel of its affective capacity is the testing of the possibilities for altering form and feature as well as our reactions to the same. But also, and importantly for my purposes, the work of this collective provides an example of how the fleshy medium is no mere vehicle for conveying a political message, but, in its composition and sensuous affect, provides for a politicised encounter.

The work of BioArt is itself an international performance, in that is dependent on the same transfers of disassociated tissues described in Chapter 3 before and after an exhibition. That is, the Tissue Culture and Art (TCA) grouping of Oron Catts and Ionat Zurr have used their 'presence' within the institutional context of the School of Human Anatomy and Behaviour to order samples from various tissue catalogues. The *Tissue Culture* and *Art(ificial) Wombs* (2000), for example, also exhibited as *The Semi-Living Worry Dolls*, is based on polymer scaffolding in the shape of Guatamalan worry dolls seeded with samples from the McCoy Cell Line, originally derived from human synovial fluid in 1955, and packaged and sold for virology studies. As an artistic medium, these cells are statically cultured in an incubator by TCA before being bathed in a nutrient-rich serum in a rotating microgravity bioreactor. Some exhibitions merely house the deceased form, or some of the documentary materials associated with the making of these; others, however, necessitate the cultivation of tissues *in situ*, requiring that these be transferred once more. According to TCA, this, "enables us to perform the duties needed to care for the Semi-Living sculptures while the exhibition is being held, in a way that enables the audience to observe and comprehend the commitment and responsibilities that we have towards the living systems we create" (*Worry Dolls*, TCA website). At the end of these exhibitions, TCA ritualistically and fatally expose all such works to a non-sterile atmosphere. Prior to the 2008 Museum of Modern Art, New York, showing of *Victimless Leather*, which uses mouse cells seeded onto a coat-like scaffolding, the ethical quandaries posed by this euthanistic practice were forcibly brought home to curator Paola Antonelli, as the jacket, "started growing, growing, growing until it became too big. And [the artists] were back in Australia, so I had to make the decision to kill it. And you know what? I felt I could not make that decision. I've always been pro-choice and all of a sudden I'm here not sleeping at night about killing a coat … That thing was never alive before it was grown" (cited in Doctorow 2008: n.p.).

In addition to their prompting of questions concerning the nature of life and death, such 'unexpected' practices source, make visible, and allow critical reflection upon the vast collections of cell lines and sublines that are stored and collected within private industry collections, such as Life Technologies, non-profit entities such as the American Tissue Culture Collection (ATCC), national collections, and a wealth of small-scale specialist collections in universities, hospitals and research centres. Larger collections, such as the ATCC, for example, tend to have more formal, restrictive licensing arrangements. A key source of materials for researchers in developed and developing countries alike because of the size of its holdings, the ATCC requires research bodies to enter into a Material Transfer Agreement (MTA) before materials can be shipped in special vapour boxes by FedEx courier. Here, as Dedeurwaerder (2010: 416) explains,

> The collection categorically affirms its 'ownership' of the materials deposited in and distributed from its collection… with the notable exception of samples deposited by the Yellowstone National Park… ATCC's MTA states that the collection and/or its contributors retain ownership of all rights, titles and interests in the distributed materials, their progeny and unmodified derivatives, including any materials contained or incorporated in modifications.

BioArt also makes visible to various publics the emergence of specialist reproductive technologies, or 'wombs,' that enable such collections. The bioreactor, for example, was developed for NASA as a ground support system that kept tissue-based experiments fresh while in transit to the shuttle. It was subsequently used in space by astronauts to cultivate and nurture tissue cells as part of a project designed to investigate and propose treatments for musculoskeletal disorders brought on by gravity-less conditions. Patented by NASA, and commercialised by Texas-based company Synthecon Inc., the microgravity bioreactor has since become a key part of experimental, therapeutic research into various cancers, HIV and, of course, stem cell development. In the hands of BioArtists, such technologies also help to 'nurture' new forms of life, but with the understanding that these are thoroughly chimerical creatures as opposed to 'natural' extensions of the corporeal body; moreover, this chimerical condition, it is implied, is actually a more 'authentic' rendering of what it is to be human.

For TCA, the ranks of the semi-living are no mere outliers; they are, instead, a modern-day portent of things to come. TCA's *NoArk* (2007-8), for example, exhibited in galleries in Perth, Madrid, Porto, Buffalo, and San Francisco, consists of tissues taken from a number of sources, grown together in a microgravity bioreactor to create an unique ensemble – the Semi-Living – and placed in the upper half of a Perspex cabinet; in the lower half are laid out preserved specimens on loan from Natural History museums within those cities where *NoArk* is being exhibited (Figure 7.1). These have included a black crow, a piglet, a kangaroo head and a mouse. Again, these tissues serve as a gesture towards the thousands of tonnes of disassociated cells produced and housed within pharmacological factories, research universities, and so on. Here, however, they are laid out in a vessel that explicitly recalls the 'world-containing' and 'end-of-the-world surviving' Ark, as well as the early modern Cabinet of Curiosity, which allowed visitors "experiential phenomena of the globe" (Benedict 2006: 701). *NoArk* and its contents evoke not a world made up of individual parts, but rather congeries of parts whose precarious relation to a host of other parts admits of no summing up.

At one level, the invocation of the Ark as a form of housing signals the valuing of a new cohort of creatures, ready and waiting to populate the world; instead of heterosexed pairs, however, we have Deleuze and Guattari's (1987) Artaud-inspired term 'Bodies Without Organs' (BWO), each expressing the manifold capacities of the flesh to be otherwise. This Ark collects and presents a reservoir of traits, relations and affects, each of which might be of use in a new world order that no longer differentiates between the social and the natural. Do we value these figures because they help to actualise such an erasure? Or, perhaps, because they indicate how best to survive in a world where each new, possible form offers an opportunity for further commodification of the flesh? While *NoArk* prompts such questions, it does not answer them. At another level, however, the creatures collected here – their flesh reassorted anew each time *NoArk* is exhibited – enact their own worldly geography, akin to the macabre exhibits of Frederik Ruysch (Chapter 5). Rusch's corpses expressed the vanity of Earthly life and time passing, as contrasted with the slower, more obdurate, tempos of the geological specimens he arrayed them against, and this emphasis upon a fleeting animation is reiterated

Figure 7.1   Details from *NoArk*, 2007-8, produced by TCA
Source: TCA.

in the death rituals of the Semi-Living. These malformed, misbegotten creatures, however, born of their artificial wombs, do not point the way to a glorious afterlife. Rather, their fate, it seems, is to become biological waste, flushed into the disposal systems of our metropolis'.

Skeleton Woman

Outside of the carefully cultivated and maintained spaces of the Semi-Living, we can find the sanctified and demonised figure of the Skeleton Woman, who, ostensibly located on the margins of economic, political and cultural life, yet insists, in quite contrary ways, upon her place at the centre of things. The first appearance of Skeleton Woman I want to draw attention to emerges in the context of the anti-globalisation demonstrations of the first decade of the twenty-first century. Propelled in large part by the widespread economic and social ramifications of the subprime mortgage debacle, as well as a wave of corporate business scandals and national and local state financial austerity measures, and inspired by diverse grass-roots, new media-savvy movements such as the Zapatistas, anti-globalisation movements, if one can label such a grouping, were operative in over 80 countries. From 2011 onwards, Occupy, for example, established a series of camps including Zuccotti Park, New York, and St. Paul's Cathedral, London, and rallied through streets protesting the fundamental inequity of a global financial system, and the anti-democratic consequences of this.

Using Twitter and Facebook to propel what Jeffrey Juris (2012) calls a 'logic of aggregation' – mediums more usually described as both evidence and help mates of a distanciated, virtual set of relations between and amongst people and place – Occupy has been characterised by the massing of bodies into physically tight spaces. These become a human wedge driven into the hugely affective as well as symbolic landscapes of both government and corporate finance. As Gertjan Dijkink (2000: 65) argues, a Westphalian state system rendered these and similar trade city's "the central symbols of the state's corporate body ... home to dominant political institutions and social classes (civil servants) with a strong stake in the regimes ruling the country." Of course these "places staged revolutionary events as well. This is not surprising since capturing the state means capturing its 'head'" (ibid.). Small wonder that Ed Soja (2010: 59) suggests that,

> Grounding the global justice movement in the right to the city creates more tangible and achievable targets than simply organizing against neoliberal capitalism, globalization, or global warming, especially as all three are primarily generated from and made concrete in the major city regions of the contemporary world.

And, that some academics have become concerned with the purification tactics of police in response, such as kettling and clearing (King 2013; Nyong'O 2012).

Some have also noted the creative play on identity within these movements, and in particular the intermittent appearance of a Guy Fawkes' mask, made iconic by the 2005 *V for Vendetta* film (Elden 2011). There is a productive anonymity denoted here, to be sure, that turns the otherwise ubiquitous, identifiable individual into the highly visible protestor. As Giorgio Agamben (1993: 86) remarks, reflecting on events in Tiananmen Square, "for the State ... what is important is never the singularity as such, but only its inclusion in some identity, whatever identity (but the possibility of the *whatever* itself being taken up without an identity is a threat the State cannot come to terms with)" (emphasis in original). But, as several feminist commentators have noted, what this masking also does, of course, is render the protestor heroically masculine (see, for example, Kilibarda 2012). It is with this denotation in mind that scholars such as Catherine Eschle (2005) have turned to another figure, whose arrival heralds not only the power of protest, but also an obdurate humanity. Zombies have promenaded at many demonstrations, but it is the arrival of Skeleton Woman, appearing in a 2000 short story by Paul Hawken titled *What Skeleton Woman Told the WTO in Seattle*, and circulated widely through Occupy's many inter-linked media sites, which I want to focus briefly on here.

Writing in response to the police operation that 'secured' the World Trade Organisation talks in 1999, Hawken (2000: n.p.) asks:

> What marched in the streets of Seattle? Slower time strode into the WTO. Ancient identity emerged. The cloaks of the forgotten paraded on the backs of our children. It is not the fast things that will prevail. In the end, that which is slow is powerful.... Skeleton woman also showed up in Seattle, the uninvited guest, and the illusion of wealth, the imaginings of unfettered growth and expansion, became small and barren in the eyes of the world. Dancing, drumming, ululating, marching in black with a symbolic coffin for the world, she wove through the sulphurous rainy streets of the night. She couldn't be killed or destroyed, no matter how much gas or pepper spray or rubber bullets were used. She kept coming back and sitting in front of the police and raised her hands in the peace sign, and was kicked, and trod upon, and it didn't make any difference.

Here, the rhythms and resilience of an elemental Earth are afforded geopolitical agency in the form of a feminised body which, whilst stripped of the flesh that confirms individuality, also confirms the possibility of a rebirth. For Eschle (2005: 1742), "feminists are the 'Skeleton Women' haunting this movement," insofar as their arguments and concerns, indeed their very presence, is barely registered. And, I think that this reminder of the specificity of bodies, and the glossing of this which takes place under a logic of aggregation, is well made. What is more, the skeletal form of this figure undercuts the easy mythos of women as mothers (and mourners) of the nation, as well as a Mother Earth. This is a feminised figure, to be sure, but it is also an alchemical one, conjured for the moment to hand.

As Eschle goes on to note, the potency of such a figure is derived from its dense and expansive mythological heritage.And, it is with this in mind that I want to point to a second manifestation of Skeleton Woman, one that also speaks to the notion of centres and margins, but in the context of a religious global imaginary that has by no means given way to a formal geopolitics. *Santa Muerte* (Saint Death) takes the form of a skeletal girl, sometimes called the 'White Girl' because of the colour of her pristine bones. Whilst her posited Aztec origins remain a matter of debate, she stands at the centre of the Holy Death sect, whose membership has grown from the neighbourhoods of Mexico City to along the US/Mexico border and beyond. As Steven Gray (2007: n.p.) rather ominously reported events in *Time* magazine, devotees have a reputation for being on the outskirts of society, whether through poverty or a predilection for crime:

> For decades, thousands in some of Mexico's poorest neighborhoods have prayed to Santa Muerte for life-saving miracles. Or death to enemies. Mexican authorities have linked Santa Muerte's devotees to prostitution, drugs, kidnappings and homicides. The country's Catholic Church has deemed Santa Muerte's followers devil-worshiping cultists. Now Santa Muerte has followed the thousands of Mexicans who've come to the U.S., where it is presenting a new challenge for American Catholic officials struggling with an increasingly multicultural population.

Certainly the vision of a dark underbelly emerging underneath the otherwise healthy US nation-state has been nurtured by the *Fox Latino News* (2011: n.p.), which, under the heading 'Drug traffickers worship 'Holy Death' Saint to keep the law away,' warns that, "Such images have become so commonplace that candles are sold in Laredo supermarkets."

This ghettoization of Skeleton Woman, however, and its attendant spatial imagery of containment and contagion, is inverted by more sympathetic commentators such as Rebecca Solnit. In a pensive piece on the drug wars that have terrorised and scarred much of northern Mexico, she recounts her visit to the shrine of Santa Muerte in Mexico City in 2007, walking through Tepito, "the black-marketeers' barrio," where "somber men were praying and lighting candles to the skeleton goddess who is the *narcotraficantes*' patron saint" (2012: n.p.). Such scenes, however, remind her of the many ways in which the drug wars in which these men play a part are not only also manifest elsewhere, but implicate a diverse array of actors. They are, she writes,

> fueled by many things, and maybe the worst drug of all is money, to which so many are so addicted that they can never get enough. It's a drug for which they will kill, destroying communities and ecologies, even societies, whether for the sake of making drones, Wall Street profits, or massive heroin sales. Then there are the actual drugs, to which so many others turn for numbness. (ibid.)

It is not often that specific relations between people and agencies, connected via these money trails, come to light, not only because of the secrecy shrouding various illegal activities and state-led policing efforts, but also the layers of privacy established around various banking systems. On 17th July 2012, however, we were afforded a glimpse of one such example when a US Senate committee (anticipating the findings of Mexico's National Securities and Banking Commission) published a report on HSBC, Europe's largest bank, detailing allegations of money-laundering for "drug kingpins and rogue nations" (Mattson 2012: n.p.). The report centred on HSBC Mexico, which, in the mid-2000s, was involved in transferring $7 billion in cash into the US, tantamount to half the overall cash flow from country to country, and went on to condemn HSBC's lack of a uniform compliance policy across its affiliates.

The image of *Santa Muerte*, whether as a tattoo, bumper sticker or charm, has been taken as a sign of criminality, to the extent that US immigration and law enforcement agents along the border are now advised to watch for her appearance as the patron saint of the *narcotraficantes*. But, if we look more closely at her iconography we see that she holds in her hands a pair of scales, testament to the demand for equity, and a globe, symbolising both her reach and her dominion (Velazquez 2007). *Santa Muerte*, does not offer a rebirth, but she does, I want to argue, remind us of the complex geographies that lie behind the *narcotraficantes*, geographies that extend through the heart of the financial system upon which so much of our daily lives depend.

Ter[r]aforming

We can glean a sense of the contingent emergence of such figurations from the above, and the extensive relations that help 'place' these over and against others. But the bigger question to be asked at this point is what kind of a world do such figures inhabit? If we no longer afford a common sense reality to those topographic representations of a globe composed of externalised physical features overlain by sharp lines that tell us where nation-states begin and end, then what other imaginaries can come to the fore as a means of configuring such an Earthly geography? For Madelaine de Scudéry, as discussed in Chapter 2, *Le Pays de Tendre* was one such possibility; at once a political medium for, and political expression of, a civilised behaviour inclusive of all, including princes, this county's citizens were also distinguished by an acknowledgement of their own creatureliness, and their kinship under the sun with a host of other soul-ful beings. Though Scudéry's *oeuvre* is not as well developed, and is certainly not as well known now as the philosophies of Leibniz or Spinoza, both of which have helped animate a feminist materialism, there is yet a generosity of touch here in regard to how a lived humanness emerges from a sensuous as well as intellectual engagement with others that resonates strongly, I feel, with what a feminist geopolitics strives to accomplish. I do not wish to pose Scudéry's work as a harbinger for a feminist geopolitics, however, but as an inspiration for thinking through this question of what kind of a world do feminist figurations occupy?

The creatureliness that Scudéry identified can be considered marginal because it flew in the face of a mechanical Cartesianism that served as a conceptual foundation for a rapidly evolving Enlightenment Natural History. And, as I hope to have demonstrated throughout this book, the importance of Nature to the formulation of a geopolitical imaginary is by no means a recent, Anthropocenic phenomenon. Rather, a progressive, modern Natural History – wherein human bodies were part of an all-encompassing Nature, yet unique and improvable – has proven crucial to the organising tenets, intellectual mission, and pragmatic concerns, of a classical geopolitics. The unchecked upwelling of the flesh has haunted such a geopolitics, from the witch hunts of Christian Europe and the emergence of a reasoned Westphalian diplomacy, to the deathscapes of the colonies and the sanitation practices of a 'One World One Health' initiative that unites human and veterinary medicine. Even teratology, whose early advocates applauded the material diversity of Nature in the making of civilisation, was to become aligned with a social Darwinism that sought to purge and scourge national bodies at the individual and collective level.

At one level, then, this marginalisation of Scudéry's geopolitical imaginary can be considered yet one more example of the insatiability of ever more quotidian forms of order. Her soul-ful chameleons join the ranks of Walter Benjamin's angelic host, Jacques Derrida's monstrous arrivant, Michel Foucault's abnormal, and Donna Haraway's cyborg, which together identify the monster as emblematic of that which exists outside of the norm, to be sure, but also as revealing of the monster-ing work of that which is proffered as common sense, normal, reasonable and ideal. And, in recent years we have come to rely on such monstrous figures to undertake a conceptual upheaval, or renewal. The longing for monstrous irruptions in social theory takes a hopeful form; it looks for, as Donna Haraway (1992) puts it, the promise of monsters. At another level, however, and in this final section, I want to invoke a teratology because of what it can tell us of an Earthly monstrousness – a ter[r]aformation if you will – predicated on an imminent material differentiation that is configured, contained and externalised by an androcentric parting of the flesh. This parting is a spatialisation that confers sharp-edges and universal metrics, such as voluminous territories and international borders, citizens and migrants (Braidotti 1996; 2000). And, it is within a ter[r]aforming that I situate geopolitics, its practice, its subjects and objects, its absences and its excess.

This is a decidedly Deleuze and Guattarian phrasing of the Earth as a geopolitical body, and it takes heed of just how influential their geophilosophy, and particularly their 1987 *A Thousand Plateaus*, has been on a feminist materialism. Immanence, or a 'for and in itself,' is posed by Deleuze and Gauttari as an empirical world that continues to emerge from material bodies and the forces they express. Underwritten by a differentiation that does not mimic an original, but continues to proliferate singularities, such a world not only precedes and exceeds our constructed systems of representation, but is fundamentally, ontologically indifferent to such an endeavour. These materialities, like the unruly stem cells of Chapter 3, assemble, multiply, disperse and congeal; and, they can be put to work in the reiterative expression of life. "It is at this moment," Ian Shaw et al. (2010: 379) write, "when the machinic productivities of materiality are translated into and integrated with practice — when worlds confronted translate into worlds to be navigated, harnessed, and managed. At the same time that these worlds are assembling and connecting ... they are also decaying, exploding, and stratifying: transcendent structures in one moment only to be collapsed into a rhizome at another." Materials combine and recombine into all manner of bodies, from the transnational surrogate womb to the blood system of an ebola host, and from the seething geochemistry of New York's Fresh Kills landfill to that of a protected Australian thrombolite, both wallowing in shallow waters and open to the skies above.

In thinking of the Earth from this perspective, what emerges is not an elemental container waiting to be filled with lifeforms, including human beings and their paraphernalia, or which can be observed in some top-down fashion as an atlas composed of parts. Rather, such an Earth is constituted from bodies – all of which are thus geopolitical in the simple sense of 'geo' as of the Earth, and bearing in mind their *puissance*, or capacity to affect and to be affected by other bodies – that emerge in the midst of their world; that is, in their *milieux*. To be sure, boundaries are part and parcel of such an engagement; these are not imposed upon the world, however, but are where materials are exchanged and organised, allowing for a unity of composition, such as a corporeality, or a territory. What is more, in the absence of an overarching spatial metric – or God's eye view – for orienting relationalities between compositions, we must needs acknowledge what Deleuze and Guattari refer to as the 'what' of connections; that is, "tactile relations" (1987: 485). This is a tactility that attends to the way in which space is 'felt' as a meshing and unmeshing of surfaces: in place of discrete objects positioned within four dimensions, and whose constituent parts can be similarly located *ad infinitum*, we orientate ourselves and others by way of shifting pressures that indicate a composite world of presences (and absences), textures and intensities. In building a new Earth that eschews sameness and nurtures differentiation, one might add (see Chapter 6), it is thus a generosity of touch that is required. The import of this line of thought for geopolitics is that its purported subjects and objects can no longer be situated solely within the categorical imperatives of either a Westphalian sovereignty or an allied Natural History. The ter[r]aformations within which these emerge, distribute and dissipate, are shifting configurations the fundamental 'profligacy' of which can help illuminate not only the power relations within which specific bodies are located (and within which they locate themselves), but of expressing how far distant each body is from the norms and mores desired by the state, capitalism and a phallogocentric order, no matter how experimental the latter are in regard to controlling the flesh.

And yet, it would be as well to heed the note of caution from feminist scholars here, insofar as the implication of this line of reasoning is that the minoritarian politics of differentiation and becoming put forth by Deleuze and Gauttari is not only more progressive than a molar politics (manifest in a rights-based feminism, for example, that presupposes a cohesive identity), but is also dismissive of the emotive relevance of a molar politics to individuals and social movements. The purported merits of a minoritarian politics – variously described as a 'becoming-woman,' or a 'microfeminism' (Deleuze and Gauttari 1987: 275) – over and against those of a molar politics has concerned a number of scholars, including Braidotti (2008) and Elizabeth Grosz (1994; 2008), even as they draw upon Deleuze and Guattari's machinic apparatus to further problematise binary logics such as real/mimic and mind/body. On a related note, Donna Haraway (2008) has noted the scorn for the homely that animates much of *A Thousand Plateaus*.

Acknowledging the salience of these debates, I want to conclude my own discussion of a feminist geopolitics by insisting that though such a molar politics can certainly help to advance women's self-determination in specific contexts, thus enhancing their capacities for action and thus their materially composed selves, it can also congeal women's possibilities of becoming, as well as the very notion of what a feminist project is. The key here is context; or, it might be said, the ter[r]aformation within which such encounters unfold. Women's bodies may well be described as 'perverse,' as Patricia MacCormack (2004: n.p.) puts it, because they, "traverse, rearrange, exceed and decrease the rigid limits culture allows us to exist within and as our bodies," but all bodies are perverse, I want to argue, because they are of the Earth. These bodies become alongside other becomings, and they further differentiate alongside the increased capacities of others, but also at the expense of stifling certain possibilities. In leaving aside such categorical imperatives, we can ask, rather: what can, and what should, a feminist theory and practice *do*? What happens when, for example, in response to gender-based exploitation, we decide to applaud efforts to actualise a sense of individualism and empowerment? What happens when, in considering the role of the state in governing reproduction, we decide to affirm rights to the body? What happens when, in illuminating a masculinist 'eye from nowhere,' we decide to own feelings? What happens when, in acknowledging the legal and medical practices that compartmentalise sex, we decide to celebrate diversity? What happens when, in delving into the embodied subject, we decide to express the visceral? And, what happens when such 'decisions' are understood to come not from a human, but a post-human, subject? If, as Elizabeth Grosz (2011: 68) argues, a feminist understanding of consciousness is that of the, "projection onto materiality of the possibility of a choice, a decision whose outcome is not given in advance" then, she concludes, it must be recognised as a capacity that spans species, even as its expression in each, and in each individual, is particular and specific. If we consider the immense breadth of feminist work in these areas, it becomes clear that there is no easy articulation of any of these pressing issues, let alone a resolution. Rather, what emerges from the literature is a sustained effort to pay care and attention to these decisions, the empirical grounds they both speak to and are drawn from, and their wide-ranging import. To paraphrase Ewa Ziarek (2001: 5), such an ethics is necessarily predicated on an infinite accountability – indeed, this is its democratic inclusiveness – but does so without the familiar reassurance of preconceived expectations and norms.

References

Agamben, Giorgio. 1993. *The Coming Community*. Translated by Hardt, Michael. Minneapolis, MN: University of Minnesota Press.
Agamben, Giorgio. 1998. *Homo Sacer: Sovereignty* and *Bare Life*. Translated by Heller-Roazen, Daniel. Stanford, CT: Stanford University Press.
Benedict, Barbara M. 2006. Saying Things: Collecting Conflicts in Eighteenth-Century Object Literatures, *Literature Compass* 3.4: 689-719.
Braidotti, Rosi. 1996. Signs of Wonder and Traces of Doubt: On Teratology and Embodied Difference. In Lykke, Nina and Braidotti, Rosi (eds) *Between Monsters, Goddesses and Cyborgs: Feminist Confrontations with Science, Medicine and Cyberspace*. London: Zed Books, pp. 135-52.
Braidotti, Rosi. 2000. Teratologies. In Buchanan, Ian and Colebrook, Clare (eds) *Deleuze and Feminist Theory*. London: Zed Books, pp. 156-72.
Braidotti, Rosi. 2008. *Metamorphoses: Towards a Materialist Theory of Becoming*. Cambridge: Polity Press.
Braun, Bruce, Whatmore, Sarah J and Stengers, Isabelle. 2010. *Political Matter: Technoscience, Democracy, and Public Life*. Minneapolis, MN: University of Minnesota Press.
Dedeurwaerdere, Tom. 2010. Global Microbial Commons: Institutional Challenges for the Global Exchange and Distribution of Microorganisms in the Life Sciences, *Research in Microbiology* 161.6: 414-21.
Deleuze, Gilles and Guattari, Felix. 1987. *A Thousand Plateaus: Capitalism* and *Schizophrenia*, translated by Massumi, Brian. Minneapolis, MN: University of Minnesota Press.
Derrida, Jacques. 1993. Politics of Friendship, *American Imago* 50: 353-53.
Dijkink, Gertjan. 2000. European Capital Cities as Political Frontiers, *GeoJournal* 51.1: 65-71.
Dixon, Deborah P. and Ruddick, Susan M. 2013. Monsters, Monstrousness, and Monstrous Nature/s, *Geoforum* 48: 237-8.
Doctorow, Cory. 2008. Curator Euthanizes Living Leather Jacket Made from *mouse* Stem-cells, *BoingBoing* Website, available at http://boingboing.net/2008/05/08/curator-euthanizes-l.html. Last accessed 25 September 2014.
Elden, Stuart, 2011. Blog Entry for the Journal *Society* and *Space*, available at http://societyandspace.com/2011/11/21/stuart-elden-v-for-visibility/. Last accessed 25 September 2014.
Eschle, Catherine. 2005 Skeleton Woman: Feminism and the Anti-globalisation Movement, *Signs: Journal of Women in Culture* and *Society* 30.3: 1742-69.

Fox News Latino. 2011. Drug Traffickers Worship 'Holy Death' Saint To Keep The Law Away, *Fox News Latino Online*, 27 June, available at http://latino.foxnews.com/latino/news/2011/06/27/holy-death-saint-making-its-way-to-us/#ixzz1V92yfpje). Last accessed 25 September 2014.

Gray, Steven. 2007. Santa Muerte: The New God in Town, *Time Magazine* 16 October, available at http://www.time.com/time/nation/article/0,8599,1671984,00.html. Last accessed 25 September 2014.

Grosz, Elizabeth, A. 1994. A Thousand Tiny Sexes: Feminism and Rhizomatics. In Boundas, Constantin and Olkowski, Dorothea (eds) *Gilles Deleuze and the Theatre of Philosophy*. New York: Routledge, pp. 187-210.

Grosz, Elizabeth A. 2008. *Chaos, Territory, Art: Deleuze and the Framing of the Earth*. New York: Columbia University Press.

Hawken, Paul. 2000. *N30: What Skeleton Woman Told the WTO in Seattle*, available at http://ratical.org/co-globalize/PaulHawken.html. Last accessed 25 September 2014.

Haraway, Donna. 1992. The Promises of Monsters: A Regenerative Politics for Inappropriate/d Others. In Grossberg, Larry, Nelson, Cary and Treichler, Paula (eds) *Cultural Studies*. New York: Routledge, pp. 295-337.

Haraway, Donna. 2008. *When Species Meet*. Minneapolis, MN: University of Minnesota Press.

Juris, Jeffrey S. 2012. Reflections on #Occupy Everywhere: Social Media, Public Space, and Emerging Logics of Aggregation, *American Ethnologist* 39.2: 259-79.

Kember, Sarah. 1996. Feminist Figuration and the Question of Origin. In Robertson, George et al. (eds) *FutureNatural. Nature/Science/Culture*. London/New York: Routledge, pp. 256-69.

Kilibarda, Konstantin. 2012. Lessons from #Occupy in Canada: Contesting Space, Settler Consciousness and Erasures within the 99%. *Journal of Critical Globalisation Studies* 5: 24-41.

King, Mike. 2013. Disruption is Not Permitted: The Policing and Social Control of Occupy Oakland, *Critical Criminology* 21.4: 463-75.

MacCormack, Patricia. 2004. Perversion: Transgressive Sexuality and Becoming-Monster, *Thirdspace: A Journal of Feminist Theory and Culture* 3.2, available at http://www.thirdspace.ca/journal/article/view/maccormack/174. Last accessed 25 September 2014.

Mattson, Jennifer. 2012. HSBC 'allowed Drug Money Laundering,' says US Senate, *The Global Post*, (17 July), available at http://www.globalpost.com/dispatch/news/business/companies/120717/hsbc-allowed-drug-money-laundering-says-us-senate. Last accessed 25 September 2014.

Nyong'o, Tavia. 2012. The Scene of Occupation, *The Drama Review* 56.4: 136-49.

Shaw, Ian G.R., Robbins, Paul F. and Jones III, John Paul. 2010. A Bug's Life and the Spatial Ontologies of Mosquito Management, *Annals of the Association of American Geographers* 100.2: 373-92.

Soja, Ed. 2010. *Seeking Spatial Justice*. Minneapolis, MN: University of Minnesota Press.

Solnit, Rebecca. 2012. An Apology to Mexico, *Salon* (10 July), available at http://www.salon.com/2012/07/10/an_apology_to_mexico/. Last accessed 25 September 2014.

Velazquez, Oriana. 2007. *El libro de la Santa Muerte* [The Book of Santa Muerte]. Mexico City: Editores Mexicanos Unidos, S.A.

Worry Dolls, TCA Website, available at http://tcaproject.org/projects/worry-dolls. Last accessed 25 September 2014.

Ziarek, Ewa 2001. *An Ethics of Dissensus: Postmodernity, Feminism, and the Politics of Radical Democracy.* Stanford CT: Stanford University Press.

Index

Aesthetics 28, 144-5, 148, 154, 155
Amazons 28
America's Conservative News (ACN) 131-3
Anatomy Act, 1832 98, 99
Androcentrism 9-10, 12, 14
Anthropocene 16, 52, 145-6, 156, 163, 165-6, 172
Antwerp 25
Art 16, 144, 145, 157-60, 173-7

Ball, Lillian 161-2
Baroque 115, 122, 135, 160, 165
Battlefields 92-3, 95
Bell, Charles 94-8, 99, 102
Benjamin, Walter 96, 103, 160, 181
BioArt 173-5
Biosecurity 142, 162
Boer War 35
Bombay 148-9
Bowman, Isiah 33
Braidotti, Rosi 6, 7, 9, 11, 17, 23, 49-50, 113, 171, 183
British India 98-9, 147-50
Buffon, Comte de 119-20, 125
Burke, Edmund 127-9, 130, 154
Butler, Judith 47, 48, 171

Cabinet of Curiosity 99, 115, 119, 175
Calcutta 98, 99, 148-50
Calvinism 25, 121, 122
Carlist Wars 102, 103
Cartesianism 13, 30-31, 59, 166
Cartography 26-7
Catt, Carrie C. 38
Chicago 37, 98, 146, 163
Cholera 142-3, 147-50, 155-6
Classical Geopolitics 2, 7-8, 11, 12-13, 14, 15, 21, 22, 23, 32-6, 41-2, 47, 51-2

Cold War 42, 104, 151
Conceptual *Personae* 6, 17, 171
Corporeal Anxiety 155, 173
Critical Geopolitics 3, 9

Dalby, Simon 23, 42, 43, 52
Darwin, Charles 34, 125-6
Deathscape 143, 147, 149, 181
Deleuze and Guattari 50, 103-4, 166, 175, 181-2
Del Toro, Guillermo 104, 135-6
Derrida, Jacques 141, 172, 181
Diprose, Rosalyn 48-9

Earth History 10, 51
Edinburgh 86, 88, 93-5, 102, 106, 150
English Civil War 117
Enlightenment 4, 15, 16, 27, 30-31, 85-9, 93-4, 98-9, 106, 116-17, 120, 127, 129, 130, 144, 181
Enloe, Cynthia 6, 43
Environmental Determinism 22
Eugenics 115, 125-6

Feminist International Relations 3, 42-3, 44
Feminist Political Geography 3, 43-5
Film 101, 104, 135-6, 178
Foetus 62-3, 101, 118
Fox News 131
Frankenstein 104, 128-9
French Revolution 4, 94, 127-8, 148
Fresh Kills Landfill 160-61, 165, 182

Gatens, Moira 49

Generalplan Ost (Master Plan East) 34-5
Geostrategy 22, 32-3, 41-2
Global Environmental Governance 11, 145-6

Gouges, Olympe de 127
Grosz, Elizabeth 4, 10, 45, 47, 50-51, 131, 155, 183

Haraway, Donna 114-15, 181, 183
Health Diplomacy 142, 146-7
HSBC 180
Huntington, Samuel P. 2, 9

Imperialism 2, 8, 13, 23, 35, 131, 146-7, 149, 151
Imperial Gothic 143, 149
Indian Wars 88, 106
International Woman Suffrage Alliance 38, 41
Irigaray, Luce 5, 47-8, 49, 51, 156, 166
IVF Technologies 60, 61, 62, 70-72

Kaplan, Robert D. 2, 9

La Fronde 28
Le Jardin du Roi 31, 119-20
Le Pays du Tendre 27-30, 180
London 32, 69, 72, 88, 94, 100, 104, 129, 177
Low Countries 13, 23, 25, 28, 115, 121

Machiavellianism 30
Mackinder, Halford 32
Mahan, Alfred T. 32
Masculinism 5-6
Maternal Anxiety 62, 70, 73-8, 79
Midwives 89, 99-100
Monsters 16, 78-9, 90, 113-15, 117-19, 121-4, 127-8, 141
Monstrousness 16, 79, 116-17, 127-8, 130-31, 141
Morrison, Toni 134
Museum Vrolik, Amersterdam 125

Narcotraficantes 179-80
Napoleonic Wars 95-6
Natural History 8, 31, 119-20, 175, 181, 182
Nazism 34-5, 36, 103-4, 126
Neo-Gothic 134-6

New York City 130, 157-8, 160, 161, 174, 177, 182

Obama, Barack 62, 130, 131-3
Occupy 177-8

Pact of Oblivion 87, 103
Paré, Ambroise 89-91, 118
Paris 26, 27, 31, 33, 35, 36, 37, 88, 89, 118, 119, 120, 148, 150
Peter the Great of Russia 121-4
Phallogocentrism 6, 10, 52-3, 171-2

Raja Serfoji 99
Rancière, Jacques 144-5, 157
Realism 22, 42, 146, 155
Realpolitik 13, 22, 30, 32, 34, 37, 38, 41, 42
Reichsfrauenführerin 35-6
Reproscapes 71-2
Ruysch, Frederik 121-3

Santa Muerte 179-80
Scudéry, Madelaine de 13, 23-4, 27-31, 47, 180-81
Seattle 178
Seba, Albertus 121-2
Semple, Ellen C. 8, 9, 33-4
Sha'arawi, Huda 41
Social Darwinism 8, 13, 16, 22, 34-5, 115, 125, 129
Spanish Civil War 87, 103-5
Spinozism 121
Spivak, Gayatri Chakravarty 11-12, 48, 149
Spykman, Nicholas 32
Stengers, Isabelle 7, 21, 161, 162
Supernatural 15, 86
Surgeon's Museum, Edinburgh 94-5, 103

Telepoiesis 172
Teratology 16, 100-101, 115, 121, 172
Ter[r]aformations 172-3, 180, 182
Territory 2, 24-6, 32, 34, 50-51, 86, 107, 142, 143, 158, 166, 182
Tissue Culture and Art 175-7
Topological 11, 59, 64, 141, 153, 155
Treaty of Westphalia 24-5, 28

Tuathail, Gearóid Ó 3, 34

Ukeles, Mierle L. 157-61

Vampires 129

Weapons 91, 95-7, 102-3
Westphalian politics 8, 13, 23, 24-6, 32, 38, 142, 151, 155, 182
Whitehead, Frances 146, 163-6
Witches 8, 90-91

Women's International League for Peace and Freedom 39-40
World War II 23, 33, 41, 87
Wounds 91-3, 95-8

Zombies 178